L U S T M O R D

L U S T M O R D

S E X U A L   M U R D E R   I N

W E I M A R   G E R M A N Y

Maria Tatar

PRINCETON UNIVERSITY PRESS • PRINCETON, NEW JERSEY

Library of Congress Cataloging-in-Publication Data
Tatar, Maria M., 1945–
Lustmord : sexual murder in Weimar Germany / Maria Tatar.
p. cm.
Includes bibliographical references and index.
ISBN 0-691-04338-8 (alk. paper)
1. Murder—Germany—History—20th century.   2. Sex crimes—
Germany—History—20th century.   3. Serial murders—Germany—
History—20th century.   4. Murder in literature.   5. Murder in art.
I. Title.
HV6535.G3T38   1995
364.1′523′09430904—dc20   94-48601   CIP

This book has been composed in PostScript Dante
Princeton University Press books are printed on acid-free paper,
and meet the guidelines for permanence and durability of
the Committee on Production Guidelines for Book Longevity of
the Council on Library Resources
Printed in the United States of America
1   3   5   7   9   10   8   6   4   2

Contents

Illustrations

Acknowledgments

I HAVE RUN UP many debts, both intellectual and personal, while writing this book. It was, in the first instance, students in my course on Weimar Culture at Harvard University who drew my attention to the steadfast critical disavowal of the material discussed in this volume. My own resistance to confronting the issue of sexual violence in Weimar Germany's artistic production began to crumble as they marshaled ever more persuasive evidence for its centrality. The many canvases by Otto Dix and George Grosz with the title *Lustmord* (*Sexual Murder*) made it impossible to continue denying what should have been evident from my reading of literary texts. Because Dix and Grosz are so prominently implicated in the representation of disfiguring violence directed at the female body, I was perhaps less reticent than I should have been to analyze a body of work that required critical tools with which I was not completely familiar. In the course of my investigations, I discovered that reaching for range and depth—casting a wide net that would catch both historical facts and fictional constructs—made sense, even at the cost of sacrificing some technical precision.

For their willingness to be enlisted in conversations that sometimes took a grim turn and for reading early versions of chapters, I want to thank the following friends and colleagues: Peter Burgard, Dorrit Cohn, John Czaplicka, Eric Downing, Sander Gilman, Peter Jelavich, and Silvia Schmitz-Burgard. Without the able assistance and energetic resourcefulness of Marielle Smith, this book would have taken much longer to complete and would have been missing many interpretive nuances. Dan Horch's expertise in the archives helped me to locate many of the newspaper articles cited in chapter 3. Challenging my arguments, along with my prose, Stephen Gauster read the entire manuscript and led me, in countless instances, to consider alternative explanations or to identify additional evidence for my analysis of a text. Finally, Annemarie Bestor and Todd Bishop have, over the years, helped to ease the burden of the process of manuscript production with their cheerful good spirits.

Colleagues from other institutions—Sabine Hake, Andreas Huyssen, Anton Kaes, and Beth Irwin Lewis—provided readings that helped me to strengthen and focus my argument at a time when I was distracted by all the trees in the forest. Mary Murrell of Princeton University Press shepherded the manuscript through the production process with remarkable dispatch and grace. Beth Gianfagna's discerning editorial eye and critical engagement with the subject matter of this book sharpened many of my arguments.

Over the years, Sanford Kreisberg, Ellen Langer, Penelope Laurans Fitzgerald, Richard Petrasso, and Larry Wolff took an interest in this project and offered wit, wisdom, and necessary distractions. My children Lauren and Daniel would have preferred that I write another book on fairy tales, but they accepted my interest in grown-up matters with unfailing good will and forbearance.

I am grateful to the staffs of Widener Library, the Houghton Library, and the Fine Arts Library of the Fogg Art Museum at Harvard University. For permission to reproduce works by Otto Dix and George Grosz, I am indebted to Peter M. Grosz and the Estate of George Grosz, Princeton, New Jersey, and to the Estate of Otto Dix. The Otto Dix Archive in Schaffhausen generously loaned me their photographs of Dix's works. Terry Geesken of the Film Stills Archive at the Museum of Modern Art provided stills from *M* and from *Nosferatu* with helpful efficiency.

Some early versions of chapters in this book appeared in print. I am grateful to the *Deutsche Vierteljahrsschrift für Literaturwissenschaft und Geistesgeschichte* for permission to reprint the essay on Döblin's *Berlin Alexanderplatz* and to the Center for International Studies at Cornell University for permission to reprint parts of chapter 3. All of the translations, unless otherwise acknowledged, are my own.

• P A R T   O N E •

Sexual Murder: Weimar Germany
and Its Cultural Legacy

Morbid Curiosity:
Why *Lustmord*?

I don't particularly want to chop up women but it seems to work.

Brian De Palma

THIS BOOK represents the long answer to a question that seemed trivial when it first arose, but that haunted me with a curious insistence. Who was that man named Haarmann in verses that I had heard sung by Germans—both in real life and in movies?

> Just you wait 'til it's your time,
> Haarmann will come after you,
> With his chopper, oh so fine,
> He'll make mincemeat out of you.[1]

In Fritz Lang's film *M*, which opens in a subtly unnerving manner when the innocent voice of a child chants this grisly rhyme, the words "black man" are substituted for Haarmann.[2] But most variants (and the one still widely known in Germany today) identify the cleaver-wielding fiend of these verses as "Haarmann." While the name Haarmann, as I quickly discovered, does not appear in the standard cultural histories of Weimar Germany, it can be found with astonishing frequency in newspapers of the time ranging from the liberal *Frankfurt Times* (*Frankfurter Zeitung*) to the Communist *Red Flag* (*Rote Fahne*) and in acclaimed novels such as Yvan Goll's *Sodom Berlin* and Alfred Döblin's *Berlin Alexanderplatz*.[3] When Lang released his film in 1931 and Döblin published his novel in 1929, both could count on general familiarity with the case of Fritz Haarmann, a serial murderer executed in 1925. They could also assume that their audiences were familiar with a range of other notorious cases—the Vampire of Düsseldorf or the Silesian Bluebeard—involving what a "medical man" in Hitchcock's *Frenzy* calls "criminal sexual psychopaths."[4] It was Fritz Haarmann who tipped me off to those cases and to the way in which they were a conspicuous presence, yet also a closely guarded secret, in Weimar's artistic, cinematic, and literary production.

Much as collective cultural memory has excluded Fritz Haarmann from the historical record and preserved his deeds in the popular imagination as something closer to lore than to fact, it was impossible to eradicate his real-life existence entirely. Of late, the Haarmann case has attracted a certain amount of notoriety, but, in one instance at least, the effort to remember turned into what was perceived to be a scandalous attempt to commemorate his deeds. In Haarmann's native city of Hanover, Alfred Hrdlicka proposed erecting a monument to Haarmann—a statue that would be a provocation to be sure—but with the hope of provoking thought. It goes without saying that the plan was never approved, but Hrdlicka still had the chance to articulate what it was that made Haarmann worthy of memorialization. Haarmann's offenses lay at the heart of "the enigmas of a nation," Hrdlicka declared. "Haarmann the mass murderer . . . was not only a lightning flash revealing the state-sanctioned mass murders that were to come; his antisocial preoccupations and drives were, above all, what made him a prototype of his time."[5] Hrdlicka may be loading the person of Haarmann with more cultural and social baggage than a single pathological case deserves, but his refusal to erase Haarmann from the historical record and his determination to investigate his deeds as symptomatic of something larger than the murderer himself guided me in my investigations.

What next caught my attention, after learning more about Haarmann, were the murder victims—not just Haarmann's, but those who began to appear as a virtually ubiquitous presence in Weimar's artistic production. The sheer number of canvases from the 1920s with the title *Lustmord* (*Sexual Murder*) ought to have been a source of wonder for Weimar's cultural historians long before now. But more startling than the way in which real-life murderers and their victims enter the referential codes of works of art from Weimar Germany is the way in which the producers of those works become personally implicated in what they put into words and images, so deeply implicated that it is tempting to give some credence to Degas's belief that a painting demands as much cunning, malice, and vice as does a crime.[6] George Grosz, who painted more than his share of what he called "ladykillers" (in the literal sense of the term) and of their mutilated victims, once had himself photographed in the pose of Jack the Ripper (fig. 1). Menacing his victim with a knife pointed at her genitals, he transforms himself from the creative artist who frames, contains, and appropriates the seductive appeal of his model into a murderer prepared to destroy the source of male heterosexual desire and of artistic inspiration. The female model—absorbed in the contemplation of her own image (note the redundant presence of both a

1. George Grosz as Jack the Ripper, *Self-Portrait with Eva Peter in the Artist's Studio* (1918). As Eva Peter admires herself in a hand mirror, George Grosz emerges from behind a larger mirror in which she is reflected to stage a mock assault on the woman who was to become his wife two years later.

hand mirror and a near full-length mirror)—puts herself on display in a gesture of serene self-sufficiency. She has, in a sense, made the artist superfluous by creating herself as a work of art, as the target of the male connoisseur's gaze. And that reason alone may be sufficient to account for the artist's impersonation of a man prepared to assault, disfigure, and mutilate the body before him.

But the photograph of Grosz does not give us the real thing. In fact, it emphasizes its own "unreality" in the proliferation of simulacra ranging from mirror images and photographs through masks and dolls. The photograph appears to represent nothing more than a witty charade, with the artist merely masquerading as murderer. Still, murder—even when it is "just" staged, as in this snapshot—is never entirely innocent. That Grosz not only drew and painted mutilated female corpses but also felt compelled to *act out* the role of murderer seems telling, particularly when we consider that there was a real erotic tie between the Grosz in the photograph and his model. (Eva Peter, the woman on display, was to become his wife two years later.) What was it that drove Grosz to open the boundaries between art and life— first, to depict killers on his canvases, then, to impersonate them in photographs? That he was engaged in mimetic practices that were violent from both an aesthetic and a somatic point of view becomes evident from descriptions of his working methods. One critic points out that he turned his canvases into "scenes of crimes," applying the knife to them and spraying them with red paint.[7] Was this part of the same syndrome that led Frank Wedekind to enact on stage the role of Jack the Ripper in a play that he had written and that had starred his wife as Jack's victim? Or that motivated Otto Dix to paint a self-portrait entitled *Sex Murderer* and to smear it with his red handprints— just as if he wanted to be caught red-handed? That real-life murderers and their victims have a habit of turning up in plays and novels or making appearances in paintings and films even as artists construct their own identities as murderous assailants suggests a strange bond between murder and art, one to which Thomas De Quincey referred in his meditations "On Murder Considered as One of the Fine Arts" (1827).[8] This book on *Lustmord* tries to define the nature of that connection and to identify how it expresses itself in a variety of ways, some self-evident and straightforward, others surreptitious and complex.

In recent years, scholars from a variety of disciplines have trained our attention on the gender politics of cultural production in Germany during the prewar era through the war years into the 1920s.[9] Their efforts have made it possible to discern the outlines of a modernist project that aestheticizes violence and turns the mutilated female body into an object of fascination and dread, riveting in its display of disfiguring violence yet also repugnant in the detail of its morbid carnality. Whether studying Rudolf Schlichter's painting *Sexual Murder*, exploring the "Sex Murderer Grotto" in Kurt Schwitters's *Cathedral of Sexual Misery*, or observing how Alfred Döblin reconstructs the psychic life of Rosa Luxemburg and sexualizes her political assassination, it becomes evident that the representation of murdered women must function as an aesthetic strategy for managing certain kinds of sexual, social, and political anxieties and for constituting an artistic and social identity.

Developing arguments about the positioning of sexual murder in the 1920s requires a close look not only at Weimar Germany's cultural understanding of the killers, but also our own ways of explaining what is at stake in cases of serial murder. This issue is addressed in the next chapter by attending to definitions and to the way in which they are shaped by the identity, deeds, and accounts of historical murderers. Our fascination with sexual murder stems in part from its mystification as a deed that, in its perversion of love into hate, could be committed only by a savage beast or deranged monster rather than a human being. Yet time and again, these murderers are constructed as sons seeking revenge against women—against mothers as agents of sexual prohibition or against women in general as icons of licentious sexuality. Similarly, those who commit murder on canvases, pages, or screens are, as I try to demonstrate, competing with the reproductive powers of women or aiming to transcend the laws of biological procreation affiliated with women's bodies. I dwell in detail on Hitchcock's representation of sexual murder, in part because it was shaped so powerfully by German cinematic portrayals, in part because it so clearly captures Western notions of what drives men to murder women. These reflections are followed by a chapter that describes actual cases of sexual murder in Weimar Germany and looks at the ways in which those cases were reported by the press, investigated by the police, and overseen by the judicial system.

The second part of this book presents case studies of works by artists, writers, and filmmakers. Looking at representations in a variety of media requires an interdisciplinary approach that turns the once closely patrolled boundaries between literature, the visual arts, and cinema into permeable borders. I examine what Louis Montrose has called the "synchronic text of a cultural system," trying to establish a kind of cultural intertextuality in which case studies illuminate artistic production even as fictional accounts broaden our understanding of social realities. If we reflect on the way in which Jack the Ripper has been featured in so many films, plays, and novels that he is now as much literary construct as cultural case history or consider the way in which Norman Bates has found his way into legal arguments and psychiatric studies, it becomes clear that the study of sexual murder requires an approach that recognizes the controversial "textuality of history and historicity of texts"[10] without, however, dissolving the line between historical fact and imaginative construct.

This study analyzes verbal and visual representations of sexual murder, or more specifically what the German language calls *Lustmord*. (I shall use that term interchangeably with the English "sexual murder," though the German term *Lust*—which implies desire and pleasure along with sexual gain—captures more precisely the multiple dimensions of the motives driving this type of killing.) It also considers the sociocultural field that shaped those images and produced, in many cases, a surprising ideological consonance among male artists who prided themselves on their highly differentiated and personalized political beliefs. Where the consonance exists, I emphasize it. But I have also resisted homogenizing constructions that would turn energetic messiness into falsely stable and stabilizing arguments about the paintings, texts, and films discussed. I have tried not to configure the material in each chapter into completely tidy, but oversimplified and inaccurate, categories—with the result that disjunctions and discontinuities emerge in the case studies. They are there because disruptive anomalies are also a part of what constitutes the work of individual artists and writers and because the anomalies are often more revealing than the signatures of a particular style.

For decades, images of the victims of *Lustmord* were suppressed in our investigations of what has come to be known as Weimar Culture—in part because of their disturbing content, in part because of their unsettling effect on our attempts to produce stabilizing definitions of modernist aesthetics by emphasizing manner over matter. Elisabeth Bronfen has stressed the degree to which overkill has also desensitized us to the image of female corpses in books, on the screen, or on canvases: "Because they are so familiar, so evident, we are culturally blind to the ubiquity of representations of feminine death."[11]

That cultural blindness often takes the symptomatic form of naturalizing rape and murder directed at women. The filmmaker Brian De Palma has insisted that "using women in situations where they are killed or sexually attacked" is nothing more than a "genre convention . . . like using violins when people look at each other."[12] To argue that images of sexual and homicidal assault are culturally innocent is to take an almost willfully naive position about the role of ideology in artistic productions. What makes woman's position as victim, either in cinema or in real life, "natural?" The violent scenes De Palma puts on screen are anything but routine, workaday images devoid of substance. They figure as arresting moments that shock us and challenge us to reflect on the complex interlocking of gender roles, sexuality, and violence.

Yet even once we agree to problematize images of sexual violence, our interpretive habits can prevent us from facing the full implications of what is represented. As twentieth-century readers and spectators, we have been trained to view violence as an aesthetic strategy funded by a powerful transgressive energy that is the mark of the avant-garde. It is seen as nothing more than a pretext for practicing the modernist art of fragmentation and disfigurement. The referential matter of modernist art is relentlessly subordinated to and effaced by its spiritualizing manner. Thus Picasso's *Demoiselles d'Avignon*, which has been characterized as depicting a "tidal wave of female aggression" and "savage, disfiguring sexual menace," has been reframed to become a modernist icon of the viewer's "collision with art" or the "emancipation of form from content."[13] Focusing exclusively on formal features and insisting on disfigurement as a purely aesthetic principle can distract from facing the full consequences of what is at stake in the pictures we see and in the words we read.

Exposure to violence breeds numerous defense mechanisms, one of the most common of which may be avoidance. It is endlessly reassuring to deny many of the unpleasant personal and cultural truths underlying the artistic construction of violent images. But while we often efface violent subject matter by dismissing it as mere convention or aesthetic strategy, morbid curiosity just as frequently gets the better of us. We may be repulsed by images and descriptions of bodily violations, yet we also feel irresistibly drawn to gape, ogle, and stare—to take a good, hard look or to make sure that we do not miss a word. When the Austrian novelist Robert Musil gave an account of press reports about the killing of a prostitute by a sexual murderer named Moosbrugger in *The Man without Qualities*, he captured the double movement from fascination to revulsion in all of us:

> The reporters had described in detail a throat wound extending from the larynx to the back of the neck, as well as the two stab wounds in the breast, which had pierced the heart, the two others on the left side of the back, and the cutting off of the breasts, which could almost be detached from the body. *They had expressed their abhorrence of it, but they did not leave off until they had counted thirty-five stabs in the abdomen* and described the long slash from the navel to the sacrum, which continued up the back in a multitude of smaller slashes, while the throat showed the marks of throttling [my emphasis].[14]

"Something interesting, for once." According to Musil, this is how those who outwardly deplore sensationalism secretly respond to reports of murderous violence and bodily violation. Yet while we may be ardent readers of such accounts, as we move from fascination to revulsion, we disavow the appeal and distance ourselves from the lurid details with a compensatory resolve so powerful that it threatens to erase the violent event once again. Thus we become complicit in ensuring an audience for an unimpeded stream of violent cultural productions and a constant blockage of efforts to understand how those productions are constituted and what they mean for us.

Deaths represented as having a spiritually or socially redeeming purpose have not met with the powerful resistance to analysis at work in images of *Lustmord*. The nineteenth-century *Liebestod* (love-death), marked by the as-

sertion of transcendent desire and the spiritualization of eros, found its most
celebrated incarnation in the musical drama of Richard Wagner's *Tristan and
Isolde*. It has not ceased to attract popular and scholarly attention over the
years and remains a permanent fixture in our understanding of a nineteenth-
century poetics of passion and death. Similarly, the Expressionist *Vatermord*
(patricide) has been subjected to unending literary and social analysis. But
whether we are reading Walter Hasenclever's *The Son* (1914) or Arnold Bron-
nen's *Parricide* (1920), it becomes clear that the murderous assault on the
father—often simply called "the father" rather than designated by an individ-
ualizing name—represents little more than a cover for an attack on authority, power, and moribund traditions. To murder the father is to liquidate the
past and to clear the way for the social renewal and regeneration championed by a generation of disaffected writers.

While it may be tempting to identify hidden symmetries in the construction of *Vatermord* and of *Lustmord*, particularly since the victims of *Lustmord*
can figure as stand-ins for mothers, the psycho-sexual dynamics are so different as to demand separate treatment. Still, as I have noted and as will become
evident in the chapters that follow, there is almost always more than a trace
of either helpless infantile rage or nervous womb envy present in the genesis,
execution, or subject matter of the works to be discussed. That the targets of
assault for sexual murderers since Jack the Ripper have been not only the
genitals of the female body, but the interior reproductive organs as well,
reveals the degree to which the murderers are driven by something more
than the perversion of sexual desire.

Lustmord seems, in many ways, less the female counterpart to *Vatermord*
than a response to the "bloodlust" of male representations of sexually preda-
tory women, the turn-of-the-century femmes fatales. The profusion of images of Eve, Circe, Medusa, Judith, and Salomé in art and literature around
1900 gives vivid testimony to an unprecedented dread of female sexuality and
its homicidal power. Whether we look at the bloodthirsty Clytemnestra in
the Strauss-Hofmannsthal collaboration on the opera *Electra*, at the licen-
tiously sultry woman in Franz von Stuck's painting *Sensuality*, or at Otto
Friedrich's triumphant *Salomé*, it is clear that women become endowed with
overwhelmingly powerful erotic energy. While most critics have emphasized how these images of seductive femininity can be read as symptoms of
male anxieties about female libidinal energy, about the unsettling of gender
roles through emancipatory efforts, or about a sense of the loss of agency,
they can also be seen as fueling those anxieties to a fever pitch.[15]

In view of the extraordinary artistic investment in representing women as
creatures of overpowering sexual evil, it is little wonder that one of Germany's most prominent turn-of-the-century femmes fatales dies at the hands
of Jack the Ripper, in a play that is unabashedly dedicated to "the Avenger."

Frank Wedekind's *Earth Spirit* and *Pandora's Box*, conceived in 1895, reveal just how short a step it is from the sexual empowerment of the femme fatale to the murderous assault on her body, and for this reason, the "Lulu plays" (as the two dramas are called) form the literary prelude to the cultural staging of *Lustmord* two decades later. Although Wedekind does not present the death of his infamous Lulu as a sexual murder in the technical sense of the term, she dies at the hands of a notorious killer of prostitutes. What is remarkable about Lulu, beyond her irresistible allure, is the degree to which she becomes endowed with a subversive power that threatens not only the integrity of the masculine subject but also the stability of the entire social order. Lulu incites her many admirers to riotous living, leaving a trail of corpses behind her. More important, her disruptive reign of transgressive sexuality destabilizes the social order. It is no accident that one character announces an uprising in France at just the moment when Lulu's husband, Schwarz, is cutting his throat (or "beheading himself," as one character reports) with a razor. Small wonder that Lulu was referred to in one production of the play as a "female proletariat" ready to mount the barricades.[16]

Wedekind himself saw Lulu as endowed with abundant natural gifts, as a "magnificent specimen of a woman" on whom no limits whatsoever are set.[17] In this theatrical empowerment of the feminine, it is difficult not to detect what Georges Balandier has identified as the "supreme ruse of power"—the tactic of allowing itself to be "contested *ritually* in order to consolidate itself more effectively."[18] By according sexual power that shades into political seditiousness to the feminine, Wedekind may have believed himself to be liberating eros from bourgeois constraints, but he also established a social rationale for controlling female sexuality by punishing transgressive behavior. Once Lulu deviates from the script that dictates self-effacing compliance with the rigid cultural codes and social conventions governing femininity, she falls prey to a variety of strategies for mortification and containment, the most radical of which is set forth by Jack the Ripper, but all of which point to her death.

While Wedekind's plays offer a compelling account of what motivated and legitimated the presence of Jack the Ripper in German "high culture," they offer little more than a hint about why sexual murder came to figure so prominently in Germany's artistic production during the war years and during the Weimar era. Let us return, for a moment, to look at the date of George Grosz's self-representation as Jack the Ripper. It was in 1918, a year when many German men might indeed be bent on revenge, that Grosz had himself photographed as "the Avenger." To my mind, it is no coincidence that this photograph was made in 1918, and not in 1914 or in 1933. Some of the writers, artists, and filmmakers in this book may never have seen a trench or inhaled mustard gas; others may not have been brutalized by the war or unnerved by the taste of defeat. Yet all of them must in some ways have been implicated in the psychic fall-out of the war years: the sense of resentment directed against victors, noncombatants, and military chiefs alike; the crisis of male subjectivity occasioned by a sense of military defeat; and a painfully acute sense of the body's vulnerability to fragmentation, mutilation, and dismemberment.

That fantasies of sexual assault on women might be driven by the combination of resentment, self-doubt, and vulnerability experienced by several generations of German men seems almost inevitable in the context of the asymmetrical effect of the war on men and on women. The amputees everywhere testified to the brutalization of men's bodies in the theaters of war. Women, who had escaped the shells and shrapnel of the trenches and survived the war with bodies intact, could easily slide into the role of a covert enemy, one that had cheered them on and had thereby become complicit in plunging them into physically devastating military combat. In addition, women's growing visibility in the labor force during the war years was perceived to be a daunting economic challenge and to some extent explains what one critic calls "the defensive reaction toward *woman* in the discourses of artists and intellectuals."[19] Advances in legal rights may have been slow— women were prohibited from attending public meetings or joining political organizations up to 1908, and they did not cast their first ballots until 1919— but that did not alter the perception that women posed a threat to the social, economic, and political balance of power.

It is not always easy to determine the extent to which the war experience motivated representations of *Lustmord* in a strange effort to balance the gender scales of carnal violence, though a number of artists speak endlessly about the brutalizing effect of the war on their psyches even as they remain entirely silent about economic, sexual, or psychological rivalries with women. But taking a closer look at military battles and at the ways in which they compare to, contrast with, or are causally linked to sexual conflict makes good historical sense, if only because the war experience left so profound a mark on survivors—among them the artists Otto Dix and George Grosz, whose work is the subject of the first two case studies in this volume.

While the violent assault on the male body unfailingly receives attentive analysis, the female corpses from the postwar era are often passed over with embarrassed silence. The carnage of World War I became the subject of numerous drawings, paintings, autobiographies, novels, films, and photographs. Veterans and non-veterans alike strained their artistic resources to present grim scenes in which combatants saw their first decaying corpse, unearthed body parts while digging trenches, or witnessed the sudden, explosive deaths of comrades. The unsparing detail of both verbal and visual accounts suggests a coercive moment based on the need to direct the reader or spectator to see with the soldier—to identify with his vision and to experience with him the profound shock, horror, and grief of combat. Some writers, most notably Ernst Jünger, but others as well, were able to glorify and aestheticize even trench warfare. Descriptions of battle might place the ravaging effects of war on display, but they also revealed combat to be an opportunity for transcendent heroism. Other writers presented the act of witnessing the human carnage of World War I as a turning point marking the conversion to a pacifist, or at least morally engaged, stance. Critical commentary on war novels or on photographs from the front almost invariably emphasizes the transformative power of representation; seeing or being subjected to graphic descriptions purportedly gives rise to revulsion against war and promotes a decisively antimilitarist position.

Our cultural willingness to face, look at, and engage in the ethical issues raised by the gore of the battlefields is paralleled by a pronounced cultural disavowal of the unheroic victims of sexual pathologies. While there appears to be a certain moral and social obligation to face up to the horrors of war or to honor its victims as heroes, no such code governs the casualties of what we call random acts of violence, particularly when, as is so often the case in real life and in fiction, the victim is a prostitute. "You have to look at that" gives way to "How can you possibly look at that?"—a sentence I found myself repeating more than once while at work on this book. In the course of this study, I try to identify the ideological factors that compel us to look at victims and to empathize with their pain or to turn away from them with revulsion and repress the feelings stirred by the sight of suffering. Yet, as noted earlier, the gesture of aversion is often coupled with its kindred opposite. Few of us can deny a voyeuristic fascination with the sight of what is our common lot. In looking at murder victims, it is easy enough to become transfixed by the sight of a body in the state of biological disintegration—to experience a secret sense of pleasure at having escaped that destiny, and to observe that pleasure turn to fear and revulsion as we contemplate the sight of the inevitable fate of our own bodies. What is particularly frightening about this fascination is the way in which it bonds us, if only for a moment, with the perpetrators of violence, drawing us into a kind of complicitous gaze at the victim.

That our ideological and cultural station determines the field of our perception and shapes our response to images and events becomes acutely apparent when we consider the range of reactions to a work like Otto Dix's harrowing *Sexual Murder* (*Lustmord*, 1922) (fig. 2). It seems almost impossible to ignore the referential aspect of this painting, yet in one instance after another art historians use the tactics to which I referred earlier in order to

2. Otto Dix, *Sexual Murder* (1922). The eviscerated corpse, the gash in the wall, and the overturned chair form a triangular space that contrasts sharply with the elaboration of a bourgeois social space marked by the hanging lamp, the table, and the window into a world of architectural order. Woman is marked here as a figure of biological dis-order and social disruption.

efface the explicit, literal image on the canvas. One critic singles out Dix's canvases of murdered women (there are many, though this one ranks among the most lurid) for their "intensely glowing colors" and "grotesque humor," which give them a "special appeal." Another treats the scene as wholly unremarkable—a mere "genre convention," to speak with De Palma—noting only that the room in which the corpse of *Lustmord* reposes resembles Dix's room as a student. He then moves on to make his real point: that the rent of fifty marks per month posed a serious hardship for the struggling young artist.[20] These two distancing gestures, the one focusing on formal features and abstract aesthetic issues, the other on extraneous biographical details about the producer of the canvas, make even the most sensational subject matter recede into invisibility.

It may be easy enough to make Dix's female corpse vanish, but it is also possible to take the full measure of the mutilated body on the canvas by squarely facing it and investigating the conditions for its representation. *Sexual Murder* freezes a moment right after death—the blood is still trickling from the body and gathering in pools. But the killer has had sufficient time to make his getaway, and the painting itself does not reveal the agent of the crime. If we look at an earlier painting by Dix, *Sex Murderer: Self-Portrait* (1920) (fig. 3), it becomes clear that one reason for the absence of a sympathetic edge to the victim's portrayal in the later painting is the unequivocal self-identification with the murderer in this portrait. In the cartoonishly surreal self-portrait, Dix depicts himself with a mock ferocious expression, wielding the bloody knife used to dismember a woman in a room with the very lamp and chair of the later *Sexual Murder*. As if to drive home his complicity with the represented murderer, Dix "signed" the self-portrait with his own incriminating red handprints. As he confided to a friend who was disturbed by the work: "I had to get it out of me—that was all!", thereby affirming murderous urges (and their link to sexual drives) even as he foreclosed, through art, the possibility of ever enacting them in real life.[21]

Dix's *Sexual Murder* of 1922 is a copycat crime in that it is based on police photographs of a prostitute murdered in Hamburg in 1900. The photographs were published, along with those of other victims of sexual murder, in Erich Wulffen's *The Sexual Criminal*, a work that was evidently studied with care by Dix.[22] Thus we can read Dix's *Sexual Murder* as conflating a referential image of the victim of a historical killing with the imaginative construction of a murder committed in the mind of the artist. Both these dimensions of the work require critical attention, particularly since references to the cultural and autobiographical are so self-consciously fashioned by the artist.

In a later chapter on Dix, I deal with the autobiographical dimensions of *Sexual Murder*, particularly those that pertain to artistic production as an expressive release for murderous urges. For the moment, however, I want to focus on some of the general issues raised by representations of an assault of this magnitude on the female body. The female body draped across the bed is turned 180 degrees from its position in the police photograph and deliberately posed in a fashion reminiscent of eroticized female bodies—Henry Fuseli's *Nightmare* comes to mind, with its idealized representation of female

3. Otto Dix, *Sex Murderer: Self-Portrait* (1920). The artist portrays himself here as a murderer, slicing body parts in a moment of savage homicidal frenzy. Notwithstanding the cartoonlike, surreal style, the painting conveys both the rage of the assaulter and the terror of the victim.

beauty. In stark contrast to Fuseli's image of ethereal plenitude or to such fetishized icons of physical perfection as Manet's *Olympia*, Dix's subject appears as a disruptive figure, the decomposing body in what might otherwise be a composition of classic order. The mutilated body, enclosed in an interior, confined space, has been violently torn open to reveal a messiness that spills out onto its surface to produce a mass of undifferentiated, physically repulsive flesh. No contrast could be stronger than the one between the gash in the mangled corpse and the framed window into the architectonic order of the outdoor space. The body of the woman, attired in such a way as to make her professional identity as prostitute unmistakable, represents a figure of biological dis-order and stands in the most forceful possible contrast to the architectural severity of the public space figured outside the window. The body, as a source of pollution, taints the interior space, covering the sheets and floor with blood, reflecting its inner gore in the mirror on the wall, spreading its disruptive power to the overturned chair, and reflecting its wound in the torn wallpaper above the bed. As Elisabeth Bronfen has pointed out, the feminine body has come to be affiliated with "the polluting world of biology, with the time-bound individual, with corrupting flesh, with the putrescence of the corpse, with a 'bad' death."[23] To represent the assault on this body is to reveal its "essence" and at the same time, through the assault, to transcend the "bad" death of femininity for the cultural organization and order symbolized in the view from the window.

Artistic representations of sexual murder usually fix on the victim, showing the female corpse in varying degrees of decay and putrefaction. Images, unable to accommodate sequential narrative, leave us with little but a blank when it comes to murderer and motive. We have only the corpus delicti, a body frozen in an unnerving moment of postmortem disfiguration. But the artist, by representing the image of bodily decay on the one hand and arresting the process of decomposition through his own composition on the other, becomes less criminal perpetrator than cultural hero. It is his biographical connection with what is represented and his artistic brilliance in representing it that eclipses the subject matter on the canvas and, as we have seen, turns him and his transcendent artistic authority into the subject of critical analysis. The corpse vanishes as the work of art and its creator enter the foreground to serve as the center of attention.

In fictional and cinematic accounts of sexual murder, by contrast, it is usually the killer and his psychosis that occupy center stage. We may see his victims, experience their terror, and feel revulsion at what happens to them, but—unless they are children—they often remain undistinguished, interchangeable figures in a series. It is only the *potential* victims, especially those who double as detectives, who become singular in the narrative. When we

do not know "whodunit," our attention is riveted on the detective work and
its elaboration of an enigma. Often we know "whodunit" from the start, and
our attention becomes fixated on the pathology of the murderer and on the
effects of the investigative process on him. The identity of the serial murderer—his motives, his own position as victim, and his dread in the face of
discovery—become the "figure" to the "ground" of his casualties in just the
way that the artist and his technique become foregrounded in discussions of
visual representations of victims of sexual murder. In both cases the victim
disappears as we concentrate on the agent of murder, on his identity, his
method, or his transgressive genius. Artistic identity and masculine identity
come to be founded on and constituted through acts of disfiguring, murderous violence.

The effacement of the victim becomes particularly problematic in light of
the way in which the agents of murder are often exonerated of guilt, positioned as cultural heroes, and declared to be the casualties of their sacrificial
victims. Paintings, novels, and films may present us with crimes committed
only in the imagination, but the defense mechanisms used to come to terms
with those crimes both shape and comment on social realities. Alexander and
Margarete Mitscherlich have written with eloquent candor about the collective denial of guilt and the positioning of the guilty self as the victim of evil
forces in Germany after World War II—though they do not explore whether
the culture of denial they identify existed long before 1945. "In these attempts
to shake off guilt," they note in their description of German efforts to come
to terms with the Holocaust, "it is remarkable how little attention is paid to
the victims, either to those on one's own side or those on the other. . . . If
somehow, somewhere, one finds an object deserving of sympathy, it usually
turns out to be none other than oneself."[24] They further note that "identification with the innocent victim is frequently substituted for mourning" and
that the Germans saw themselves as victims of "evil forces: first the evil Jews,
then the evil Nazis, and finally the evil Russians."[25] Thus even if one takes the
view that the imaginative enactments of crimes served a prophylactic purpose, as they seemingly did for Dix, a question remains: To what degree is
the disfiguring violence presented in a sympathetic light, drawing attention
to the perpetrator's entitlement to discharge his "evil" urges and effacing the
suffering of the victim? To what extent do these works legitimize murderous
violence, providing for it a socially acceptable outlet? Do the "aesthetically
pleasing" images of fictive victims contaminate our perception of the real-life
victims, leading us to look at their corpses as works of art? Why else would
Joyce Carol Oates, in an essay on serial killers, write of the "nude, violated
corpses of abducted boys and girls" that appeared like "nightmare artworks"
in affluent Detroit suburbs?[26]

While this study is concerned with making victims visible and understanding the cultural significance of the violated female corpse put on display or shielded from sight, it also probes both the aesthetic and psychological questions raised by looking at the motives of the agent—the agent as an artist who puts murder on the written page, on the stage, on the screen, or on a canvas, or the agent as a man who commits murder in fact. It also questions whether the representation of violence can shade into real-life violence and whether the production of violent images is not in some ways predicated on the desire to violate real-life bodies. Does art, as Dix claimed it did, have a preventive function, foreclosing on the desire to commit murder in real life, or does it feed what criminologists call the twentieth-century epidemic of violence? To what extent do stories about sexual murder polarize gender roles and perpetuate notions about sadistic male violence inflicted on passive female victims? These and other issues are raised as I look first at the real-life killers, then at the artists who saw in them kindred spirits, and finally at their fictional and cinematic counterparts. My discussion of serial murderers and representations of *Lustmord* in Weimar Germany begins only after an inquiry into our own cultural understanding of sexual killers.

"Ask Mother": The Construction
of Sexual Murder

A boy's best friend is his mother.

Anthony Perkins as Norman Bates in Psycho

I SHALL BEGIN by looking at the killers—Jack the Ripper, the Lipstick Killer, the Vampire of Düsseldorf, the Boston Strangler, Son of Sam, to name just a few—and at the ways in which we have read and probed the minds of fictional and historical sexual murderers to produce a composite image that straddles the line between mythical construction and psychological realism. The figures discussed in this chapter commit what forensic experts variously call sexual murder, serial murder, mass murder, recreational murder, and rape-murder. Alfred Hitchcock's term for the agent, "criminal sexual psychopath," names the three most important areas implicated in the deeds that mark these men as deviants. Although that designation is too cumbersome to adopt here—and for some too controversial (note that the American Psychiatric Association substituted the term "sociopath" for "psychopath," then replaced the latter term with "antisocial personality disorder")—it forcefully reminds us of the ways in which cases of compulsive murderers who derive some measure of sexual satisfaction from their crimes muster a full range of problems touching on laws and their transgression, on gender and sexual violence, and on the pathology of mental life.[1]

Sexual murder, as Cameron and Frazer have argued, is a *"fuzzy* category with unclear boundaries," for it is never really possible to determine the degree to which sexual gratification is at work as a motive. Furthermore, one could assert that any murder has a sadistic, hence erotic component, to it.[2] In Norman Mailer's *An American Dream*, Stephen Rojack, a professor of existential psychology "with the not inconsiderable thesis that magic, dread, and the perception of death were the roots of motivation," sees murder as an eroticized release for hatred: "There is something manly about containing your rage, it is so difficult, it is like carrying a two-hundred-pound safe up a cast-iron hill. The exhilaration comes I suppose from possessing such strength. . . . Murder offers the promise of vast relief. It is never unsexual."[3]

In Rojack's logic, violence becomes not only a substitute for sexual activity, but a superior mode for releasing the ultimately unbearable tension generated by the "manly" act of containing rage. Here is Rojack's description of his feelings as he is murdering his wife Deborah:

> I released the pressure on her throat, and the door I had been opening began to close. But I had had a view of what was on the other side of the door, and heaven was there, some quiver of jeweled cities shining in the glow of a tropical dusk, and I thrust against the door once more. . . . I was driving now with force against that door: spasms began to open in me. . . . Some black-biled lust, some desire to go ahead not unlike the instant one comes in a woman against her cry that she is without protection came bursting with rage from out of me and my mind exploded in a fireworks of rockets, stars, and hurtling embers.[4]

Desire has been inverted in this frenzied rage that mimes and intensifies the orgasmic intensity of sexual contact. Murder affords a transcendent rather than a bodily experience ("my mind exploded"). Instead of feeling mere physical gratification, the murderer has an unmediated vision of what lies beyond life ("a view of what was on the other side of the door"). The female body in its death throes becomes the site of a transcendent experience that negates sexuality even as it uses it as a vehicle for a privileged moment of insight.

Sexual murderer and serial murderer are probably the two most common designations for the figures discussed in this chapter—the one term emphasizing the nature of the pathology (violence is eroticized to become a substitute for sex), the other the compulsion to repeat. Mass murderers, by contrast, have an array of motives for their killing sprees (foremost among them revenge and a need to take justice into their own hands) and do not necessarily labor under the compulsion to repeat at intervals. Acting out of desperation, they kill their victims en masse, as many as possible as quickly as possible, and often commit suicide or expose themselves to gunfire once they have let loose their rage.[5]

For serial murderers and sexual murderers (I will use the terms virtually interchangeably since the latter is a subcategory of the former and each term captures different aspects of the killer's pathology), flouting the law and terrorizing a specific group targeted for revenge constitute nothing more than secondary gains. While the term serial murder reduces the killer's victims to mere links in a chain and thereby suggests that they are all ciphers for a concealed target of homicidal rage, the term sexual murder captures the passionate mixture of desire and cruelty that drives the killer. "These were crimes of passion, not profit," the psychiatrist in *Psycho* sanctimoniously, but also correctly, declares. Coterminous with sadism because of the sexual pleasure derived from a savagely brutal act, sexual murder is also often linked with necrophilia through the symptom of erotic attachment to dead flesh.

It will, then, come as no surprise that sexual murderers are flanked by sadists and necrophiles in one of the earliest accounts of sexual murder. Richard von Krafft-Ebing, author of the *Psychopathia sexualis* (1885), drew special attention to sexual murder (*Lustmord*) and marked it as a distinctive type of crime characterized by savage physical assault on an object of desire and morbid fascination with the body's interior:

> The presumption of a murder out of lust is always given when injuries of the genitals are found, the character and extent of which are such as could not be explained by merely a brutal attempt at coitus; and, still more, when the body has been opened, or parts (intestines, genitals) torn out and are wanting.[6]

What makes the sexual murderer particularly horrifying is his drive to mutilate the body he desires, to violate the biological integrity of his victim, to become the destructive counterpart to the lover/healer. It is this need, what Foucault has called an "insane dialogue of love and death," that differentiates him from other killers and gives rise to a unique moral, legal, and psychiatric discourse about his crimes.[7]

According to Colin Wilson, Jack the Ripper "inaugurated the age of sex crime."[8] But who was Jack the Ripper? To this day the identity of the man who murdered and mutilated five prostitutes in the Whitechapel area of London's East End remains so shrouded in mystery that it has been easy to construct countless fictional Jack the Rippers. There is Jack as deranged physician—only a man practiced in surgical skills could have disemboweled the corpses so swiftly; there is the Jewish Jack—as social agitator, ritual butcher (*schochet*), or as polluter who murders sexual pariahs; there is Jack the socialist crusader and agent provocateur whose murders were designed to call attention to the squalor and poverty of the East End; there is Jack the decadent aristocrat, who satisfied his lust on miserable and defenseless women.[9] This multitude of identities has contributed to the creation of what one "Ripperologist" has called the legend of Jack the Ripper, a man who is "part–folk hero, part-myth."[10] Because Jack the Ripper lacks a stable social and historical identity, he can be reinvented by each age to stand as the most notorious example of male sexual violence. That he is endlessly refigured, as the spooky stalker of Paul Leni's *Waxworks* (1924) or as General Jack D. Ripper in Stanley Kubrick's *Dr. Strangelove* (1964), reveals the degree to which cultural production is invested in depictions of murderous aggression against women. Though there was once a real person who terrorized the East End from August to November of 1888, "Jack the Ripper" has become more fictional construct than historical figure; he seems in his natural element when flanked by Dracula and Frankenstein's monster, rather than by the sexual murderers Peter Kürten or Peter Sutcliffe.[11]

While the deeds of Jack the Ripper are by no means unprecedented, there is a way in which his reputation has entered the collective cultural conscious-ness in a singular way to produce a well-defined profile for the sexual mur-derer: a lone male who preys on powerless or socially marginalized figures and whose violent mutilation of the body becomes a substitute for sexual release. It was, however, not just the mystery of the killer's identity, the social status of his victims, and the grisly mutilations that created a sensa-tional cultural identity for Jack the Ripper. The real murderer communicated to the public through the newspapers (along with many pretenders who aspired to his name—the files of Scotland Yard hold some 350 letters from Jack the Ripper, of which two or three at most are from the hand of the actual killer), and the press engaged itself with unprecedented intensity in his crim-inal career. The *Illustrated Police News*, a penny weekly, devoted a total of 184 cover pictures to the Ripper crimes and was still writing about the case in 1892.[12] As early as October 1888 the *Lancet* denounced the sensationalizing of the murders in the press:

> Today, the press takes care to report at inordinate length, and often with objectionable minuteness, the details of the latest murder, divorce or fash-ionable scandal. The Whitechapel tragedies have afforded a typical case in point—what with gruesome descriptions of the victims, elaborate conjec-tures as to the precise mode and motive for the crimes, and interminable theories as to the best means of discovering the criminal, one would think that the thoughts of the entire nation were practically absorbed in the contemplation of revolting wickedness.[13]

Punch also took the high moral ground when it fretted about "the effect of these gigantic pictures of violence and assassination by knife . . . on the mor-bid imaginations of imbalanced minds" and declared news coverage of the murders to be "a blot on our civilization."[14] What bothered the writers for the *Lancet* and for *Punch* most was the fear that newspaper accounts would "infect" Britain's youth and inspire copycats with a craving for the kind of attention received by Jack.[15] Jack the Ripper thus figured as a double menace: he created a state of alarm in the East End but also promoted a kind of moral panic among the upper social classes about the effect of crime reporting on the young and on the working classes.

The preoccupation with the sensationalism surrounding the murders was, in a sense, a not so subtle pretext for endless opportunities to read up on the murders and to talk ceaselessly about them as a symptom of degeneration and as a source of constant danger. The "ruinous effect" of reading histories of murder, the Lancet reported, "cannot be denied. . . . Youth, untrained in right principle, perhaps overworked, physically and mentally morbid from the want of fresh air and sufficient house room, affords a ground already prepared to receive the tares of this injurious teaching."[16] This discourse of danger in turn intensified the need for further pontifications and fulminations.[17] But all the talk generated by the murders, whether it went into grisly anatomical detail or veered off into anxious pronouncements about urban degeneracy, may have had a deeper meaning, one that Judith Walkowitz has proposed as an alternative explanation for appreciating the significance with which the Ripper murders were invested. The Ripper episode, she argues, "covertly sanctioned male antagonism toward women and buttressed male authority over them. . . . Women were relegated to the interior of a prayer meeting or their homes, behind locked doors; men were left to patrol the public spaces and the street."[18] In reinscribing the notion of female vulnerability and male dominance (with men figuring simultaneously as threatening presences and as necessary protectors), talk of the Ripper murders created, whether consciously or not, powerfully stabilizing arguments about gender roles.

Sexual murders arouse both curiosity and anxiety. Unlike most homicides, they present us with a stubbornly enigmatic and threatening constellation of events, even after they have been solved. This is not to say that all other types of murders are transparent and lend themselves readily to coherent accounts of their motivation. But they are often committed within the familiar parameters of greed, revenge, sexual jealousy—feelings to which most people have fallen prey at one time or another, even if not to a murderous degree. These homicides may be repellent and disturbing, yet they usually do not defy comprehension, instead offering a link between killer and victim so direct as to secure a sense of protection from further harm. By contrast, few can fathom the compulsion to which the sexual murderer is a slave. His crimes become terrifying precisely because they seem to be gratuitous acts with no self-evident material profit or psychological gain. Since the killer strikes "without reason," he creates a reign of terror in which everyone feels at risk because anyone can be the target of his homicidal mania, even when in practice the victims may be predominantly prostitutes or homosexual men.

It is not only the apparent or real randomness of the homicides that creates an exaggerated sense of public danger when a sexual murderer is on the loose. Because the murderer often shows no signs of derangement and because he does not display the conventional marks of criminal behavior, it is impossible to identify him, to anticipate his moves, or even to perceive any risk. So-called psychological profiles remain almost worthless, for they do little more than emphasize the gravity of the threat or the deceptively benign facade offered by the killer to the world. "You're dealing with a very danger-ous psychopath," warns the psychiatrist called in to advise the police about the serial murderer in *Basic Instinct*, a film virtually unique in its identification of sexual murder with a female assailant. Equally penetrating wisdom is offered in Fritz Lang's *M*, when an official declares that the murderer is probably a person who "looks harmless" and who "probably wouldn't hurt a flea" under ordinary circumstances.[19] Everyone remains at a loss when it comes to identification. In real life, most killers, one study concedes, are caught by sheer chance. David Berkowitz, for example, was called in for police questioning only after his illegally parked car was ticketed near the scene of a murder; Joel Rivkin was arrested after officers stopped him for a traffic violation and found a woman's body in his pick-up truck.[20] The signs that normally alert the citizenry to peril are absent (Hitchcock delighted in the fact that the notorious John Christie was a "bald, mild, little man, very calm"), thus making every person a potential suspect and creating an atmo-sphere conducive to mob rule and paranoid behavior.[21] Because the sexual murderer can both kill anyone and be anyone, he is able to terrorize a com-munity, to create a palpable sense of panic that contrasts starkly with the quiet invisibility of his own psychosis.

Adding to the dread and hostility stirred by the sexual murderer's random choice of victim and by his ability to blend into the crowd is the horror aroused by the crimes themselves. The mutilation and maiming of the vic-tims goes against nature, transgressing all moral and social laws. Here again, Jack the Ripper provides the precedent:

> It is probable that he first cut the throats of his victims, then ripped open the abdomen and groped among the intestines. In some instances he cut off the genitals and carried them away; in others he only tore them to pieces and left them behind. He does not seem to have had sexual intercourse with his victims, but very likely the murderous act and subsequent mutila-tion of the corpse were equivalents for the sexual act.[22]

The offense lies not only in the nature of the violation but also in the scandal-ous perversion of erotic urges, in which sexual satisfaction is achieved through the violence of murder. While the criminal can be caught and brought to "justice," it is rarely possible to fathom fully the source of his pathology, to read his mind and understand exactly what drove him to murder.

The challenge of understanding the sexual murderer, along with other

criminals who commit seemingly gratuitous acts of violence, was responsible for what Foucault has called the "psychiatrization of criminal danger"—a
development that becomes fully manifest in cinematic narratives about sexual murder, which all seem to include at least one obligatory appearance by
a psychiatrist and sometimes culminate in a parodistic twist when the psychiatrist *is* the killer, as in, most recently, *Dressed to Kill*, *Silence of the Lambs*, and
Basic Instinct (which adds a further twist by making the killer a woman).[23] In
all these films, we have an ironic reversal of the notion that deviant behavior
produces the psychiatric profession. Despite the intervention of psychiatry
into the legal profession, in courtroom practice, there is a steadfast resistance
to accepting the insanity plea at the very outer limit of criminal behavior.
When criminality and insanity collapse into one category, the call for expert
psychiatric testimony nearly always turns out to be a charade, for a morally
outraged jury invariably responds to the brutality of the deeds by convicting
a defendant on criminal charges.

Branded a maniac, beast, monster, or vampire, the sexual murderer often
escapes psychiatric and legal definition by moving into a special category
beyond human terms. He does not need to be analyzed in conventional ways
because he represents a "unique" deviation from the norm, an anomaly that
can become less troubling than it should be because it is defined as "other"
and "alien" rather than as the product of a familiar social reality. In speaking
of the Yorkshire Ripper, Colin Wilson has pointed out how easy it was to
label him a creature of nightmare, even when the real mystery had to do
with "what peculiar pressures turned this quiet man into a maniac who stole
up behind women in the dark, smashed their skulls with blows from a ball-
headed hammer, then pulled up their skirts and blouses and carefully inflicted dozens of wounds with a specially sharpened screwdriver."[24]

This need to mount a special discourse for talking about sexual murderers
and to construct a disease-ridden, subhuman stereotype of them made it all
the more shocking when such murderers were apprehended and turned out
to be "everyone's next-door neighbor."[25] In the face of the sexual murderer's
ordinariness, the elaborate construct of an infectious monster collapses, giving way to a second attempt to deflect attention from continuities between
the murderer and his milieu, one implicit in Colin Wilson's description of
how the Yorkshire Ripper turned from "a quiet man" into a "maniac."

Commentators at the trials of mass murderers frequently account for the
aura of sanity that surrounds the accused by theorizing about a split personality. While the sane persona routinely goes about his business in the everyday
world—delivering mail, sweeping floors, or attending law school classes—a
crazed self periodically emerges to commit horrifying deeds completely alien
to the other half of the self. Once again continuities between "normal" and

"insane" are denied, and the notion of a beast in human garb is reinscribed; the "diseased," evil side of the killer's personality emerges in the form of a maniac without any relation whatsoever to the ordinary, human self. The murderers themselves, once apprehended, often eagerly embrace the idea of two selves: Peter Sutcliffe *and* the Yorkshire Ripper, Peter Kürten *and* the Vampire of Düsseldorf, or Albert DeSalvo *and* the Boston Strangler. An exception (if only until the full opportunistic possibilities of the Jekyll and Hyde plea became evident) can be found in the case of the Chicago serial murderer John Wayne Gacy. Here is how Gacy's biographer reports the murderer's reaction to the proposal that he was suffering from a split personality:

> At first John wouldn't accept any of this crazy crap. He told the docs he didn't want to apply that Jekyll and Hyde shit to himself. He didn't even want to think about it because "that's running away from reality." John was committed to honesty in analyzing himself, and he hoped the docs would see that. He told them he wasn't going "to blame somebody else" for something he did.[26]

Gacy's statement succinctly explains the instant appeal of the Jekyll/Hyde theory for apprehended murderers, some of whom feign split or multiple personalities in order to exculpate their "true" selves, and most of whom suffer from dissociation, what Gacy called the "Other Guy tilt" of his personality.[27]

Once we move beyond the stereotypes of the killer as a degenerate, a diseased monster, or a split personality to an exploration of the "peculiar pressures" that allow the man and the maniac to coexist, the experts all seem to disagree, today as at other times. There are biological explanations relying on studies of everything from chromosomes through hormones to body type; there are pop-psychological accounts and orthodox psychoanalytic considerations; and there are social explanations that investigate victimology, subcultures of violence, the effects of capitalist economies on human behavior, and so on.[28]

A narrow focus on any one particular avenue of inquiry reveals just how deeply flawed monocausal explanations can be. No one has yet found the biological, psychoanalytic, or sociological key to decoding the mystery of sexual murder. What we can clearly identify, however, is the way in which our culture mystifies the notion of sexual murder and constructs a stereotypical perpetrator on the basis of what we read in the paper, what we find in books, or what we see at the movies rather than on the basis of the actual historical cases.

Let us begin with the view, disseminated in its most popular form in the films of Alfred Hitchcock, that sexual murderers are driven to their crimes either by hostile mothers who torment their sons by regulating their every move or by seductive mothers who undermine the efforts of their sons to achieve masculine autonomy.[29] I shall take this view as my point of departure because it is the most prominent explanatory model in our own culture and because it is deeply rooted in representational practices surrounding serial murder in Germany in the 1920s. As we shall see, depictions of *Lustmord* in the era following World War I frequently become implicated not only in issues of sex, violence, and gender but also in issues of maternity, mastery, and (pro)creation, with artists and writers entering into competition with the reproductive powers of the maternal body or striving to contain the unruly sexuality of the female body and appropriate its seductive allure by placing it on display.

Accepting the logic of arguments about the hostile and/or seductive mother as the source of homicidal urges directed at women means that even Adolf Hitler can be exonerated of guilt for his cold-blooded brutality, for he becomes nothing more than the victim of a perversely sadistic mother. Karl Menninger, for example, asks:

> Who can look fairly at the bitterness, the hatefulness, the sadistic cruelty of Adolf Hitler without wondering what Hitler's mother did to him that he now repays to millions of other helpless ones? We must remind ourselves again and again that the men by whom women are frustrated are the grown-up sons of mothers who were chiefly responsible for the personality of those sons.[30]

Menninger never specifies "what Hitler's mother did to him"—he can only "wonder" about it, never once taking the trouble to investigate the factual basis for his claim. Whatever it was, she becomes "chiefly responsible" for the personality of her son. We happen to know that Klara Hitler lost three children to diphtheria about a year before Adolf was born, but we know virtually nothing about how she actually treated her son. Most biographers report only that she indulged him (a claim so general and so stereotypical as to be meaningless) and quite sensibly do not try to forge an explicit link between maternal indulgence and filial pathology. The case is quite different for Hitler's father: we know that he regularly beat his son, though one biographer dismisses this fact by noting that "in the Austria of those days severe beatings of children were not uncommon, being considered good for the soul."[31] We also know that Hitler believed his father to be an alcoholic and recounted scenes of "abominable shame" in which he had to pull his father out of "reeking, smoky taverns."[32] This autobiographical recollection, whether true or not, never found its way into Menninger's speculations.

As I have noted, mother-hating and its perceived effect, woman-hating, has become our culture's most prevalent mode for explaining the murderous rampages of sexual killers. Take the case of Albert DeSalvo, the Boston Strangler, for whom a psychiatric committee constructed an "expert" profile of "an impotent male bearing an unendurable rage toward his mother and all women like her." Susan Brownmiller summarizes their report:

> The Strangler's mother was probably dead, they agreed, but during his childhood she had walked about "half-exposed in their apartment, but punished him severely for any sexual curiosity." Consumed by mother hatred, the psychiatrists divined, the Strangler had chosen to murder and mutilate old women in a manner "both sadistic and loving."[33]

The so-called experts showed little interest in DeSalvo's father, whom Brownmiller indicts for the criminal behavior of the son:

> The consuming rage DeSalvo bore was uncompromisingly directed against his drunken, brutalizing father, who had regularly beaten him, his mother and the other children during a wretched youth. DeSalvo's father had engaged in sex acts with prostitutes in front of his children, had taught his son to shoplift, had broken every finger on his wife's hand and knocked out her teeth, and had gone on periodic rampages where he smashed up all the furniture in the house. As a final act of rejection he abandoned the family when Albert was eight.[34]

Despite the flurry of attention directed at the domineering mothers of serial killers by psychiatrists, the press, and filmmakers, the murderers themselves tell a story that resonates with paternal abuse. Here is the voice of "Son of Sam," a man whose self-fashioned moniker points to a paternal connection with his murderous rages:

> When father Sam gets drunk he gets mean. He beats his family. Sometimes he ties me up to the back of the house. Other times he locks me up in the garage. Sam loves to drink blood.
> "Go out and kill," commands father Sam. . . .
> "Mr. Borreli, sir, I don't want to kill anymore. No sur [sic], no more but I must, 'honour thy father.'"[35]

Here is Tim Cahill's effort to enter the mind of John Wayne Gacy—exceptional in its assignment of blame for the crimes of a serial murderer to an abusive father:

> Maybe drugs and alcohol set loose the Other Guy tilt to his personality. . . . There was, John told the docs, a lot of the Old Man in the Other Guy tilt. Now, take the Other Guy tilt during a blackout and apply it to some greedy

little hustler. You would get an angry, punishing father, an irrational alcoholic father who had to strike out. . . . The corpse would be found in the
morning with the dawning of sobriety, and it would be hidden in a father's
hiding place, in the basement, to be covered over and forgotten, like a
father's helpless drunken ravings.[36]

Rather than simply speculating on what drove Gacy to murder, Cahill recon-
structed what passed through Gacy's mind through extensive interviews and
investigative reporting. But his linking of paternal behavior with a grown
son's pathology may also miss the mark by seeking a monocausal explanation for a complex syndrome. While there is robust statistical evidence documenting that serial murderers as a group suffer traumatic neglect or abuse as
children, there are also many neglected and abused children who do not
express their sense of abandonment and rage by killing. In reviewing actual
case histories of sexual murderers (bearing in mind that some of the killers
deny abuse where it existed while others exaggerate it), it becomes clear that
abusive parents—tyrannical fathers at least as often as overbearing mothers—figure prominently, but they may be more correlate than cause.[37]

Cinematic constructions of sexual murderers have, to a remarkable degree, shaped our understanding of real-life killers, with the construction
sometimes eclipsing or eradicating the facts. Ever since *Psycho* (1960), the link
between overbearing mothers and male sexual rage directed against women
has become so strong that a filmmaker has only to evoke the name "Mother"
to explain a murderer's crazed actions. Hitchcock's *Frenzy*, made a dozen
years after *Psycho*, requires no more than a few brief allusions—a picture of
Rusk's mother in his apartment, a few passing references to her, and the sight
of her head at a window—to establish just who is really responsible for the
deeds of the notorious "tie-murderer."[38] I use the term "responsible for"
advisedly, for the psychiatric gloss to *Psycho*, included as a coda to the film,
makes it clear that "Norman Bates" was not the killer: it was, rather, the
"mother-half of Norman's mind" that committed the murders. Norman's
mother, we learn, was a "clinging, demanding woman" who forged a pathologically intense bond with her son, but then, when she "met a man," failed
to meet the needs she had fostered. Not only did she deserve her death
(Norman presumably poisoned her and her lover), she can also be held ac-
countable for the deaths of Norman's victims ("Mother killed the girl," the
psychiatrist declares). In the end, she takes over ("The battle is over, and the
dominant personality has won"), as signaled in the eerie superimposition of
a grinning skull over the incarcerated Norman's face.[39]

"Mother" has not only invaded Norman's mind, she has also entered his
body, turning him into an effeminate male who, though not technically a

transvestite (as the cinematic psychiatrist gravely declares), dons women's clothing when he commits violent acts and begins to merge bodily with the victim of his matricidal deed. (*Psycho*-imitators, most notably *Dressed to Kill* and *Silence of the Lambs*, have gone a step farther than Hitchcock to turn their killers into transvestites and frustrated candidates for transsexual surgery: Bobbi/Dr. Robert Elliot of *Dressed to Kill* is described as "pre-op transsexual," while "Buffalo Bill" in *The Silence of the Lambs* skins and flays his female victims in order to make what is described in the novel on which the film is based a "girl suit out of real girls."[40]) Unable to separate himself from his mother and to establish an adult male identity, Norman Bates is represented as both childlike and effeminate. He sleeps in a child's bed surrounded by toys and stuffed animals, remaining "permanently locked in childhood" even as he tries to escape it by assuming mother's identity.[41]

While the author of the novel on which the film *Psycho* is based wanted to write a story along "Freudian lines" and was determined to develop a hero who "had a thing about his mother," Hitchcock was also working in a cinematic tradition of feminized sexual murderers that reached back to the early 1930s when Fritz Lang, a director to whom he repeatedly paid homage, was making films in Weimar Germany. Lang's *M* (1931), which Hitchcock obviously knew long before 1936, when he made *Secret Agent* with Peter Lorre (who had also starred in *M*), features a murderer with a pudgy, childlike face and with what has been described as an "effeminate" look.[42] Like Norman Bates, who nervously snacks on candy corn while conversing with his next victim, the murderer in *M* is shown as a creature of regressive orality, always chewing on something. While we know nothing of Beckert's personal history, we quickly learn how his behavior is profoundly implicated in a need to win maternal attention by provoking maternal wrath. We would do well here to remember how Julia Kristeva writes of food as "the oral object (the abject) that sets up archaic relationships between the human being and the other, its mother, who wields a power that is as vital as it is fierce."[43] Of Beckert's deeper affiliations with mothers (it is no coincidence that the mother of one of his victims is named Frau *Beck*mann), I shall have more to say later.

Fritz Lang's *While the City Sleeps* (1955) reaffirmed both the feminization of sexual murderers and the way in which maternal behavior shapes the perverse drives of the murderer. "Ask Mother": these are the words tellingly scrawled with lipstick (hence the term "Lipstick Killer") on the walls of his victims' homes by Edward Mobley, the demented killer of Lang's film. As the killer reads *Strangler* magazine, he hears a radio broadcast in which a newscaster taunts him with these words: "You're a Mama's boy. The normal feeling of love that you should have toward your mother has been twisted into hatred. For her and all of her sex." Just who has done that twisting becomes clear when a knock on the door introduces "Mother," a pathetically timorous woman, on whom Mobley finally vents his anger, almost killing her, as he reveals the source of his psychosis:

> When you adopted me, you wanted a girl, didn't you? And he wanted a
> boy.... I remember once when I was eight years old. I was helping you
> dust the house and that woman from across the street came over and said,
> "My, my." And you said, "Yes, I know. He's exactly like a little girl, isn't
> he?"[44]

Norman Bates and Edward Mobley, the two principal pre-1960s cinematic models for sexual murderers are both men whose "twisted" mothers have so arrested their psychosexual development that they remain boys whose maternal attachment is marked, in the one case, by fatal excess and morbid identification, in the other, by an equally fatal depletion of affect and distancing. Not Norman Bates, but rather the "mother-half" of his mind, is the agent behind the mysterious disappearance of Marion Crane—it is "mother's" sexual envy that provides the motive for the murder and it is "mother" who gives Norman the pretext for wielding the knife in the shower. As for the "Lipstick Killer," the press has already made the diagnosis long before the murderer is apprehended: "You're a Mama's boy." Here again, the man who has been permanently locked into a feminine position through his identification with mother is the man who kills, though this time, instead of succumbing to the delusion of being mother and murdering her sexual rivals, he resists the delusion and attempts to eliminate her by killing "all of her sex."

For Norman Bates and his like (those who introject the "clinging, demanding" mothers they want to murder), a powerfully durable connection with sexuality is what turns women into targets of murderous assaults. Because Marion Crane moves and arouses Norman, she must be punished by "Mother" and becomes his next victim. Edward Mobley has very different motives when he kills. Because women incarnate femininity (the very quality he so loathes in himself), he labors under the compulsion to eradicate them and thus to remove the source of his sense of perpetual humiliation. Sexuality and femininity, both of which threaten the notion of autonomous masculinity held up as a social ideal, create unmanageable anxieties for these cinematic "mama's boys," who are unable to negotiate a "successful" Oedipal transition to adult heterosexuality. It is almost as if we have an inverted Oedipal situation, with a young male who wishes to kill his mother or succeeds in killing her and (in the absence of a father) will live in the company of men in a world he will have purged of women. Or we have a failed triangulation of desire, with mother and son locked in a relationship in which affect is so intensely polarized as to produce murderous rage along with abject self-effacement. Here, it is important to emphasize the degree to which these screenplays seem written directly out of Freud and perpetuate cultural stories about essentialist gender roles and family constellations that often do not square with the patterns that emerge from an analysis of real-life case histories of serial killers.

Recent psychoanalytic accounts of male developmental patterns and the formation of gender-identity also offer mother-centered explanations for sexual murder. Male gender identity, it has been argued, is more likely than its female counterpart to be invested with ambivalent or negative feelings for women, since boys must follow a path of development that requires radical separation from their early close identification with a female figure. A sense of loss through separation, fear that the separation will never be accomplished, and rage that the separation must be made in the first place can combine to create powerful feelings of resentment and fantasies of revenge.[45]

This foregrounding of a boy's feelings of loss, inadequacy, and rage reminds us of the degree to which our culture has fixed its attention on the maternal role as *the* determining factor in male pathology. How or whether a boy can negotiate the path from dependence to "masculine autonomy" becomes determined by a mother's relationship to her son. His feelings and his developmental patterns are orchestrated by her behavior alone. Hitchcock's line of thinking, which has played a powerful role in shaping popular psychology, goes so far as to erase the son's subjectivity completely—in the end he is nothing more than the secret agent of his mother's wishes.

In *Male Fantasies*, Klaus Theweleit has reflected on sexual murder, not as an act provoked by women, but as a natural corollary of the cultural construction of femininity. Through her association with the body, bleeding, and birth, woman becomes uniquely linked with mortality and provokes anxious fears even as she arouses erotic desire.

> It's as if two male compulsions were tearing at the women with equal strength. One is trying to push them away, to keep them at arm's length (defense); the other wants to penetrate them, to have them very near. Both compulsions seem to find satisfaction in the act of killing, where the man pushes the woman far away (takes her life), and gets very close to her (penetrates her with a bullet, stab wound, club, etc.). . . . Once she . . . is reduced to a pulp, a shapeless, bloody mass, the man can breathe a sigh of relief.[46]

For Elisabeth Bronfen, woman's link with birth and procreation, rather than connecting her with life, binds her to decay and makes her an object of dread rather than veneration: "The paradigmatic coupling of Woman and body serves to allegorize the aspect of corruption, vulnerability, and disembodiment inherent in human existence. . . . The conjunction of woman-death-womb-tomb reduces to the ambivalence that the mother's gift of birth is also the gift of death."[47] The cultural dread of women as agents conjoining corporality and death becomes a pretext for the effacement of the feminine in the service of male biological and psychological survival, along with transcendent aesthetic creativity. In this formulation, agency, responsibility, and guilt are shifted back from the female/feminine victim to the murderous subject, whose psychological needs and psychotic deeds become his own doing and undoing.

◆ ◆ ◆

This book seeks to map the cultural consequences of crimes—crimes enacted in real social settings and regulated by the legal and penal codes, then represented in the popular press, on the screen, on canvases, or in books. It will also study crimes fantasized in imaginative contexts, then reworked and produced as artifacts judged for their aesthetic and ethical value. As we move along a Moebius strip, with historical experience on one side and cultural production on the other, there will be many moments when the one imperceptibly shifts into the other, effacing itself on one side even as it inscribes itself on the other.

It was Karl Marx who displayed the broadest vision when it came to discussing the effects of criminal deeds. Just as a philosopher produces ideas and a poet poems, he argued, a criminal produces crimes. But beyond that the criminal also produces the entire criminal justice system (constables, judges, hangmen, juries, and so on), along with ancillary agents of social regulation ranging from psychiatrists through probation officers to journalists. An entire discursive space opens to accommodate "scientific" statistical studies, press reports, confessions, forensic documents, medical studies, and psychiatric evaluations, each serving to reinforce consensual positions on crime and creating a collective memory that reinforces the "truth" of those positions.[48] The criminal has an impact not only in the social and economic arena, but in the ethical and aesthetic realms as well:

> The criminal makes an impression, partly moral, partly tragic, as the case may be, and thus renders a "service" to the stirring of moral and aesthetic feelings in the public. He produces not only compendia about criminal justice, not only penal codes and thus also a judicial apparatus, but also art, belles-lettres, novels, and even tragedies, as Müllner's *Guilt* and Schiller's *Robbers*, as even *Oedipus* and *Richard the Third* demonstrate.[49]

While it is true enough that the depiction of transgressive behavior has always captured the imagination of creative writers, it is only since the romantic era that the criminal mind has proved a source of seemingly endless fascination. As Theodore Ziolkowski has convincingly demonstrated, the criminal in literary works has become less "an object of aesthetic contemplation" than "a projection of the artist's own subjectivity."[50] But while artists may have identified with the psychology of the murderer—with what Joel Black has called a "passionate spirit of rebellion," "unfulfilled fantasies and desires," and an "overworked imagination"—few have ever openly declared a real sense of empathy or identification with "femicidal" maniacs.[51] Yet these maniacs and their "works" were displayed with unsettling sympathy and frequency by writers, artists, and film producers in Germany between the two world wars.

To understand the attraction for artists of *Lustmord*, I will return, for a moment, to a very different intellectual climate to illustrate the degree to which representational practices license violence in order to erase all traces of femininity from a masculine "text" produced by a self-sufficient male creator. Hitchcock's *Psycho*, more openly than almost any other work, reveals the degree to which its producer becomes one with the murderer, repeating, through his film, an assault on a body. In the marginal notations for the description of the notorious shower scene in *Psycho*, Hitchcock wrote: "The slashing. An impression of a knife slashing, as if tearing at the very screen, ripping the film."[52] The assault on Marion Crane's body is duplicated in an assault on the screen itself, an assault that seems to have as its target not only the "feminized" audience seated before the screen, as one critic asserts, but also the cinematic product itself, a product that Hitchcock repeatedly affiliated with women ("Movie titles, like women, should be easy to remember"; "Suspense is like a woman") and in whose origins a female movie star was often implicated.[53] The producer of on-screen images of murder operates with a double economy, at once eliminating the female source of disturbance for the male killer in the movie and assaulting the disruptive feminine elements in his own work.

The production of *Psycho*, along with that of other representations of sexual murder, reads almost like an enactment of Walter Benjamin's description of artistic creativity:

> The genesis of great works of art has often been captured with the image of birth. This image is dialectical; it takes the process in two directions. One has to do with creative conception, and its genius is feminine. This femininity exhausts itself in accomplishment. It gives life to the work of art, and then it dies. What dies in the master artist once the creation has been completed is that part of him in which the creation was conceived. But the work of art, once completed—and this takes us to the other side of the process—is not a dead thing. . . . The creation, in the process of being com-

pleted, gives birth once again to its creator. Not in the feminine mode, in which the creation was conceived, but rather in its masculine element. Reanimated he exceeds nature: for the existence which he acquired the first time around from the dark depths of the womb he now owes to a more radiant domain. His home is not where he was born; instead he is coming to life where his home is. He is the masculine first-born of the work of art, which he once conceived.[54]

Benjamin's gendered division of labor, with a feminine self conceiving, giving birth, then expiring from the effort of giving birth and a masculine self that experiences a second, spiritual birth through the production of a work of art, reveals exactly what is at stake in textual production. "Not only is a text created over a dead, feminine body," Elisabeth Bronfen observes, "but this sacrifice also gives a second birth to the artist."[55] This second birth bears none of the biological traces of decay associated with female procreation; it transcends the "feminine" and "exceeds nature" to produce not only the perfect text (a wholly masculine one) but also the perfect woman (a dead, silent body). Can it be an accident that Hitchcock formulated the obstacles to finding the perfect "title" in the following way? "I fear that the perfect title, like the perfect woman, is difficult to find. . . . Any woman can be [a woman of mystery] if she keeps those two points in mind. She should grow up—and shut up."[56] In a macabre cinematic elaboration of this statement, *Psycho* shows us that the only way to shut a woman up is to open her up.

Through the production of images in which female bodies are obliterated, the male artist also effaces the feminine aspects of his labors and spiritualizes the work of art to which he gives birth and which, in turn, rejuvenates him and makes him "masculine." We can see at once, then, that the projects of historical serial killers and of the artists who represent their "work" are both defenses against the fantasmatic double threat of sexuality and death conjoined in the feminine. If artistic creativity seems less of an immediate peril to real-life women in its assault on nothing more than representations, we would do well to remember that the circulation of these images produces the very conditions that secure a conjunction between death and femininity so strong as to engender the need to kill.

The representation of violence cannot but become deeply implicated in the violence of representation.[57] What I have in mind is more than a play on words, for there are ways in which both the production process and the critical reception of violent images result in a blurring of the boundaries between inside and outside and between "fantasy" and "reality." Let me return to the example of Hitchcock, not only because of his deep indebtedness to the cinematic fantasies of Weimar Germany, but because there is a kind of unparalleled richness of detail in accounts of how he set about making films and how audiences responded to the violence in them.

The thematic centrality of murder in Hitchcock's films already points to the way in which violence is inscribed in the filmmaker's role. Hitchcock, as William Rothman points out, represents "the threat of murderous violence," a threat that plays itself out not only in the cinematic fantasy but also in the off-screen realities of the production process and at the moment of viewing the film.[58] Characters on the screen, actors in the studio, and viewers of the film alike are scripted as passive victims or as silent witnesses to a "staged" violence that breeds a culture of abject subordination or tacit complicity to the desires of the "auteur." As we accustom ourselves to that position in our role as viewer, it becomes almost "natural" to respond to violence in a voyeuristic manner—one that precludes interventionist efforts.

"Assaultive gazing," a position in which the audience is invited to collude with the camera and to experience sadistic pleasure in a character's physical or emotional torment, has been tellingly contrasted with a "reactive gazing" that looks at and empathizes with the pain of the on-screen victims or indeed sees itself as the target of cinematic terror.[59] These categories, also known in film theory as the projective gaze and the introjective gaze, have been shown by Carol Clover to be resolutely gendered—with the assaultive gaze figured as masculine/sadistic and the reactive gaze figured as feminine/masochistic. Clover further observes that in the horror genre "assaultive gazing . . . is by and large the minority position and that the real investment of the genre is in the reactive or introjective position, figured as both painful and feminine."[60] These theoretical elaborations, though they do not take into full account the way in which sadistic cruelty can be funded by masochistic anguish or vice versa, can help us understand the degree to which artistic representations of violence imply a double assault, first on the models for the represented images, then on the audience for whom they are intended.

Let us return to Hitchcock, who—despite an intense desire for public adulation and commercial success—displayed a remarkable disdain for film audiences, likening them on one occasion to a "giant organ to be played."[61] But the filmmaker's most sincere contempt was reserved for actors and, even more emphatically, for the "leading ladies" of his films. "On the set he's a sadist," one observer remarked. "It had long been my conviction . . . sustained by working with Hitchcock, that a good director must have something of a sadist in him," another noted. The director of *The Birds*, a third commented, was "a sadistic son of a bitch."[62] Susan Sontag has emphasized that the act of photographing implies violation and that capturing images is fueled by murderous aggression. "To photograph someone is a sublimated murder," she writes. And again: "The act of taking pictures is a semblance of appropriation, a semblance of rape."[63] While this may seem a powerful over-statement of the sadistic element in photography, it turns the violent on-screen assaults in Hitchcock's oeuvre into further symptoms of the film-maker's sadistic aggression. Even at the very end of his life he was writing a rape-murder scene, this time to open what was to be his next film, *The Short Night*.[64]

Nowhere is Hitchcock's sadism more evident than in the directing of Tippi Hedren, a moderately successful model with no acting experience whatso-ever, whom Hitchcock chose to star in *The Birds*. For this film, Hitchcock had used a combination of live, trained birds, mechanical birds, and animation to render the avian assaults. In the scenes with children, he relied exclusively on the mechanical birds and on animation, but for the two minutes of screen time during which Tippi Hedren was assaulted, he had no reservations about sacrificing her personal safety to cinematic realism and "integrity." Those two minutes of screen violence were crafted with the same loving detail devoted to the shower slaying of Marion Crane in *Psycho*. Is it any wonder that François Truffaut felt that Hitchcock filmed scenes of murder as if they were love scenes, and love scenes as if they were murder scenes?[65] The two-minute assault scene required a full week of eight-hour days of shooting, days that left Tippi Hedren on the brink of emotional and physical collapse.

Witnesses to the shooting and those who constructed accounts of it speak in glowing terms of Hedren's "courage"—a type of courage that enabled Hitchcock to construct a technically flawless product with a powerfully real-istic moment of cinematic violence. Donald Spoto (Hitchcock's biographer), for example, writes about the filming in a way that legitimizes the relentless assaults on Hedren's body in the name of cinematic brilliance. I quote his words at length because they naturalize and authorize the violence against the actress in so revealing a fashion:

> One must admire the courage of Tippi Hedren. . . . Miss Hedren was placed daily in a cage-like room on the soundstage, an opening was made for the camera, and two men, with heavy gauntlets protecting them from fingertips to shoulders, opened huge boxes of gulls which they threw di-rectly at her, hour after hour. The girl is seen fending off the birds, and that is just what Miss Hedren did for what she has called "the worst week of my life." The use of real birds for this scene was a surprise to Miss Hedren, who was initially told that mechanical birds would be used. . . .
>
> At the end of the attic sequence, when Melanie is on the floor being pecked by birds, elastic bands were tied around Miss Hedren's legs, arms and torso. Attached to these bands were nylon threads, and one leg of each of several birds was tied to this string so the birds would not fly away. . . .

Eight hours daily, for an entire week, she was subjected to this nerve-racking experience. Birds flew at her, and birds were tied to her. "Finally, one gull decided to perch on my eyelid, producing a deep gash and just missing my eyeball. I became hysterical."[66]

In a final stroke of irony, we hear that, on each day of shooting, representatives from the Humane Society were present to see that the birds were not mistreated; they insisted, for example, on enforcing a strict quitting time of five o'clock.

I have already alluded to the way in which cinematic violence is not only directed at the characters within the cinematic frame but also invades the real world outside the frame. The hand wielding the knife in *Psycho* is aimed both at Marion Crane and at the audience, seeming to enter the space of the real in much the way that the birds, in the film of that title, flutter into the frame from behind the camera, or the oversized gun in *Spellbound* seems ready to fire straight at the viewer.[67] As Slavoj Žižek notes of the latter shot in Bodega Bay: "Here Hitchcock mobilizes the feeling of threat which sets in when the distance separating the viewer—his/her safe position of pure gaze—from the diegetic reality is lost."[68] Dissolving the boundaries between cinematic fantasy and off-screen reality reveals the degree to which Hitchcock was invested in threatening the viewer in a way that moves one step beyond encouraging identification with a terrorized character.

"I always believe in following the advice of the playwright Sardou," Hitchcock declared. "He said, 'Torture the women!' . . . The trouble today is that we don't torture women enough."[69] The assaultive gaze, whether fixed at the lens of the filmmaker's camera or in the mind's eye of the novelist and artist, is so often located in a male body and takes as its target a female or feminized body that it becomes virtually impossible to gender that gaze as anything but masculine. What we shall see in the works that follow is an affirmation, perpetuation, and naturalization of the notion that sadistic violence emanates from male bodies and that that violence drives a solid wedge of difference between the two sexes. Statistics bear out the notion of sexual murder as a "distinctively male crime," for women who kill are generally motivated by jealousy or revenge—only in the exceptional cases that prove the rule do they murder strangers in an act of eroticized assault.[70]

The last two decades have witnessed an unprecedented outpouring of literature by both male and female writers on the ways in which sexual conflict is engendered by male violence. Male brutality toward women, so the argument runs, is the one stabilizing difference between the sexes. "Critical eloquence on the subject of male sadism," as Carol Clover observes, "holds the gender bottom line" and gives us "our ultimate gender story."[71] In a sense, then, efforts to add yet another volume to the evidence that men brutalize women through rape, battering, or other forms of abuse ratify the notion that sadistic violence is a permanent part of the male psyche and turn the sexual politics of specific cultural moments into a transhistorical phenomenon wholly resistant to change. By looking at male sexual violence in the context of artistic production in Germany in the 1920s, I try to reveal the degree to which that violence was in fact "unnatural"—conditioned by certain social practices and cultural stories prominent at the time and buttressed by collaborative work between agent and victim.

The journalistic prominence of stories about sexual murderers is a telling fact about our collective cultural consciousness. While the victims of serial murderers account for only a tiny percentage of homicides, they become the subject of endless daily conversations, receive prominent media attention, and repeatedly figure as the objects of cultural representation. Thanks to this discursive fullness, the press becomes a rich source of documentation for cases of sexual murder. In the chapter that follows, I analyze the journalistic practices of various newspapers, periodicals, and magazines in order to clarify our understanding of Weimar Germany's construction of sexual murder and to chart public responses to the personal and social disruptions engineered by the sexual murderer. Moving from a definition of our own cultural position with regard to sexual murder to a clarification of what is at stake in these crimes for Germans living in the 1920s will take us one step closer to decoding the many issues that arise in the case studies comprising the second part of this book.

CHAPTER THREE

Crime, Contagion, and Containment:
Sexual Murder in the Weimar Republic

The social milieu is the culture fluid of criminality;
the microbe is the criminal, an element which only acquires
importance the day it finds the fluid which makes it ferment.

Alexandre Lacassagne (1885)

You criminals are the disease. I'm the cure.

Sylvester Stallone as Marion Cobretta in Cobra (1986)

"OH COUNTRY of opposites and of extremes!" writes the narrator of Yvan Goll's *Sodom Berlin* as he reflects on Germany, a place that brought forth both the poet Friedrich Hölderlin and the psychopath Fritz Haarmann. The one figures as a model of empathetic self-sacrifice, the other as an exponent of sacrifice in the name of self-aggrandizement. Both are linked by blood: "Hölderlin, who opened his veins in his derangement, to water a rose tree. . . . Haarmann, who drank the blood of his blonde boy-loves from the softest spot on their necks."[1] Berlin is the city where German pathologies converge and flourish: it is a "diseased, stinking" place, the site of pestilence, corruption, decay, and of death engulfing life. And it is also a woman, "an old ogre" [eine alte Menschenfresserin], whose alluring beauty rapidly fades. I shall return later in this chapter to some of the powerful associations evoked in Goll's apostrophe to the city of Berlin, but first we must look at the less familiar term in the unorthodox pairing of Hölderlin/Haarmann in order to establish exactly what it was that made Fritz Haarmann so fitting a symbol of the demonic, destructive side of Germany.

The homosexual serial killer, Fritz Haarmann, was executed in 1925 for committing nearly thirty murders in Hanover. Many of his victims (all male) died when he bit them in the throat, presumably after they had fallen into what the prosecutor termed "youth's deep sleep."[2] Haarmann disposed of the bodies by dismembering them, then burying the body parts or throwing them into the Leine, a river running through Hanover. It was rumored that he had sold the flesh of some of his victims, but no proof was ever adduced to that effect. It was probably either the notorious Wilhelm Grossmann or the equally infamous Karl Denke whose deeds gave rise to the popular German rhyme about the axe-wielding Haarmann who makes mincemeat or goulash of his victims. Grossmann, who came to be known as the Bluebeard of the Silesian Railway, was charged in 1921 with the murder and cannibalization of fourteen women.[3] Denke, called the Mass Murderer of Münsterberg, lived in seclusion for years and, in a grim foreshadowing of state-sanctioned crimes in the decade to follow, kept detailed records on the body weight of his victims, but he nevertheless enjoyed an unblemished reputation in his neighborhood, where he was known as "Vater Denke." For some reason, the buckets of blood that he poured out into an open courtyard on a regular basis, along with the strange smells and sounds emanating from his living quarters, failed to arouse suspicion.[4] Denke committed on the order of thirty murders over a period of twenty years and hanged himself shortly after being arrested on *suspicion* of attempted murder (a young man begging at his door managed to ward off a murderous assault and went to the police). It was only after Denke's suicide in jail, just days after Haarmann had been convicted, that the police grasped the full extent of his criminal activity. In his quarters, they discovered human bones, chopped-off fingers, pickled flesh, teeth, suspenders made of human skin, and a host of other grisly items.[5]

The Haarmann, Grossmann, and Denke cases captured the headlines in the early part of the 1920s. Just when the shock of the Haarmann murders was wearing off, the Denke case hit the newspapers and gave rise to endless expressions of incredulous revulsion. The coverage given to those cases paled, however, by comparison to that accorded in the latter part of the 1920s to the crimes of Peter Kürten, a man who admitted to killing thirty-five people in Düsseldorf, almost all women and children. He was convicted in 1931 of nine murders and of various attempted murders, along with other crimes ranging from arson to rape. Unlike Denke, who lived in studied isolation, Kürten was employed and married. He regularly courted the press with provocative letters designating the location of buried corpses and dropping ominous clues about the next murder. Since many of his victims were young children, his crimes made the news almost as soon as they were committed and terrorized the city of Düsseldorf in a particularly intense way. (Haarmann had also murdered children, but the youngest was thirteen years old, and nearly all of his victims were runaways, drifters, or derelicts, whose absence did not raise suspicions.) After Kürten was arrested, he acknowledged his need to seek notoriety when he averred that he had committed his crimes in order "to agitate the public" and to create a state of "turmoil."[6] The notoriety, in turn, fueled his criminal ambitions to such a degree that he credited journalists with inspiring him to reach new heights of offensiveness. At a press conference, he bowed to the assembled reporters and congratulated them on their role in his criminal career: "I have already observed that the sensational reports in certain scandal sheets turned me into the man who stands before you today."[7]

The very medium that registered, narrated, and dramatized the crimes of Kürten also played some role in relaying the criminal impulse back to him and shaping his identity. The newspaper coverage must have been especially satisfying for a man whose professed ambition was to be "the most celebrated criminal of all time."[8] Even those papers that made a point of avoiding the sensationalizing accounts gave detailed coverage to the murderer's victims and to the reign of terror he was imposing on the city of Düsseldorf.[9] Kürten's trial, staged to satisfy "the people's need for justice" [das Rechtsempfinden des Volkes], was in itself something of a spectacle held in a building designed to accommodate fifty physicians, psychiatrists, and educators along with some one hundred reporters and foreign correspondents, for whom fifteen telephone booths had been specially installed.[10]

After Kürten's arrest, and especially during his trial, interest in the crimes continued to run high, but there was a nearly studied indifference to the murderer himself, that is, to the motives and to the psychosis that had driven him to kill. In its front-page coverage of Kürten's arrest, the *Frankfurter Zeitung* found Kürten's punctuality—his neighbors reported with some admiration that he regularly went to work at precisely 6:45—more compelling than an exploration of his motives (this may not surprise some familiar with the cultural importance of punctuality in Germany). The few vague attempts to explain the murderer's pathology remained unconvincing. That Kürten's wife was a few years older than he does not, for example, offer any clear evidence of too strong an attachment to his mother, as one writer asserted.[11] Most often a diagnosis (e.g., sadism) was substituted for analysis: thus one legal commentator "explains" Kürten's psychotic behavior by diagnosing him a schizophrenic.[12] Evidence of fetishism (the murderer had tied the stockings of a victim around his waist shortly before he was arrested) and the murderer's habit of using cosmetics (a fact that evidently led witnesses to underestimate his real age) are noted but not pursued. It was apparently sufficient to refer to "that enigma, man" [das Rätsel Mensch] and to leave it at that.[13]

The resistance to exploring Kürten's psyche and the consequent mystification of his crimes may seem astonishing from our own perspective, but it is typical of most journalistic accounts of serial murderers in the 1920s. The respected *Frankfurter Zeitung*, for example, fixated on personal survival in economic hard times as the motive for Denke's killings—the pots of fat and tubs of preserved human flesh in Denke's kitchen were evidently there because he needed the food. It documented Denke's losses during the Great Inflation of 1923 and posited a direct connection between the murders (Denke kept the victims' clothing and consumed their flesh) and Denke's financial ruin during the inflation: "Denke probably began his criminal activities during the inflationary period, since he had sufficient resources for himself up until then."[14] An American reporter covering the Kürten case found this account wholly plausible, refining it somewhat by turning the combination of war and economic hard times into the source of Denke's madness: "It is possible that as a small bourgeois living on his property, he had become maddened by the starvation and hardships entailed first by the war and then by the inflation which made the rent due from [his tenants] Gabriel and Voigt worth nothing overnight."[15] The two reporters had evidently never stopped to ponder the fact that numerous other victims of the German inflation had not turned to murder and cannibalism to ensure their physical survival in bad economic times. Almost anything seemed preferable to serious analysis of the motive and the complex psychological, social, and cultural issues raised by crimes of this magnitude: witness the way in which one police investigator finds Denke's reading of *Robinson Crusoe* the most compelling piece of information about how the murderer came to be drawn to cannibalism.[16]

Again and again newspapers served up phrases about serial murderers as "beasts," as victims of the desperate postwar conditions (a favorite rhetorical gambit of the extreme left and right alike), as persons tainted by their heredity ("ein Opfer erblicher Belastung"), or as "morally and mentally defective." Programmed responses like those made it easy to evade the social and cultural issues at stake. Only the most vague references are made to the childhood of these men and to the milieu in which they grew up. That Kürten's father was an alcoholic who admitted that he beat his son and that he exercised restraint only for fear of incurring medical expenses is mentioned merely in passing, if at all.[17] Kürten himself spoke of a reign of domestic tyranny in which his father battered the mother in front of the children and brutalized the children in various ways—tearing their clothes to shreds, smashing furniture to bits, and, on more than one occasion, terrorizing all the children by sharpening a kitchen knife while threatening to cut the eldest son's throat. Of Kürten's mother we know little ("gutmütig," a vintage cliché for describing the good nature of the German *Hausfrau*, is the term used to describe her), but frequent reference is also made to her strong sensual nature. No reporter ever offers any evidence for either judgment.[18] Kürten himself traced the source of his psychosis to the relentless humiliations he suffered at home, at his father's workplace (where his indignities were doubled because he was also a mere apprentice), and at various prisons where he was subjected to bodily restraint and put on display. The press, by contrast, repeatedly referred to Kürten as a biological, psychological, or moral anomaly or resurrected empty phrases about man in general and Kürten in particular as an enigma.

Before Kürten's capture, press reports focused on the victims and the way in which they were murdered, on police efforts to identify the killer, and on the public reaction to the presence of a mass murderer. The liberal-republican *Frankfurter Zeitung* rarely gave much space to criminal cases, but for the serial murders committed in Düsseldorf, it made an exception. On 16 November 1929 a lengthy editorial, occasioned by the discovery of a nineteenth corpse, speculated on the identity of the killer and voiced concern about the agitation of the public. Readers are told that "fantastic assertions" are being made and learn that the public is in a state of "nervous overstimulation": "tips" from private citizens had apparently led to the arrest of several dozen men. This is still a far cry, however, from the "state of hysteria" attributed by the *Daily News* to the women of Düsseldorf. The very day of that editorial, the evening edition of the *Frankfurter Zeitung* recorded the public's overwhelming sense of alarm ("ungeheure Erregung") and observed that if the murderer continued to run free, the psychotic fears of the public ("Angstpsychose unter der Bevölkerung") would become more widespread than ever. Two weeks later, an update on the murders bore the caption "Düsseldorf Murderer-Psychosis" [Düsseldorfer Mörderpsychose], referring not to the killer's psychosis but to the public's. It was not the discovery of another corpse that prompted the article, but the arrest of another innocent suspect, in this case a hapless fellow described as innocuous ("harmlos"), who had the habit of dressing up in women's clothes. Attention was evidently shifting from the deranged killer and his innocent victims to the "demented" public and its innocent victims.

Almost imperceptibly, then, the press had succeeded in transferring signs of the murderer's "disease" to the public, which was in a fever-pitch about the murders ("Düsseldorf fiebert!") and circulating "the wildest rumors" [die tollsten Gerüchte]. The attributes ascribed to the public are charged with sexual overtones—the Rhineland is said to be "trembling with excitement" [zittert in Spannung], and the country is in a state of constant alarm. *Erregung*, the term most frequently recruited to describe the anxious population, implies a highly emotional state of anxiety, but can also denote sexual arousal. Ironically, and not coincidentally, it was also the very word Kürten had used to describe his state of mind before murdering.[19] The population at large was thus seen as duplicating the psychosis of the murderer, partaking of his sexualized frenzy in its desperate attempt to defuse the general sense of anxiety by finding scapegoats. The real threat derives from the close resemblance of the psyche of the killer to the collective mentality of those he is terrorizing. The motives of the serial killer are, in one sense, not at all enigmatic; rather they sound an all too familiar chord, one that finds a strong resonance in the general population.

Each of Kürten's crimes was doubly directed and had a double gain: the act of murder not only claimed a victim, but also consolidated the basis of the murderer's power to achieve the effect of terror. Kürten claimed to derive as much, if not more, sexual satisfaction from the response to his murders as from the actual killing.[20] In transcripts of an interview with a court-appointed psychiatrist named Sioli, Kürten declared that the excitement (*Erregung*) and outrage (*Empörung*) expressed by participants in a spontaneous protest staged after the discovery of another corpse had aroused him sexually and led to ejaculation. Time and again Kürten disputed the sexual nature of his crimes, though he did not deny that sexual arousal and satisfaction coincided with the act of assault and murder. He sought to rationalize the killings by asserting that the urge to kill was funded by a need to even the score for his public humiliations—above all to retaliate for the many instances of abusive treatment while incarcerated—by creating an explosive event (*Knalleffekt*) that would terrorize, impress, and forever make him the object of abject dread. His chief motive, he claimed, was "revenge on mankind."[21] Only an endless succession of murdered bodies could deliver the desired effect of hysterical obsession with the perpetrator.[22]

The public was right to be terrified of the murderer and terrorized by his deeds, especially considering the number of victims who were children and the number of murders committed within a matter of months. As one account of the killings pointed out, an atmosphere of tense anxiety was a necessary condition for keeping the public vigilant, thus protecting potential victims and facilitating the capture of the killer.[23] Yet the press insisted on emphasizing the peril that came directly from the population of Düsseldorf—a mob of deranged citizens (feminized through their hysteria) developing all manner of psychoses, laboring under various delusions, and pressing for the arrests of innocent men. The more it focused on the pathologies of the general population, the less necessary it seemed to talk about Kürten and the source of his deranged behavior.

In a retrospective analysis of the murders in Düsseldorf, the director of the homicide division for the criminal police in Berlin revealed just how "tainted" the public had become when he identified a number of psychoses that had evolved during Kürten's reign of terror. There was, to begin with, the assault psychosis, then the missing-person psychosis, and also the letter-writing psychosis.[24] Inspector Gennat cited a number of cases in which women fabricated stories about assaults in order to get police sympathy or to attract the attention of aloof husbands and adds that some children manufactured similar tales when they came home late from school. For this unusually sober observer, however, it was not a sign of derangement that reports of missing persons would proliferate; parents were right to feel apprehensive and were justified in turning to the authorities when their children failed to arrive home on time. The letter-writing psychosis, in Gennat's view, was fostered by the press, for nearly every newspaper wanted to sign the murderer on as a regular correspondent. But even when various symptoms of fear were shown to have a rational basis or were attributed to provocative journalistic practices, the public was branded psychotic and *its* pathologies came under close scrutiny. That a police investigator would choose to focus his energy on emergent collective psychoses rather than on the mentality of the murderer is a telling commentary on the need to turn away from the crime, to deflect attention from the cultural and psychological complexities of sexual murder by looking at its social effect rather than its causes.

After the murderer had been apprehended, the public's state of mind still remained a central concern. One legal journal even referred to the outbreak of a "psychotic fear of clemency" for Kürten.[25] This is not to say that the press lost complete sight of the killer—to the contrary it scrupulously documented the legal twists and turns of judicial proceedings against Kürten and closely followed the trial, which one reporter described as a "colossal spectacle" staged for the people.[26] Heated debates about capital punishment took place, but they stood in the shadow of concerns about the deranged state of the public. Reporters repudiated their own responsibility in the promotion of public hysteria by pointing the finger of blame at pulp novels, at the rumor mills, or at radio broadcasts. Nevertheless, despite their best efforts, the role of the press in covering murder cases became part of the debate about the threat of "criminal contagion," the power attributed to a single diseased person to ravage an entire population.

The press came to be perceived as boosting the "toxic" effect of these killers, not only by giving the murderers precisely the kind of attention they craved and thereby spurring them on to ever greater atrocities, but also by inspiring those who were eager for notoriety to commit copycat crimes. Evidence that plenty of people were yearning for the limelight of criminal fame, even if they were not capable of committing the deeds, can be seen in the fact that no fewer than two hundred people rushed to take credit for the murders in Düsseldorf by turning themselves in to the police. Approximately 160 letters from "the killer" arrived at police stations and newspapers.[27] One prominent contemporary criminologist declared that it was possible to be "psychologically infected" by newspaper accounts about killers and by dime novels about serial murderers.[28] Kürten himself emphasized how riveting he had found a fictionalized account of Jack the Ripper and the Whitechapel murders, and he also stressed at his trial that the deeds of that serial murderer had played a profound role in his fantasy life.[29] The degree to which the press's reports about murders, in particular sexual murders, had an effect on social mores became a much debated issue in the late 1920s and early 1930s. The *Frankfurter Zeitung* devoted an entire page to the effect of crime-reporting on youth, with essays by a judge, a doctor, and the head of an orphanage. Some held that sensationalizing articles in the press infected youth; others believed that they innoculated them against the crimes reported. These metaphors of disease, which belonged to the writers at the *Frankfurter Zeitung*, so permeated and organized every attempt at social analysis that they quickly degenerated into clichés—without, however, surrendering any of their ideological power.[30]

That criminals were widely believed to spread a psychosis capable of infecting an entire population and of taking on epidemic proportions became clear in the context of cases other than Kürten's. Theodor Lessing's study of Fritz Haarmann and his trial describes what one observer recalled about the citizens of Hanover when it began to dawn on them that the bones and rotting flesh in the river Leine belonged to human beings: "You became convinced that you were seeing a psychotic population, a hideous epidemic that had previously broken out here and there during the war years."[31] Once again attention is deflected from the unspeakable deeds of the killer to the traumatized public, with the public marked as the deranged double of the criminal. During and after Haarmann's trial, observers made the point—as in the Kürten case—that Haarmann's deeds had fostered all kinds of delusional behavior in the public, including the dread of eating meat for fear that it had human origins (*Menschenfleischpsychose*).[32]

Disease metaphors permeate our own discursive practices about violence and its social effect. Consider the words of U.S. Surgeon General C. Everett Koop, who declared: "Violence is every bit a public health issue for me and my successors in this century as smallpox, tuberculosis, and syphilis were for my predecessors in the last two centuries. Violence in American public and private life has indeed assumed the proportions of an epidemic." Or think of the "Violence Epidemiology Branch" at the federal Center for Disease Control in Atlanta, Georgia.[33] But the metaphorical logic of these two examples is rooted in the notion that epidemics of violence are symptomatic of a profound social malaise rather than the effect of a single toxic individual. If the epidemic can indeed be traced to a single human source, then the only cure for the ailment is the elimination of that person. To some extent, this latter model of toxic contagion must have guided Theodor Lessing's thinking about Haarmann, for despite his discerning and sophisticated analysis of the legal, social, and psychological implications of the murderer's trial, he came to the conclusion that, for real justice to prevail, Haarmann had to be eliminated in one of two ways: the one allowing the criminal to gain the high moral ground by destroying himself, the other licensing the mothers of the victims to repeat the violence of the crime on the body of the perpetrator. "Suicide (as a form of self-indictment for someone who is prepared to repent for having sinned against the human community in the most monstrous way) or—a swift lynching carried out by offended humanity. . . . What I would do? Give the thirty mothers of the dismembered boys the chance to break through the bar and to tear Haarmann to pieces."[34] By suggesting that the moral score can be evened by turning the physical violence directed at the victims against the body of the perpetrator, Lessing enmeshes himself in the discourse of contagion that he otherwise tries to resist in his commentary on the trial.

The only form of relief from the crimes of a Haarmann, so it appeared, was the eradication of the man. To pave the way for his elimination, the legal machinery of Hanover needed to emphasize that Haarmann was a case so special (not difficult given the circumstances of his crimes) as to nullify the need for due process. The trial was over within a matter of days. "Quarantine" was followed by a swift execution closed to the press and public. It was, however, not only public outrage and the need for retribution that led to a speedy conviction and to a verdict prescribing the death penalty. As Lessing pointed out, local officials in Hanover had a special stake in the Haarmann case, for the man had been on the payroll for a number of years as a police informant. Any attempts to understand what made Haarmann tick, to situate him in the social network of "normal" humanity, were rebuffed by the court as maneuvers to block the quickest possible execution of justice. "What sort of psychological questions could possibly be asked?" was the response to Lessing's plea to call in expert testimony from Ludwig Klages, Alfred Döblin, Sigmund Freud, or Alfred Adler. The presiding judge berated Lessing for his attempt to sidetrack the proceedings: "Psychology has no place in the courtroom," he declared.[35] Were the court to concede that it was worth taking a close look at the criminal and examining how he had escaped detection for so long, it would also have to admit that he was a human being who had operated in a specific milieu—not just a source of defilement that had to be eliminated. That specific milieu, already troubled by social unrest and political upheaval, had a vested interest in quietly doing away with a criminal rather than protracting and deepening the discussion about him.

One of the few newspapers to come out against the death penalty for Haarmann was the Communist daily *Die rote Fahne* (*The Red Flag*). For its writers, Haarmann was yet another symptom of the widespread corruption under the Social-Democratic regime. It was the republic that had made a Haarmann possible, that had installed and legitimized criminal violence when it authorized capitalistic enterprise: "The beast Haarmann, a bloodsucker who works on his own in a primitive way, lives in the shadow of the bloody weapons used by the capitalist state." What Haarmann had done on a small scale, the state practiced on a grand scale with its cold-blooded murders of communist dissenters. (The same sort of thinking could be found among pacifists who asserted that Haarmann's crimes were trivial compared to those of the real butchers and bloodletters, the World War I generals Hindenburg and Ludendorff.)

The links between Haarmann and the police were not at all a surprise to *Die rote Fahne*; they merely confirmed the suspicion that "bloodhounds and criminals" were collaborating with the police to persecute communists. The "bourgeois press," it declared, had a desperate need to make Haarmann singular, to designate him as a psychopathological case, a radical, perverse deviation from the norm. That press frantically sought to describe Haarmann as "sick" and "isolated" in his role as "bloodsucker" and "flesh-eater," then "ran out of things to say." What particularly enraged *Die rote Fahne* was the attempt to bury the Haarmann case, to gloss over the crimes that were flourishing under the Weimar regime and thus to quell critical voices and to forestall any kind of preventive action along the lines of social change. In this regard, the death sentence was felt to be particularly absurd, for it was important to study Haarmann, to establish that the man was mentally ill (*geisteskrank*) rather than monstrous, and to identify and understand the source of his pathology.[36] For *Die rote Fahne*, the death penalty served only political ends—it meant getting rid of a frighteningly visible symptom while ignoring its more subtle, deeper social causes. And it had the further advantage of stifling commotion in places like Hanover, where anger at the police was bound to stay alive as long as the criminal was not yet dead.

When it came to the trial of Peter Kürten, held over a nine-day period in April 1931, the press took two very different positions.[37] On the one hand, the *Lokal-Anzeiger* in Berlin, along with numerous other papers, focused on the heinousness of the crimes and adopted the line familiar from the Haarmann case. Kürten is described as a beast and a vampire, then becomes the target of a seemingly endless string of imprecations:

> And now you can look behind the curtain and see this horrifying thing, this thing that has never before appeared, this monstrosity of a sadistic abortion.... His soul is a chamber of horrors filled with the most awful things.... He is nothing but a heap of garbage, permeated with loathsome things about to explode.... This man Kürten is the most frightening person ever to come before the court. This man Kürten is one of the most abominable persons that mankind, the lower reaches of mankind, has ever born out of the morass.[38]

That this monster is put on display and granted the privilege of a trial rather than being exterminated is an outrage to the citizens footing the bill.

The *Berliner Tageblatt*, by contrast, showed great restraint in its coverage of the trial; there, Kürten is treated with a certain amount of affective detachment and never demonized. Instead the paper stresses the innocuous appearance and mild-mannered, well-spoken demeanor of the defendant: he is a textbook case of the banality of evil, to borrow a phrase first coined by Joseph Conrad.[39] In a thoughtful post-trial editorial, the *Frankfurter Zeitung* tried to explain how a man who had committed such horrifying deeds could appear so "normal" and make such a decent impression in the courtroom.[40] Kürten was not out to hoodwink the public, the editorial insisted. What had happened in the course of preparations for the trial, as Kürten confessed his crimes and responded to a range of interrogations about his life, was tantamount to psychotherapy, according to the paper. The pressure to recall childhood memories, to narrate events from his family life during the official psychiatric evaluations conducted to determine whether Kürten was legally sane—along with the constant framing and reframing of the murders during police questioning—had effected a "talking-cure," thus creating a unique moment in which the legal establishment had cured the criminal as it prepared him for trial. In presenting Kürten as a human being gone wrong rather than as a monster, the *Berliner Tageblatt* and *Frankfurter Zeitung* (notwithstanding its astonishingly reductive version of what constituted a psychiatric cure) offered alternatives to the prevalent model of quarantining and exterminating criminals. Their advocacy of full due process seemed to derive from a conviction that the brutality of the deed is a signal of human psychosis rather than a sign of bestial behavior. That point, it should be noted, was only rarely made in the Haarmann case—perhaps because of the far more severe physical mutilation of the corpses and the rough-hewn, working-class demeanor of the defendant in that trial.

The two ways of managing deviant behavior that became evident in press coverage during the trials for Haarmann and Kürten—the one based on Pasteurian notions about germs and the transmission of disease, the other based on naive psychiatric views about the scientific value of case studies and the therapeutic possibilities of recollection and confession—organized discursive practices about criminal behavior. But it was also evidently possible to see the violence of sexual murder as an effect less of toxic or psychotic behavior than of "normal" male rage at women. The *Berliner Tageblatt* chose to print an unusual editorial about sexual killers in connection with the Haarmann murders. This essay by Franz Blei, an "interesting voice" in debates about the Haarmann case, was a near apologia for the ghastly deeds committed by those who are described as *Lustmörder*. Blei's views may seem outlandish, but they are not at all idiosyncratic and thus worth summarizing in full. Blei begins by asserting that there has never been a female sexual murderer, for sexual murderers bite their victims in the throat, an act that registers itself as "the active, aggressive principle of male love." From the start, Blei is intent on maintaining a strict polarization of the two sexes, making sadistic violence the marker of masculinity and its absence a sign of femininity.

Blei describes the act of biting as an "escalation of affect" so great that what begins as a normal, human impulse turns into a murderous reflex. Sexual murderers are, then, not at all monsters, just men who cannot limit and contain an urge. "What man has not wanted to murder his beloved in a moment of silent rage?" Blei casually asks, thus betraying his belief that the true motive of *Lustmord* is the release of frenzied hatred. Women are always trying to show how dependent men are on them, he grouses. "Nine-tenths of a woman's involvement with a man consists of showing how essential she is and insinuating herself into his life. Usually the man lets himself be duped and tamed: he marries." Is it any wonder that irritation at their relentless fussing and fault-finding ("You knotted your tie badly again!") turns to unrestrained rage? When we read further to find that the mutilation and dismemberment of the victims' bodies is less a sign of derangement than of sound pragmatism (the killer has to get rid of the evidence), we begin to realize the extent to which Blei's attempt to identify extenuating circumstances for men who murder itself borders on the pathological. His analysis is telling in that, once again, it suggests that the crimes of serial murderers are driven by rage at women, in particular at "motherly" women.[41]

Gender issues did not by any means escape the attention of the contemporary popular press, and, according to Blei's line of reasoning, *Lustmord* could easily be framed as justifiable homicide. The *Berliner Illustrirte*, for example, in the context of an essay on a "modern Bluebeard" (the Frenchman Henri D. Landru), speculated on the motives of sexual killers and came to the conclusion that "the revenge of men against women" drove them to murder. That phrase not only reinscribed the division between the sexes by insisting upon an us-against-them mentality, but also reconstituted male sadism—the initial marker of that division—as nothing more than a defense against female attachment to the carnal and material.

> The struggle and battle between the sexes is the obverse of what makes the world go 'round, not only out of a sense of betrayal and disappointment but also out of a general sense (felt only dimly by men of a lower order) that men, who represent the principle of spirituality and striving for the divine, constantly have their wings clipped and are debased by women, who represent the principle of earth and matter.[42]

The reporter for the *Berliner Illustrirte* was probably relying to a great extent on ideas popularized by Otto Weininger in his influential study *Sex and Character* (*Geschlecht und Charakter*, 1903). This work, which left its mark on the writings of, among others, Hitler, asserted the chief difference between the sexes to be the "greater absorption of the female in the sphere of sexual activities." Women, according to Weininger, are in fact fixated on the body, wholly devoted to sexual matters, "to the spheres of begetting and of reproduction," whereas men are free to pursue matters of the spirit—science, art, religion, philosophy.[43] For several hundred pages, Weininger recycles nineteenth-century gender stereotypes, rambling on nearly endlessly about the single-minded preoccupation of women with procreation, a preoccupation that handicaps them physically, morally, and intellectually.

The ideological pressure to view women as fettered to the carnal and to see men as spiritual beings engaged in a noble struggle to free themselves of biological needs explains why Blei found it so easy (in the abstract at least) to exonerate the *Lustmörder* and to see him less as a deranged monster than as a frustrated and (justifiably) enraged man. This tendency to exculpate men who murder certain kinds of women (especially those whose role it is to minister to bodies) played a prominent role in literary texts of the time—Döblin's *Berlin Alexanderplatz* is a cardinal example—but it also showed up with varying degrees of emphasis in reactions to the real-life cases. When Peter Kürten confessed to his wife that he was the Düsseldorf murderer, she was stunned. "What, those innocent children too?" she asked, half entreating him to diminish the scandal by admitting only to the murders of the "not-so-innocent" women, who had, for the most part, been killed after they had agreed to a walk in the woods, a rendezvous, or a tryst with her husband.[44] So long as a killer's victims are drawn from what one contemporary observer termed "that unfortunate class of women who have always been the prey of the criminal," there was not much cause for alarm. The Whitechapel murders, because they involved women believed to be prostitutes, were felt by some observers to be less a source of terror than of lurid entertainment.[45] As one letter to *The Times* declared, "Statistics show that London . . . is the safest city in the world to live in. . . . In that particular class of murder now confronting us, however, the unfortunate victims appear to take the murderer to some retired spot and to place themselves in such a position that they can be slaughtered without a sound being heard."[46] Only when it became clear that the victims were not necessarily prostitutes or women of "easy virtue" did the police and the public sit up and pay attention to the crimes.

The moral status of the victim shapes the ideological construction of the killer in a decisive fashion. We have seen how responses to the deeds of sexual murderers move along the spectrum from horrified contempt to undisguised empathy. When the victims are "innocent children," the serial killer is demonized and discursive strategies building on metaphors of disease and pollution are mobilized to target the murderer as a source of contamination and to advocate his elimination. When the victims are prostitutes—women marked with the signs of corrupt and corrupting sexuality—the killer is not infrequently judged to be a normal person provoked to an act of violence or his victims are seen as complicitous in their murders. Is it, then, any wonder that many sexual killers perceive themselves to be guardians of a higher moral order, ridding the world of polluting influences? "The women I killed were filth, bastard prostitutes who were standing round littering the streets. I was just cleaning up the place a bit," claimed Peter Sutcliffe, the "Yorkshire Ripper" who referred to himself as the "Streetcleaner."[47]

The association between filth and prostitutes, the construction of a fantasmatic threat of pollution parallel to that of criminals, is embedded primarily in an urban culture, a culture with a social periphery that represents not only a sanitary peril, but a moral and political one as well. As Charles Bernheimer has shown in the context of Balzac's literary oeuvre, the *putain*, the putrid woman, is the emblematic figure of Paris, a city whose "cruel miasmas" and "fetid sludge" made it both pestilential and excremental.[48] The prostitute, representing instability, excess, and corruption, stands in for the entire array of evils associated with the city. To murder her is to cleanse and purify, to cure all the symptoms of modern urban plagues. Yvan Goll's observations on Berlin reveal the degree to which that city, like Paris, was also personified as a corrupt female body that posed a sanitary and moral peril—it was the female body that became the source of pollution rather than the men who were engaged in "cleansing operations" or who had some less deadly kind of economic, social, or sexual stake in prostitution.

Franz Blei and Otto Weininger had no difficulty condemning the female victims of many serial killers, but they would have run into trouble trying to pin the blame for Fritz Haarmann's crimes on his victims. If they had, they would have found themselves in the awkward position of pointing the finger at boys and men. Yet there was an interesting way in which gender issues—when the victims were male—were reconfigured in such a way as to pathologize the feminine once again, this time by turning the male perpetrator into what one criminologist of the time called "a caricature of a woman."[49] Here is how one observer, Theodor Lessing, described Haarmann, a man who, judging from contemporary photographs, is unambiguously masculine in his physical presentation: Haarmann's hands are "soft" and "white"; his chest, back, and posterior are "feminine" in their pudginess; his body is rugged, but "womanly"; and his voice is like that of an old woman. The general impression is that of an "androgynous being," at once "like a man, like a woman, like a child." We are told that Haarmann enjoys cooking and that he darns his own socks—sure signs, for Lessing and no doubt for his readers, of gender confusion. Significantly, Lessing adds that Haarmann is raw matter ("ein Stück Natur"): he lacks the ability to reason or to behave morally. This statement, as much as the recitation of effeminate traits and the fact of his homosexuality, places Haarmann squarely in the domain of the feminine.[50]

The sexuality of the heterosexual serial murderer's female victims and the femininity of homosexual serial murderers become pathologized in discussions of numerous case histories. Just as important, the positions of violent agent and suffering victim are unsettled by ideological issues turning on gender. The "normal" heterosexual male who murders streetwalkers is not infected with the same corrupt, contaminating, and contagious powers of the effeminate homosexual male who kills other men. He can easily slip into the role of suffering victim, at the mercy of murderous female evil. Once he chooses to kill men or children, however, he becomes marked as a figure of unmitigated evil and absolute otherness, crossing over into the category of deranged monster.

As George Mosse has observed in the context of Nazi racism, it was important to "brand" any deviation from the Aryan norm, to make the outsider "readily recognized as a carrier of infection threatening the health of society and the nation."[51] Given that medical theory of the time held that homosexuality could spread like an infectious disease, then how much more quickly, for example, could the gender confusion of a serial murderer race through a town? Like the beasts and monsters of the tabloids, these socially constructed serial murderers took on the infectious character of outsider figures that signified far more than isolated instances of aberrant behavior. They figured as threats of monumental proportions, imperiling not only the survival of individuals (the potential victims of the murderer) but also the well-being of the larger community (which could become infected by the murderer).

That more than the issue of criminal pathology was at stake in discussions of serial murderers becomes painfully evident in a pamphlet published in 1924 on the Haarmann case. For the anonymous author of "The Insane Asylum or the Gallows? The Truth about the Mass Murderer Haarmann of Hanover," there was more to the Haarmann case than met the eye. A conspiracy of far-reaching consequences was evidently at work—one spearheaded by the Jews, who were protecting and promoting deviant sexuality and criminal behavior, all in the name of greater social tolerance. According to this writer, homosexuality was socially rather than biologically determined. Those who condoned it or advocated its decriminalization were creating conditions under which it could flourish, and they could thus ultimately be held responsible for the existence of men like Haarmann. "H. [Magnus Hirschfeld] and his allies, with the conscious backing of the Jewish press, are unleashing a contagious plague."[52] The pamphlet is revealing in the urgency of its need to find a way, however tenuous, to blame Haarmann's crimes on the Jews, to see them as the secret agents of criminal behavior in general, and to link criminality and Jewishness through metaphors of infection and disease. By 1929, the official Nazi newspaper was declaring that "Jews are forever trying to propagandize sexual relations between siblings, men and animals, and men and men." These efforts, it added, are "nothing but vulgar, perverted crimes" that should be punished with "banishment or hanging."[53]

We have seen the degree to which fear of becoming a serial killer's victim was shadowed in a powerful way by the fear of turning into his double. In the folkloric and literary imagination, the one figure capable of infecting his victims, turning them into duplicates of himself, was the vampire, the dreaded creature who drained his victims of their lifeblood and enlisted them in the legions of the undead. Is it any coincidence that in newspaper headlines and in casual conversation alike Kürten was referred to as the Vampire of Düsseldorf? Kürten himself had testified to drinking the blood that spurted from his victims' wounds, though it is possible that he fabricated this piece of information in order to realize his ambition of becoming the world's most notorious criminal.[54] "Like the vampire of legend," one contemporary account observed, Kürten "first sates himself on the blood of his victim, and then returns to silence and oblivion."[55]

The infamous Haarmann, through his mode of murder, had made the analogy between vampires and serial murderers almost inescapable. He came as close as was humanly possibly to being a vampire, so much so that Theodor Lessing diagnosed his illness as "vampirism."[56] Unlike Kürten, who used hammers and knives to murder, Haarmann, as I have noted, killed by biting his victims in the throat and drinking their blood. The term vampire, when applied to Kürten, seemed less a mark of his literal bloodthirstiness than a sign of his power to spread a disease that threatened to infect the entire population with the desire that drove him to shed blood, a desire that is encoded in novels such as *Berlin Alexanderplatz*, with its haunting repetition of the refrain from a Nazi song ("Blood must flow, blood must flow, blood must flow thick, fast, and strong"), and that must have permeated a culture in which men were to sing enthusiastically about sharpening "long knives" to plunge into "Jewish bodies" or about the moment when Jewish blood purls over knives ("wenn Judenblut vom Messer spritzt"). In this context, it is somewhat chilling to note the parallels between Kürten's efforts at self-vindication and Nazi defenses for murderous ideological programs. In prison, Kürten declared: "I just wanted to get revenge. Human blood would have to flow because of my martyrdom and travail."[57]

The discursive strategies developed for reflecting on killers like Kürten and Haarmann did not have to be invented by the press. Looking at Friedrich Murnau's film *Nosferatu* makes it clear that the tropes for representing the "pathology" of otherness had already been installed by 1922 (the year the film was released) and that they received nothing more than fuller elaboration as the decade drew to a close. The vampire Nosferatu eerily sets the terms for the double threat of serial killers: he murders on a scale small and large. Not only does he suck the lifeblood of individual victims, he also, through his noxious presence in a community, unleashes a disease of epidemic proportions. To the question posed in the opening title—"NOSFERATU! Was it he who brought the plague to Bremen in 1838?"—the answer is a decisive "yes."[58] At the very moment when Nosferatu's coffin is being loaded onto a ship en route to Bremen, we see the earth around it swarming with rats and witness the beginning of the transmission of the disease when one of the rats bites a workman's foot. Shortly thereafter the entire ship's crew succumbs to the plague, and the craft enters the German city to infect new victims. The shot of a newspaper feature recounting the outbreak of the plague informs the audience of the path of the illness, which follows Nosferatu's moves: "NEW PLAGUE BAFFLES SCIENCE—A mysterious epidemic of the plague has broken out in Eastern Europe and in the port cities of the Black Sea, attacking principally the young and vigorous."[59] One of the more vicious pieces of Nazi propaganda (one to which I will return in this chapter), the film *The Wandering Jew* (*Der ewige Jude*), sets up alarmingly similar parallels between foreign agents and vermin, this time with the Jews as invaders from the East whose paths and patterns of "infestation" are represented as coinciding with those of plague-infected rats (fig. 4).

While critics of *Nosferatu* have anxiously sought to protect Murnau's name by insisting that the resemblance between Nosferatu and caricatures of Jews in the Nazi newspaper *Der Stürmer* are purely coincidental, a reading of the original screenplay for *Nosferatu* suggests that Murnau must have been fully

4. Nosferatu peers out from the hold of the ship carrying him to a German port. The rat on his arm is a sign of the plague that he carries with him from foreign parts.

aware that he had chosen a text that portrayed vampires as creatures affiliated through stereotype with Jews.[60] Note that the most compelling reason to travel to Nosferatu's castle is the prospect of financial gain. When Hutter arrives in the Carpathian mountains, he is warmly greeted by a Jewish innkeeper, who monitors his moves and prevents him from missing the carriage that transports travelers to Count Orlik's castle. The original screenplay includes an unfilmed scene in which Hutter has one last chance to escape the encounter with Nosferatu, but fails to heed the warning of a local woman—significantly, while she is worshiping at a shrine to the Virgin Mary. Jews are represented as allies of Nosferatu, facilitating the visit to the Count's castle, while the folkloric custom of taking protective measures against the demonic vampire by executing Christian ritual gestures (e.g., making the sign of the cross) is repeatedly emphasized.[61]

As Elisabeth Bronfen has pointed out, *Nosferatu* shows us how illness "comes from outside, where it is carried by a 'dehumanized being,'" who must be eradicated in order for the community to return to a state of purity and health.[62] Vampires in general (but Nosferatu in particular), being serial murderers *par excellence*, offered perfect models for thinking about men like Haarmann and Kürten. The peril to a population, in both cases, comes from an indeterminate creature—disruptive because it appears to blur semantic oppositions such as human/bestial, masculine/feminine, and dead/alive (fig. 5). Indeed, the term "undead" reflects the way in which the cinematic vampire introduces a third, blurring term into such otherwise stable oppositions as dead/alive. What always remains clear, however, is that a return to the purity, integrity, and wholeness of the world as it was before the invasion from outside can be accomplished only by eradicating the source of pollution. When Nosferatu goes up in smoke, the plague vanishes with him, and we return to a world made whole and holy.

The intense emotional investment associated with efforts to destroy sources of pollution becomes especially evident in Fritz Lang's *M* (1931), when Schränker, the leader of the city's crime ring, declares the murderer to be an outsider (*Außenseiter*) who is destroying his business and who hence must be eliminated: "This beast has no right to exist. He has to go. He has to be searched out and destroyed! No mercy or pity for him!"[63] It may be coincidence that Schränker's greatest concern stems from the economic threat posed by the outsider Beckert and that he describes his plans for exterminating this "beast" in precisely the terms (*ausrotten* and *vertilgen*) that the Nazis used to frame their genocidal campaign against the Jews. But that Lang chose the Hungarian Jew Peter Lorre to play the role of Beckert (much is made of this casting decision in the film *Der ewige Jude*) can only deepen the suspicion that what had been perceived to be a cinematic indictment of the Nazis (the film's subtitle was *A Murderer among Us*) became ensnared in a discourse that Lang himself eventually resisted even as he seems to have unwittingly absorbed it in the 1920s.[64]

The language used to describe serial murderers both fed off and played into the discourse about all "aliens," whether living within German borders or outside them, whether marked by ethnic difference or by deviant behavior, whether classified as mentally defective or physically diseased. The terror engendered by these foreign agents stemmed less from their real or projected individual traits and deeds than from their imagined ability to pollute in such a way that no one and nothing is spared.[65] The vampire image was repeatedly invoked by exponents of various ideological persuasions to designate the irresistible power of alien intruders to enfeeble and infect—in such a way that all who belong to the "pure," indigenous race are turned into the victims of a bloodthirsty monster.[66]

The press reports on the likes of Haarmann and Kürten were symptomatic of a pervasive fear of pollution, but they also validated all the anxieties

5. Nosferatu's elongated hands and fingernails and his eerie gaze give him the look of an indeterminate creature, ready to attack his next victim.

aroused by deviant behavior (real and imagined) and intensified them. When films like *Nosferatu* configure the source of the plague as a bloodthirsty foreign intruder with features that match the stereotypical drawings that were to appear in *Der Stürmer* and when the press writes about serial killers as if they were vampires who will spread the lethal disease of hysteria, it becomes easier for a Hitler to tap into national fears about the power of bloodthirsty monsters (those who sapped the real lifeblood or the economic lifeblood of the Aryan race) to contaminate and destroy an entire population.

Artur Dinter's 1919 novel *Sin against Blood* (*Die Sünde wider das Blut*) enacted nearly all of the Nazi clichés about Jews as devilish vampires who both drain the Germans of their vitality and taint the race through sexual contact with Aryan women. The blonde, Nordic protagonist, Hermann Kämpfer, marries an equally "racially pure" woman who inexplicably gives birth to a child "authentically Jewish," down to its "curly black hair, dark skin, and dark eyes." Hermann, who was aware that his wife, years earlier, before their marriage, had given birth to a stillborn child sired by a Jew, learns from a "medical friend" that it takes no more than a single sexual contact to permanently pollute the blood of an Aryan woman. He murders the Jewish officer and, at his trial, adamantly defends his deed on the grounds of protecting German blood from Jewish vampires:

> If the German people cannot soon manage to rid itself completely of the Jewish vampire that it has unsuspectingly suckled with its heart's blood . . . then it will perish before long. The Jew imperils Germany's future more powerfully than our enemies on foreign soil, because he cannot be conquered with sword in hand. I committed this deed only in order to sound a warning from my heart, from this very place out into the world. With firm resolve I shall sacrifice my life for the fatherland, and I hope that I will not have done this in vain. May my death become the signal for the assault against the archenemy of the German people.[67]

There are many remarkable rhetorical leaps in this passage, but two are particularly notable. First, the speaker manages to elevate himself to the status of prophet by launching the genocide he has predicted. Second, he twice positions himself as a victim—first as a casualty of the "Jewish vampire" that has been feeding on the German people (one of whose representatives he has just dispatched), then as a man who, in murdering a Jew, has sacrificed his life for the fatherland.

The rhetorical sleight-of-hand evident in Dinter's anti-Semitic tirade became commonplace in Nazi propaganda, which figured the Jews as malicious aggressors even as they became the targets of intense vilification and murderous assaults. *Der ewige Jude* (1940)—in English *The Eternal Jew* or *The Wander-*

ing Jew—opens by enunciating the master trope associated with the Jews: they are the source of a plague, an illness that "threatens the health of the Aryan peoples."[68] We hear how the Jews constitute a foreign body, a parasite living off its German host. Wherever rats show up, there also is the Jew, carrying plague and leprosy. But the Jews, who, in the film, become the targets of a barrage of vicious words, are imbued with the classic traits of the perfect victim—the deserving victim who validates the deeds of the killer. The film represents Jews as corrupt (Wagner is quoted to support that racial characteristic), dirty (*schmutzig*), diseased, and nomadic. They conduct their business in the streets ("The main part of Jewish life takes place in the street"), figure as experts in the art of mimicry, and are engaged in trade yet produce nothing, feeding off the body of their "hosts."

Because the metaphors of disease and vampirism linked with criminal violence were or became part of the discursive strategies applied to Jews, it became all the easier to figure the Jews as murderers who operated, surreptitiously, to be sure, with the same bloodthirsty brutality as sexual killers. Let us look first at the homicidal aspect of the "Jewish threat." The coda to *Der ewige Jude*, prefaced with a warning to all "sensitive" (presumably Aryan) viewers, offers "original footage" of Jewish ritual slaughter. "The following pictures are genuine," the viewer is told. "They are among the most horrifying that a camera has ever recorded. We are showing them even though we anticipate objections on the grounds of taste. Because more important than all objections is the fact that our people should know the truth about Judaism."[69] These slaughterhouse images had a significance that went far beyond the issue of cruelty toward animals. A children's song that appeared in print in 1938 reveals how quickly the collective unconscious seemed to free-associate from Jewish ritual slaughter to manslaughter:

> It's in the blood of the Jews:
> Anger, envy, hate, and rage
> At every nation in the world
> That doesn't count as "chosen."
>
> They slaughter animals, slaughter people,
> Their bloodthirstiness knows no bounds!
> The world will return to health
> If we save it from the Jews.[70]

The quick mental leap from butchering to homicide was based in part on a centuries-old belief that Jews engaged in the ritual murder of children in order to use their blood for healing purposes.[71] But that relationship was further cemented by the affiliation of Jews with criminal violence and the practice of framing their deeds in the same terms as those used to describe the slayings of the most brutal murderers.

Jews came to be linked not only with the perpetrators of sexual murder, but with the victims as well. Like the prostitute, the Jew is seen to represent a serious threat to the moral, fiscal, and sexual economy of the social body. As Sander Gilman has pointed out, both prostitutes and Jews have been linked by what is seen to be a sexualized relation to capital—they have "but one interest, the conversion of sex into money or money into sex."[72] Unable to find value in transcendent spiritual matters, their interests remain fixed on the material and financial. More important, prostitutes and Jews, because of their spiritual corruption, are considered carriers of sexually transmitted diseases, a view clearly articulated in Hitler's *Mein Kampf*:

> Particularly with regard to syphilis, the attitude of those who guide the nation and the state can only be described as total capitulation. . . . In this case the only way to proceed is to attack the causes, not to remove the symptoms. The cause lies primarily in the prostitution of love. . . . This Jewification of the spiritual life and mammonization of the mating instinct will sooner or later destroy all our descendants.[73]

By turning Jews into polluters and carriers of an infection that threatened to taint not only individuals but also what Hitler referred to as the social body (*Volkskörper*), the Nazis were able to position the victims of their genocidal project as dangerous aggressors who had to be exterminated. In *Mein Kampf*, Hitler incessantly returned to the matter of the Jewish "plague" [Seuche] or "pestilence" [Pest] and its poisonous effect on the racially pure blood of the German people. The imperial city of Vienna, with its "repulsive racial mix of Czechs, Poles, Hungarians, Ruthenians, Serbs, and Croatians" along with "Jews and more Jews," struck him as "the incarnation of *Blutschande*."[74] The Jews took on all of the characteristics of the demonic other—the criminals, psychopaths, homosexuals, prostitutes, and victims of physical disease who were threatening the lifeblood of the German people. When the fear of otherness finally took hold in its most frightening form during the Third Reich, it was ironically the mass murderers who cultivated a hysterical fear that their victims would first infect, then finally destroy them.

During the 1920s, criminality was figured in such a way that it became enmeshed in a complex discursive network connecting various facets of what was perceived to be urban culture. Klaus Theweleit has pointed out that "syphilis" was one name given to physical incarnations of threats from within—"it is a particularly apposite name, a rich code, containing as it does the corrosions of femininity, Jewishness, epidemic disease, criminality (the contagion is international), and emasculating death."[75] But each of the items in Theweleit's catalog of social evils can also serve as a rich term for encoding the *Unrat* (filth) of urban culture that Hitler relentlessly denounced. The boundaries between femininity, Jewishness, disease, and criminality became so porous in the 1920s that it was almost impossible to talk about the one without implicating the others. Ultimately, the loss of these boundaries produced a kind of discursive homogenizing or *Gleichschaltung* that could be put into service by the Nazis to tap into profound anxieties about threats from the outside to the self and to provide the illusion of order and control in a world marked by complexity and instability.

· P A R T   T W O ·

Case Studies

WHILE Weimar Germany has often been glamorized as a period of alluring decadence or idealized as the breeding ground for modernist culture, it also figured as a bridge connecting two cataclysmic historical events. That the bridge was not freestanding, but anchored in the momentous events located at each end is a fact that, until recently, was often conveniently overlooked by cultural historians. In what follows, I have tried, when appropriate, to understand how the work of a particular artist, writer, or filmmaker is rooted in the war years or anticipates, in however indirect a manner, the ideological configurations of the Nazi years. I have deliberately avoided using the term "case history" to characterize the individual studies because each analysis turns as much on cultural enigmas as on issues of individual pathologies. Why, for example, did Otto Dix paint one canvas after another with the title *Lustmord* yet never directly address what was at stake for him in the production of images of murdered and disemboweled women? That critics avoided discussing the issue is even more telling. Why did George Grosz, who was his own severest critic, never question the asymmetrical nature of the representational practices he applied to the men and to the women in his drawings? Why did there seem to be a conspiracy of silence when it came to the role of women in Alfred Döblin's novel *Berlin Alexanderplatz*? And how is it that a man who murders children could become the target of our sympathetic identification in Fritz Lang's film *M*?

As the answers to these puzzles emerged, unexpected patterns appeared as well, the most important of which touches on the complex issue of agency in sexual violence. While the victim/agent relationship is never uncomplicated in any of these studies, one aspect of it reveals a surprising stability. Just as the German soldiers who invaded foreign territories in 1914 saw themselves as possessing *Opfermut* (the courage to sacrifice oneself) and *Opferbereitschaft* (readiness to sacrifice oneself), so the Nazis constantly figured themselves as victims—either of traitors at home who had stabbed them in the back or of parasitic and diseased foreign agents. In this context, it is worth noting that the German language collapses the notion of "victim" and "sacrifice" into a single term (*Opfer*). In the cultural production of the 1920s, we will see how agents of aggression and terror place themselves ever more emphatically into the role of victim even as the victim becomes an *agent provocateur*, if not agent pure and simple. This inversion has obvious ideological consequences that go beyond—but are not entirely divorced from—the issues of gender conflict addressed in this book. I shall refer to some of those consequences in the pages that follow.

Fighting for Life: Figurations of War, Women, and the City in the Work of Otto Dix

Everywhere the mystery of the corpse.

Max Beckmann

WHETHER they fought in the trenches or escaped military service, German artists, writers, and filmmakers of an entire generation were marked by the war experience and produced works colored by the mud and blood of World War I and its battlefields. For the painter Otto Dix, who experienced combat at first hand, four years at the front led to fundamental shifts in personal convictions and aesthetic positions. When an artist produces work as complex, contradictory, and at times aggressively disturbing as Dix's, it is not always easy to construct tidy arguments about new inflections of old themes and to chart a clear, direct route through ideological developments. Nonetheless, Dix's postwar artistic production—whether it takes the form of bloody battle scenes, mutilated female corpses, grotesque urban streetscapes, or serene neoclassical portraiture—seems singlemindedly devoted to working through primal fears aroused in combat situations, both military and sexual. It is to the subterranean working through of gender conflicts in this war experience that I will first look for a key to understanding an array of issues at stake in Dix's oeuvre, most notably the drive to disfigure the female body—a representational practice that becomes evident in the many post–World War I works bearing the title *Lustmord*.

What we find in Dix's postwar artistic production might be called a continuation of war by other means and with a very different adversary. It is as if the war functioned as an event that released the creative energies of artists and legitimized the represention of brutal violence directed at the female enemy on the domestic front rather than the male adversary on the military battlefield. But the gender trouble we see in Dix's work is fueled by more than the war experience. As noted earlier, emancipatory efforts in matters social and economic raised the stakes in the battle of the sexes and intensified hostilities. Yet for both Dix and his contemporary George Grosz, World War I becomes a kind of pre-text for staging sexual conflicts—an experience of violent excess transferred to the domestic area.

No two works illustrate more clearly the transformative power of war on Dix's artistic output than *Walpurgis Night* (*Walpurgisnacht*, 1914) (fig. 6) and *Flares* (*Leuchtkugeln*, 1917) (fig. 7). The brush and pen-and-ink *Walpurgis Night* displays a scene of frenzied exhibitionism, with five female figures riding unambiguously phallic broomsticks in lewd postures suggesting their sexual availability. Commingling erotic energy with demonic sexuality (this is, after all, a witches' sabbath), the drawing represents female sexuality as both seductive and threatening. We seem to be at once in the realm of a pagan fertility rite and at the site of a licentious, self-indulgent orgy.

Even the most cursory glance at *Flares* reveals striking compositional congruities with *Walpurgis Night*. But the grounds for comparison go far beyond compositional elements, particularly when we consider that Dix viewed war as a decidedly diabolical affair—something of a military Walpurgis Night ruled by the death drive rather than the pleasure principle:

> Lice, rats, barbed wire, fleas, shells, bombs, underground caves, corpses, blood, liquor, mice, cats, gas, artillery, filth, bullets, mortars, fire, steel: that is what war is! It is all the work of the Devil![1]

Flares presents a male counterpart to the devil's work of *Walpurgis Night*, with an assembly of bodies in death throes rather than in the throes of sexual abandon. Not only are the expiring soldiers drawn in skeletal white outline to emphasize the morbid hopelessness of their plight in the war-torn landscape, their heads resemble nothing more than skulls decaying on the battlefield. Despite the bleak and grisly character of the military carnage on display, it is not without sensual beauty. Its brilliant colors and compositional accomplishment point to an aestheticization of martial violence, with the explosive deaths of the soldiers producing an ornamental effect against the vivid hues of earth and sky. As if to signal that there is more to the battle scene than carnal mayhem and wanton destruction, the soldier at the center of the canvas is less cadaverous or skeletal than infantlike in his soft, rounded forms. From the ruins of the terrain, the earth seems to give birth and renews life in the midst of spectacular deaths. What is particularly striking about the contrast between these two works is the way in which the feminine comes to be associated in the earlier work with dissolution, excess, and sexuality in the service of self-gratification, while the masculine becomes affiliated in the later work with heroic self-sacrifice in the service of rebirth. Is it nothing more than coincidence that the ladies of *Walpurgis Night* vanish to give way

6. Otto Dix, *Walpurgis Night* (1914). This orgiastic witches' sabbath demonstrates the degree to which Dix invested the naked female body with demonic sexual power. The explosive energy of the naked bodies in the service of sexual frenzy marks an interesting contrast with scenes of war carnage displaying male bodies exploding on battlefields.

to a new order in which men engage in regeneration as they expire on the battlefields?

The displacement of the female body and the appropriation of its biological functions through the creative energies of male autogeny becomes a regular fixture of Dix's postwar artistic production. Consider his *Portrait of the Painter Karl Schwesig with His Model* (*Bildnis des Malers Karl Schwesig mit*

7. Otto Dix, *Flares* (1917). The skeletal bodies of soldiers in their death throes are set against a backdrop of stunning visual effects.

Modell, 1925) (fig. 8) and *Self-Portrait with My Son Jan* (*Selbstbildnis mit dem Sohn Jan*, 1930) (fig. 9). In this case, compositional congruities are not readily apparent, for the painter Schwesig and his model do not give us the full frontal view of painter and model in the later self-portrait. Yet a closer look reveals that the arms of both models are posed in similar fashion, just as the furrowed brows and hands of both artists, poised with a brush, closely resemble each other. But there the resemblances end. The painter Schwesig cowers in a corner as he paints a hefty woman who occupies four times the canvas space devoted to the artist and dwarfs him with her overwhelming

8. Otto Dix, *Portrait of the Painter Karl Schwesig with His Model* (1925). The fleshy figure of the model dominates the canvas, with the artist Schwesig nearly cowering in the corner. That the canvas is still blank seems to suggest a crisis of artistic performance in the face of the overwhelming sensual power of the model.

9. Otto Dix, *Self-Portrait with My Son Jan* (1930). The artist celebrates both his paternal and artistic identity in a work that resonates with allusions to biblical themes and religious painting. With brush in hand, Dix proudly faces the viewer as he exhibits the son to whom he has given life and the brush with which he has created a work of transcendent spiritual purity.

fleshiness.[2] The painter Dix, by contrast, proudly faces the viewer as he puts his creation on display. While Schwesig struggles to reproduce the contours of the corpulent female body, Dix exhibits the toddler to whom he has given life and on whom he has conferred immortality through artistic representation. In an act of artistic triumph, Dix erases the link between sexuality and creation, negates human mortality, and recreates himself as the artist who stands as the source of life and immortality. Here, the sensual woman who threatens to overwhelm and crush the creative artist is effaced to make room for the autogenous artist who has appropriated the procreative powers of women and gone them one better by producing a work of transcendent spiritual purity.

Yet even as Dix moves toward displacing female fecundity and plenitude with images of male artistic autonomy, he relentlessly invests the feminine with exaggerated biological, social, and political power. In a diary kept at the front during the First World War, Dix asserted that war had to be considered "a natural event." "Money, religion, and women," he added, may create "occasions for combat," but none of them figures as war's basic cause (Grundursache), which Dix cryptically identifies as an "eternal law." That "eternal law," as it turns out, has more to do with women than Dix initially admits, for the war diary elsewhere records this pronouncement: "In the final analysis, all wars are waged over and because of the vulva."[3] Many of Dix's most acclaimed paintings remind us of just how central that particular part of the female anatomy was to his oeuvre, but none more strikingly than the right panel of his triptych Metropolis (Großstadt, 1927–28) (fig. 10), which turns the garments of a lady of the night into an enlarged representation of what Dix sees as the cause of war. The Seven Deadly Sins (Die sieben Todsünden, 1933) (fig. 11) shows us the figure of Voluptas wearing garb that again takes the shape of enlarged female genitals.[4] In a less sensationalizing mode, Dix also produced a series of paintings based on the tradition of the clothed male artist with his nude female model. In one canvas after another, he configures and reconfigures this basic pair as self-portrait with muse, as client and prostitute, as murderer and victim, as death and the maiden, or as old man and young lover. Always on display, the female body is foregrounded and relegates the male body to the "negative space" of background even as its self-presentation undermines—in ways that will become evident through an analysis of Dix's oeuvre—the hierarchy constituted by the figure-ground relationship.[5]

It may be easy enough to document Dix's obsession with the female nude and with female genitalia in particular, but that obsession does not necessarily translate into an explanation for a causal link between war and woman. Even a long, searching look at Dix's many war drawings offers little evidence for constructing arguments about either sexual envy or gender rivalry as the

10. Otto Dix, *Metropolis* (1927–28). The garish excesses of urban life are revealed at the center of a triptych that displays the marginalization of the war veteran in spatial terms. The prostitutes, with the opulent fabrics of their dress and display of flesh, overwhelm the compositional space of the two panels.

hidden cause of war. What we see in those drawings are, for the most part, energetic, futuristic depictions of trench warfare or bleak, desolate landscapes of war-torn terrain. Yet Dix himself, somewhat disingenuously, insisted that he was bent neither on aestheticizing war nor on issuing passionate pacifist statements with his art. He had no explicit ideological program, he claimed, and wanted only to capture what he believed to be war's essence.[6] In the process of representing the battle scenes of World War I, however, Dix uncovered for himself something that was less timeless and universal than specific to the culture in which he lived.

For Dix, war meant more than combat between men. Unsparing in their depiction of human casualties, his war drawings and gouaches often focus in an unusually detailed way on a battleground scarred by trenches, barbed wire, and shellholes—on a terrain, in short, that has been ravaged by soldiers. The drawing *Trench with Barbed Wire* (*Graben mit Drahtverhau*, 1915) illustrates the degree to which men and war matériel disfigure the earth, turning it into a bewildering landscape of labyrinthine obstructions, with only small pockets of safe refuge. Dix seems fascinated by what one critic, in telling metaphorical language, calls the "surreal dismemberment of the earth"; what another critic describes as the transformation of the earth "from its organic fullness and diversity . . . into hideously mangled innards"; and a third terms the "mutilation of the earth."[7]

However hideously savage war may be, with "hunger, lice, mud, all those insane noises," exposure to it seemed vital to Dix the artist: "I could not

11. Otto Dix, *The Seven Deadly Sins* (1933). The personified vices proceed down the path of destruction. Note that Lust is represented as a woman, whose costume bears a resemblance to the frontal pose of the prostitute in *Metropolis*. The Hitler moustache was added later to the dwarf (Envy) riding on the back of Avarice.

12. Otto Dix, *Shellhole with Flowers (Spring, 1916, outside of Reims)* (1924). The war-torn landscape regenerates itself. Unlike the invalid soldiers who survived but whose bodies remained mutilated, the earth shows signs of recovering from the ravages of war.

possibly miss it. You have to see man in an unbridled state in order to know something about him."[8] What is extraordinary about Dix's war portfolio is the way its contents display an unspeakably brutal aggression trained on the earth—the very place that shields the soldiers from enemy attack—rather than on the enemy soldier. While we rarely catch a glimpse of man-to-man combat, we repeatedly see orgies of *another* kind of violence: wounded soldiers struggling with the earth, male corpses embracing the earth, and male casualties draped over the landscape in a ghoulish *Kriegestod*, a grim modern reprise of the nineteenth-century *Liebestod*. So charged are Dix's battle scenes with erotic energy that the artist seems to experience war "sensually like a lover."[9]

Once the earth is recognized as an active participant in the war drama, it becomes possible to construct an explanation for why Dix assigns blame for war to the vulva. Let us begin by looking at one of the few war sketches that is neither a stylized battle scene nor a snapshot of systematic devastation. *Shellhole with Flowers (Granattrichter mit Blumen*, 1915) (fig. 12), and a later drawing of 1916 with the same title, show the earth recovering from wartime shelling and regenerating itself. One critic, in a now familiar interpretive leap, describes the earlier drawing as a depiction of "the damp belly of the earth," torn open by a shell but on the road to recovery.[10] Dix's representation of the earth is less benign in the context of *Shellhole with Corpses* (*Granattrichter mit Leichen*, 1917) (fig. 13), which shows the earth exploding from the blast of a shell, expelling the bodies of soldiers from its center. Mother Earth thus becomes not only the site of regeneration but, more important, despite the womblike protection it offers soldiers, the locus of an explosive, violent death.

That Dix saw Mother Earth and the human maternal body as homologous entities becomes evident from his 1919 painting *Pregnant Woman* (*Schwangere Frau*). Here earth and woman become one, with the planet serving as the belly of a cosmic female figure painted in rich red, blue, and gold Renaissance hues.[11] Whenever Dix draws pregnant women or depicts scenes of birth— violating with unprecedented frequency what Hélène Cixous has called the "taboo of the pregnant woman"—the women are invariably described by critics as earth mothers (*Erdenmütter*).[12]

Dix's equation of Mother Earth with human mothers, his focus on the regenerative powers of earth and the procreative capabilities of women, becomes especially significant in the context of cultural myths about male combat as a virile form of reproduction. The gulf between maternal and military service, as Nancy Huston has pointed out, is not as great as it might first seem. But the parallels go beyond the Gnostic conundrum and its answer: "How long will men make war? As long as women have children," though the answer has an interesting double meaning in implying that men compete with women's procreative powers by making war. As Huston points out, "reciprocal metaphorization" has cemented the enduring cultural analogy between war and childbirth:

> It is impossible to determine whether men decided to confer social prestige upon labor pains so that women might partake, at least to some extent, in the glory of battle—or whether, conversely, they strove to invent for themselves a suffering as dignified, as meritorious and as spectacular in its results as that of childbirth.[13]

For Dix's contemporaries, this metaphorization came to be less reciprocal than unilateral—procreative metaphors were relentlessly pressed into service to endow men with the capacity to do precisely the opposite of what their military missions really accomplished. This new ethos of male (pro)creation was nowhere proclaimed with greater rhetorical confidence than in the works of Ernst Jünger. "War, the father of all things, is also our father," Jünger declared. "It has forged us, chiseled us, and hardened us to make us what we are." This second birth from a male parent, even if on "female" soil, in turn creates a soldier who is able to sire his own father: "War

13. Otto Dix, *Shellhole with Corpses* (1917). This futuristic depiction of warfare, with soldiers dying as they are expelled from the earth, suggests the powerlessness of Mother
Earth to protect the soldier from an explosive death.

is not only our father but also our son. We created him and he created us."[14]
For Jünger, reproduction is completely in the hands of fathers and sons who
constitute each other in an endless series of invigorating conflicts that create
impermeable bodies of steel. What is born is "a new relation to the elemental," one purchased at the expense of "Mother Earth, whose soil has been
blasted away in the rekindled fires of material battles and fertilized by
streams of blood."[15]

Even once the illusions about the rejuvenating energy of military combat
were shattered by the brutal realities of trench warfare, there were still many
who desperately wanted to see something rise out of the ashes, and who

therefore continued to affirm cataclysmic destruction as the only real guarantee of renewal. Hermann Hesse's best-selling novel *Demian*, published in 1919, tried to uphold the notion of the "Great War" as a mortal struggle for rebirth: "A huge bird was struggling out of its egg. The egg was the world, and the world had to be destroyed."[16] Jünger's combat pains and Hesse's birth pains both seem to underwrite the belief that the only way to manage the trauma of a military conquest is to transform the manifest tyranny of a "feminine" position (struggle, conquest, and submission) into an experience that emphasizes the procreative advantage of that position.

That the success of a masculine reproductive project rests on the dismemberment and annihilation of a feminine entity squares with the "facts" of numerous myths of creation in which a male god murders and dismembers a female before giving birth to a new order.[17] If, as Freud has suggested, myths are projected psychology, then the possibility of womb envy as an important component of psychosexual dynamics becomes all the more evident on the basis of these and other similar cultural stories. Melanie Klein and Karen Horney have written convincingly about men's awe and envy of women's capacity for giving birth—for Klein, Freud's phallocentric thinking is little more than a defense against womb envy.[18] By making war instead of love, as Jünger's military rhetoric reveals, men can not only appropriate but also improve on the procreative process, producing a species untainted by the primitive biological process through which women give birth to helpless infants and also eliminating the nuclear family, perceived by the prewar generation as that most oppressive and stifling of all social institutions.

The notion of achieving male autogeny through a displaced ruination of female procreative powers made a belated appearance in Dix's work. During the war years, and for a good part of the immediate postwar period, Dix represented mobilization less as a glorified fitness mission that turned the male body into a hard, chiseled form than as an enterprise that led almost directly to physical immobilization. When it came to the battlefield, Dix remained a realist. With unrelenting candor, he revealed that combat, rather than creating indestructible bodies, depleted, paralyzed, and mutilated the body of the soldier.

While Dix's war drawings represent nature as self-healing and fertile, they show the male soldier as victim, suffering a thousand deaths in combat or simply rotting away, as in the sketch *Dead Soldier* (*Toter Soldat*, 1922). The soldiers who survived the Great War (one thinks of the mutilated men in Dix's *Card Players* [*Skatspieler*, 1920]) often fare little better than their dead comrades, for they are trapped in bodies beyond repair. Leading a shadowy existence, they are virtually overwhelmed by the fleshy plenitude of those figures for the sake of whose sexual organs they had evidently entered the war. In *Soldiers from the Front in Brussels* (*Frontsoldaten in Brüssel*, 1924), the voluptuous carnality of the preening streetwalkers is so prominent that one easily overlooks the figure of a soldier, whose gaze lingers enviously on the parade of prostitutes. The soldier in *A Visit to Madame Germaine in Méricourt* (*Besuch bei Madame Germaine in Méricourt*, 1924) is similarly dwarfed by a bone-crushing prostitute whose fetishized body stands in sharp contrast to the patched military uniform of her client. While maimed invalids cower in corners or abjectly beg in the streets, prostitutes strut past them in poses that flaunt their robust vitality and physical superiority. *Street in Prague* (*Prager Straße*, 1920) sharpens the plight of war veterans by situating them on an avenue famous for its expensive boutiques and restaurants. A shopwindow displaying artificial limbs is directly adjacent to another with an array of wigs for ladies. The contrast between depleted soldier and fetishized female is further underscored by the fleshiness of a well-padded female derrière fleeing the scene to escape the sight of the emaciated war survivors.

Despite the fact that invalid soldier and corpulent prostitute are constructed as opposites, or at least placed in an asymmetrical power relationship, they are also, in some respects, homologous with one another. Nowhere is this more directly illustrated than in a drawing by Dix, which was given the title *Two Victims of Capitalism* (*Zwei Opfer des Kapitalismus*, 1923) (fig. 14).[19] There, prostitute and veteran (the one bearing syphilitic facial sores that look like bullet wounds, the other displaying war wounds that resemble female genitals) are reckoned as the casualties of a society that harnesses bodies into service for pay. In more subtle ways too, Dix equated those enlisted in the urban struggle for survival and those conscripted for military battle even as he marked the distinctions between the two. His two great triptychs, *War* (*Der Krieg*, 1929–32) (fig. 15) and *Metropolis* (*Großstadt*, 1927–28), may seem unlikely doubles of each other, particularly in light of the macabre gloom of the one and the garish colorfulness of the other, but they have more in common than immediately meets the eye.

What links the two paintings goes beyond surface similarities, but those connections deserve mention. To begin with, there is a remarkable study in contrasts between the nobility of fallen men and the corruption of fallen women.[20] The left panel of *War* shows soldiers marching into the war zone, while the left panel of *Metropolis* shows prostitutes sauntering through a red-light district (what Boston calls its "combat zone"). The central panel of *War* displays a corpse presiding over a full panoply of military devastation; *Metropolis* shows a garishly dressed woman striking up the band. Both right panels mark a return from the combat zone. There is a powerful likeness between the face of a courageous soldier rescuing a comrade in the right panel of *War* and the face of the invalid in the right panel of *Metropolis*—both are self-portraits of the artist.

War is rich in "intertextual" references to paintings of Christ's passion and

14. Otto Dix, *Two Victims of Capitalism* (1923). That the prostitute and soldier are both victims—one operating for pay in urban combat zones, the other enlisted for military service, is revealed by their representation as casualties. The syphilitic facial scars of the prostitute resemble bullet wounds, while the war injury of the soldier has a shape resembling female genitals.

martyrdom. Much as Dix was self-consciously working in opposition to a literary trend of the late 1920s that sought to recuperate war as a valiant military effort, he was unable to escape the need to find some redeeming value in the destruction and carnage of the battlefields.[21] That even scenes

15. Otto Dix, *War* (1929–32). The triptych with predella has been read as both an indictment of war and as an idealization of male heroism. Allusions to Christ's martyrdom
abound in these war scenes.

from World War I—which he deliberately painted in grey (*grau*) tones to
emphasize their horrifying (*grausam*) aspects—offered some opportunities for
heroics becomes evident from the master sub-narrative of Christ's passion
and suffering told in the war triptych.[22] The soldiers in the left panel marching to war, in this account, are bearing their arms like a cross; the central
panel shows a crucifixion scene with one soldier impaled on an iron bar (his
loincloth is borrowed from a Grünewald crucifixion scene) and another
whose body is riddled with bullet wounds that bear an unmistakable resemblance to the sores covering Christ's body in another Grünewald crucifixion;
the right panel frames a heroic figure (the self-portrait of the artist) pulling a
comrade out of the firing zone in a tableau that mimes the deposition. Numerous critics have pointed out that the predella, with its three soldiers
sleeping underground, is modeled on Hans Holbein's *Dead Christ* (1521).

Martyrdom played a prominent role even in Dix's prewar artistic production. There are numerous pen-and-ink sketches showing the mocking of
Christ, his torture, and the deposition from the cross. The mortification of
male flesh seems a recurrent obsession from 1910 until the outbreak of the
war, with crucifixions and circumcision scenes abounding. The body of Saint

Sebastian, wracked with pain from arrows piercing his flesh, is a common theme in Dix's work from the same years. In stark contrast to these images of corporeal torment is a typically serene Madonna of 1914, which shows Virgin and child at the center of an admiring crowd. Even in the prewar work, Dix seems intent on configuring conventional religious themes in such a way as to contrast the stoicism of men in the face of physical adversity with the elation of women in the blissful throes of a spiritualized form of procreation. The adoration brought to images of female plenitude stands in stark distinction to the lonely anguish of male figures, depleted and humiliated in the face of defeat.

Paul Fussell has documented how Christ's sacrificial suffering impressed itself on the consciousness of military men fighting the battles of World War I. "Reminded of the Crucifixion all the time by the ubiquitous foreign calvaries and by the spectacle of uniformed miscreants immobilized and shamed with their arms extended," Fussell writes, "the troops readily embraced the image as quintessentially symbolic of their own suffering and 'sacrifice.'" Robert Graves, Wilfred Owen, and Siegfried Sassoon were among the many British poets who drew analogies between the passion of Christ and the sufferings of military men. During the Battle of the Somme, Graves noted, Christ was being invoked by Germans and Allies alike as a model for their heroic martyrdom. Thus Dix's *War* must have had a special resonance for veterans. What Dix captures on his canvas is both the real carnage of battle and the soldier's hope for salvation through tribulation—a hope that persisted into the postwar years.[23]

Though not directly represented by Dix in his military drama, resurrection and the afterlife are implicit in the emphasis on a transcendent heroism. "I simply wanted to describe and show—in a manner resembling reportage— all my experiences from the years 1914–1918, to show that true human heroism means surmounting the senselessness of death," Dix stated.[24] Dix's triptych presents itself as a secular altarpiece that concedes death's invincibility even as it validates the heroic struggle to resist it through the grim determination of the soldier pulling his comrade out of the carnage. The helmets, rifles, bayonets, and shell holes may anchor the scenes in the specificity of the First World War, but, for Dix, the struggle staged in the triptych reaches beyond that particular conflict with its hostile factions to a more general struggle confronting man with his mortality.

Dix turns the war into a zone where mortals battle for their lives in the face of the devastatingly powerful machinery of death. Unlike the combatants in earlier works by Dix, the soldiers in the war triptych are not at all consumed by the desire to couple with the earth in a torrid *Kriegestod*. They are engaged in an existential battle more than anything else, with soldiers pitted against a disembodied destroyer. Here, it seems, Dix's universal cause of war has been effaced, or perhaps repressed, for female sexuality does not seem to figure at all into the ruinous scenes of devastation in *War*. Yet, I would argue, it is there nonetheless, for *War* and *Metropolis* can be read in tandem as documents of the way in which Dix, in the 1920s, unsettled the gender roles and hierarchies established in his early work and divested many of his female figures of their procreative powers (representing them as cadaverous prostitutes with diseased bodies) even as he transformed the "negative space" of male suffering into a redemptive arena of transcendent heroism (artistic as well as military). A look at Dix's *Metropolis* can clarify some of the common underlying cultural anxieties of the two triptychs and reveal what led Dix to channel those anxieties into polarized visions of war and the city.

Beneath the surface glamour of boa feathers and fox stoles in *Metropolis*, there lurks a grim *danse macabre*. For all its garish colorfulness, *Metropolis* represents, in the context of Dix's oeuvre, a covert doubling of the morbid scenes of mutilation, decay, and death in *War*. The left panel of Dix's triptych of urban pathologies already forges a link between it and *War*: the dead invalid across whose body prostitute and war veteran gaze at each other figures, despite his role as a war combatant, as a casualty of urban life. In the right panel we see another invalid, hatless and with stumps for legs. Excluded from the field of vision of the prostitutes who parade past him, this figure is more dead than alive to the world. Reading this panel alongside the right panel of *War* points up the striking contrast between a male gesture of heroic defiance (a refusal to surrender a comrade to death, even when death so clearly commands the battlefield) and female indifference to suffering (with an invalid left for dead, even as a horse on the canvas is comfortably settled with a feedbag). While war moves men to mount heroic resistance to death even when the landscape is littered with corpses, the city is the site of a battlefield on which men surrender to a squalid life of mute passivity and a demeaning death.

Berlin as Whore of Babylon, as the incarnation of voracious sexuality, was precisely what captured Dix's imagination. We know the extent to which Dix was fascinated by the book of Revelation (the Bible was one of two books he had in his knapsack during his years in combat) and the degree to which he seemed to labor under a compulsion to juxtapose images of carnal pleasures with those of death and dissolution.[25] For Dix, the body of the prostitute became the site of intersecting discourses on urban corruption, murderous sexuality, and grotesque corporality.

Metropolis sets up so stark a contrast between invalids and prostitutes that it becomes almost impossible to imagine affinities between the two. Yet a closer look at the figures in *Metropolis* reveals that Dix, for all his self-proclaimed artistic naïveté, worked hard to encode some resemblances and congruencies. The dominant figure of the left panel in *Metropolis* is undeniably the invalid/beggar who has his back to us, but whose visage is visible and reveals itself to be a self-portrait. His compositional counterpart in the right panel is the prostitute who, with a body that takes the form of female genitals, looks out frontally at the viewer. Dieter Scholz was the first to discern that the position of this prostitute's hand on her fur coat exactly duplicates that of Albrecht Dürer's hand in his *Self-Portrait in a Fur Coat* (*Selbstbildnis im Pelzrock*, 1500). Scholz could easily have emphasized the elongated visages of both figures as well, and he fails to register that this particular "intertextual" reference is only one of many nods and bows in Dürer's direction, the most striking of which can be found in Dix's *Self-Portrait with Carnation* (*Selbstbildnis mit Nelke*).[26]

On the face of it, it is odd to find the very artist with whom Dix identifies in an early self-portrait associated with the menacing feminine presence in *Metropolis*. To further complicate matters, that figure crosses gender lines to emerge not as the predictable threatening father in an oedipal scenario, but as a coldly disdainful woman. Michael Fried has shown us the extent to which oedipal conflicts can lie buried beneath layers of paint,[27] and Dix's *Metropolis* works hard to mask that conflict, despite its figuration of a helpless male (barely able to walk) "exposed" to a woman of commanding arrogance, whose iconographic significance is figured in glaringly sexual terms. Yet the invalid and prostitute of *Metropolis* are also powerfully linked to each other, not only through their resemblance to two German artists, but also because the bodies of both signify lack—the invalid with his two stumps for legs (the German *Kriegsverletzter* and *Kriegsversehrter* capture the notions of woundedness and depletion), the prostitute with the woundlike opening to which she points. One is led to the inescapable conclusion that Dix meant to associate all three—artists, invalids, and prostitutes—with vulnerability, lack, castration and that the term opposed to these signifiers of femininity is the overpoweringly fecund phallic woman.

Dix's prewar drawings of female figures unequivocally celebrate the voluptuous beauty of the female body, often erasing the line between the maternal and the seductive. These powerful nudes glow with radiant energy; there is nothing in the least sinister about them, even when they represent prostitutes.[28] Beginning in the 1920s, many of Dix's female nudes lose their earthy, erotic qualities and begin to turn into skeletons of themselves, in some cases literally so. For Dix, women not only challenge male biological superiority through their reproductive labor, they also stand as the source of a lethal urban pathology affiliated with the unreproductive sexuality of the prostitute. By the 1920s, Dix's female nudes convey a frontal view of death, with the voluptuous banished to the margins of his canvases. In *At the Mirror* (*Am Spiegel*, 1922) what we first see is a haggard prostitute preening before the mirror—only a careful second look reveals the clever cosmetic deceptions that make the hag appear to be an attractive young woman from behind. Death and decay can come to dominate a canvas completely, as in what is probably the most unnerving "still life" ever painted, *Still Life in the Studio* (*Stilleben im Atelier*, 1924). There, Dix juxtaposes the literal still life of a moth-eaten female dummy with the overwhelming corpulence of a pregnant woman, mocking the power to give life by inserting the gravid body into a funereal scene. Few artists can be credited with as many portraits of pregnant females as Dix, but these images become more and more disturbing over time, slipping into a macabre mode that erases the voluptuous sensuality of the pregnant body and turns it into a de-eroticized site of grotesque carnality.

Dix's attention to the two unspeakable extremes of our existence becomes especially prominent in a series of six graphic works grouped together in 1923 under the mordantly ironic title *Death and Resurrection*. Included is a suicide dangling from the ceiling before the ghost of himself, seated on a chair reading the newspaper (perhaps a report about his own death) with obvious pleasure. Another work in the group shows the decaying body of a soldier killed in combat; flowers sprout around him while mice, birds, and centipedes sport about his corpse. *Sexual Murder* (*Lustmord*, 1922) (fig. 16), the piece designated as second in the series of six, is perhaps the most graphically horrifying of all the images. In it, the "comic relief" from the grisly scene of death is more ghoulish than in all the others. On a bed lies the spread-eagled corpse of a woman whose body has been mutilated in the style of Jack the Ripper. At the foot of the bed, dogs copulate in a grim parody of the notion of "resurrection" through reproduction.

Why would Dix, after suffering through the bloodbath of World War I, fix his attention so intently on the carnage of urban crime—on murders, slashings, and rapes? Was he simply by nature so preoccupied with mutilated bodies and rotting corpses that his artistic production could move seamlessly from the battlefields of World War I to the sites of urban crime? Why is it that the male project of self-destruction through an explosive *Kriegestod* coupled with heroic defiance in the face of death gave way to the male project of maiming, mutilating, and murdering female bodies? More than a keen resentment of conscription into a battle for the "home" front, a brutalization of men through the war experience, or a crisis of male subjectivity stemming

16. Otto Dix, *Sexual Murder* (1922). This etching appeared in a cycle of graphic works entitled *Death and Resurrection*. The corpse is the most grisly of all the images in that collection.

from a humiliating defeat seems to be at stake here, for the relations between
women and war, regeneration and destruction, desire and death—conditioned by all manner of social, economic, and biological realities—are constructed in a manner so complex as to resist stabilizing statements.[29]

It is not always easy to fathom why an artist who painted one of the most
powerful indictments of war (notwithstanding his denial of its ideological
significance) and who (ex post facto) valorized resistance to devastation and
death would return from his years at the front to cover his canvases with
scenes from a latter-day battle of the sexes producing carnage as repulsive as
that of the trenches. One postwar canvas after another displays the corpse of
a woman violated and murdered. These urban *Lustmorde* generally show the
victim alone, though *Murder* (*Mord*, 1922) preserves the face of the criminal
killer as he exits from a room in which a dead naked women is sprawled on
the floor next to a bed. The male figure bears a distinct resemblance to the

enraged pimp in Dix's *Fose and Lui* (1921), which captures a moment that could easily figure as the prelude to a *Mord*, if not a *Lustmord*. But for Dix sexual murder is not just symptomatic of a barbaric urban culture: to be sure, pimps kill whores, but more reputable citizens are also murdering women. Dix's *Sex Murderer: Self-Portrait* (see fig. 3) is, despite its surreal style, a confessional self-portrait that makes the act of murder something of a human, all-too-human fantasy rather than the result of a perverse derangement.

Why did Dix do it? What drove him to incriminate himself, to present himself as a man with knife in hand, slicing through the neck, breasts, and limbs of a nude woman? Why did he "sign" this painting with red prints from his own hand? Why would he mime the stabbing gestures of a murderer for friends or declare that he depicted himself as a murderer to avoid committing a sex crime in real life? A self-portrait drawn a year later shows the artist surrounded by figments of his imagination—among other things we see a female torso covered with sores, a disemboweled female corpse, and a close-up of that secret agent of war known as the vulva. And in 1922 Dix painted another *Sexual Murder* (see fig. 2), his most graphic representation of a mutilated female corpse. It is interesting to observe how Dix sets himself up here too as the perpetrator of this most horrifyingly realistic of all the sexual murders he painted. Not only does the scene of the crime bear a distinct resemblance to Dix's room as a student, the site of the murder (as the lamp, bed, and chair reveal) is the very same room represented in the surreal self-portrait as sex murderer. What remained a sketchy fantasy in the self-portrait becomes a luridly realistic representation in *Sexual Murder*.

Paul Fussell has argued that it was not until after World War II that the "ritual of military memory" of the First World War was "freed from all puritan lexical constraint and allowed to take place with a full appropriate obscenity."[30] By the 1960s and 1970s, he argues, censorship had so eased, both in the public realm and the private imagination, that full expression of the massive obscenity of war became possible at long last. For Fussell, Pynchon's *Gravity's Rainbow* and Mailer's *American Dream* offer up examples of "adequate remembering and interpreting" of war's horrors. Yet the passages Fussell sees as so perfectly capturing the realities of war have nothing to do with combat—instead they consist of scenes of intense sexual depravity and perversion dictated, in one case, by what Fussell calls a "filthy slut" who becomes "the spirit of military memory in all times and places." What Fussell fails to note is that the postwar imagination seems to have found it convenient to manage traumatic military memories by converting them into sexual nightmares in which women emerge either as orchestrators of unspeakable atrocities or as abject victims of male violence. "It is after recalling the sadistic, bloody details of his shooting of four Germans in Italy that Stephen

Rojack proceeds to sodomize the 'Kraut' Ruta," Fussell notes in his praise of *An American Dream*—a work that reveals the "full obscenity of the Great War."[31] Without reflecting on the weighty consequences of the transfer of physical violence and bloodshed from the arena of male military action to the sphere of heterosexual encounters or on the way in which a traumatic memory of violence against men becomes the occasion for an act of sexual aggression against a woman, Fussell implies that the private perversions of human sexuality are far more compellingly horrific than anything in the public realm of warfare.

Anyone who looks at Dix's postwar drawings and paintings will find it hard to believe that standards for censorship in Germany were not sufficiently relaxed to accommodate sexual violence until the 1960s. While it is true that Dix was several times brought up on obscenity charges, he was never convicted, and he seemed more inhibited by the negative voices of art critics than by official threats of government censorship—at least until the Nazis came to power. The authorities, as in the case of George Grosz, were so unnerved by Dix's depictions of mutilated male bodies (which might weaken German "military resistance") that they failed to pay much attention to pictures of women disemboweled, with their throats slashed. In a parallel move, art historians wax eloquent about the horrors of combat in their commentaries on Dix's *War*, but do not register much shock at the number of sexual murders in Dix's oeuvre.

Dix's canvas serial murders are, in a sense, overdetermined by a profusion of culturally specific experiences (above all combat in the First World War) and by more general psychic anxieties (among them womb envy and dread of engulfment). Yet there is another issue at stake here as well—an aesthetic one that cannot in any sense be divorced from the cultural and psychic but that deserves special attention on its own terms. Susan Gubar, among others, has pointed out the way in which much of Western artistic production has been locked into a system with two fixed coordinates: male creators and female creations. Ovid's story of Pygmalion, with its male artist who usurps women's procreative powers to give birth to the ideal woman, stands as the paradigmatic myth of "male primacy." (Note that Pygmalion is driven to create an idealized alternative to a real woman because of his revulsion with prostitutes and with "the many faults which nature has implanted in the female sex.")[32] It is perhaps telling that Dix produced a self-portrait framed by the words "I, Dix, am the Alpha and the Omega" [Ich Dix bin das A und das O] and that he often signed his works with an "A" and "O," as if to stress in the most emphatic possible terms his own generative powers and position as supreme creator.[33]

17. Otto Dix, *Self-Portrait with Muse* (1924). Dix, paintbrush and maulstick in hand, resists and represents the sensuality of this muse. Through the gaze trained on her and through the transcendent power of his craft, the artist is able to contain the threat embodied in this decidedly unethereal figure.

Dix's entire oeuvre, with its many inflections of fertility, reproduction, pro-creation, and artistic creativity, is profoundly implicated in issues of origins and agency, with an implied dividing line established between male creative spirits and female reproductive bodies. A look at virtually any random sam-ple of the artist's paintings, etchings, and drawings will document a profusion of works focused on male artists (including numerous self-portraits) and on their female models (studio models, muses, prostitutes, wives, and mothers). Dix's *Self-Portrait with Muse* (*Selbstbildnis mit Muse*, 1924) (fig. 17) is perhaps the most complexly revealing of all his studies that pair artist and model. That canvas displays Dix at work on a painting that seems to come to life in part because the canvas within the canvas has no borders and becomes the ground for both representer and represented. Dix's muse, as we know from the paintbrush that the artist is in the process of applying to her, is—in the context of the painting—nothing more than a representation, yet she and her creator come to occupy the same space; he breathes life into the very agent who is to inspire him and breathe life into his art. The muse, with wings attached to her decidedly unethereal body, strikes a pose reminiscent of an angel, but it is she who, in a radical twist, is conceived by the artist and delivered through his labors.

Critical opinion has not held the physical appearance of this muse in particularly high esteem. When Diether Schmidt, in a phrase that is more than a play on words, writes that this woman is both "terrifying" and "fecund" [furchtbar und fruchtbar], he registers the prevailing view of her.[34] Whether it is the dark hair on the upper lip, the protruding eyes, or the full breasts that disturb critics is not clear. But details aside, this muse is a powerful physical presence—one that has been created and contained, notwithstanding the absence of a frame, by the artist who stands before her, his eyes fixed on her, with the symbols of his double control: paintbrush and maulstick.[35] Here the artist has taken the female model/muse and turned her into his own creation through an act of inspired sublimation. It is not through her "fecund" body that life is given but through the disciplinary gaze and powerful brushstrokes of the artist who resists and tames the aggressive sensuality of the phallic woman. *Portrait of the Painter Karl Schwesig with His Model*, to which I referred earlier, serves as a pointed contrast to the mastery of the model implied in the portrait of Dix with his muse. The Schwesig portrait flies in the face of a strong "masculine" representational tradition in which male artists subdue and possess their female models through a form of creative artistry fueled by erotic energy. In the context of Dix's work, it becomes the parodistic exception that proves the general rule.[36]

Dix's critics have repeatedly asserted the artist's control of his models through the power of his "clinical" eye. The medical term is in many ways more apposite than immediately seems apparent, for Dix himself—despite the implied desire in his work to spiritualize (re)production—cultivated metaphorical equivalences between surgical operations and artistic practices. Like physicians, artists study human anatomy, passing beyond what meets the eye to learn the ways of the human body inside and out.[37] Dix was fascinated by external appearances, but he valued the outer precisely because it offered access to what was on the inside, both in a spiritual and physical sense. His fascination with surgical intervention, with the opening of the human body, becomes evident in his portraits of Dr. Andler, a physician whom he shows at work in the operating room in *Portrait of the Surgeon, Professor Dr. R. Andler, Singen, in the Operating Room* (*Bildnis des Chirurgen Professor Dr. R. Andler, Singen, bei der Operation*, 1943) (fig. 18) and in *The Operation* (*Die Operation*, 1943) (fig. 19). We have seen the extent to which Dix identified with the menacing aspect of surgical intervention by representing himself as wielding a knife, gleefully opening up bodies that become the subject of his creative artistry.

A look at Dix's self-portraits reveals that the artist, when painting, made a habit of wearing real surgical gowns purchased from a medical supply company.[38] A photograph of Dix in 1927 seated before a portrait of Theodor Däubler shows him with stains that look more like blood than paint on his surgical gown; a self-portrait of 1933, in turn, suggests a medical student rather than an artist. But the picture that really tells a thousand words—the one that points up the willful parallels set up by artists between the art of painting and that of surgery—is a photograph of Dix and his colleagues at the Dresden Art Academy in 1930 (fig. 20).[39] Here the young male artists, with sleeves rolled up, confer with the professional verve of interns as they labor to reproduce the female human body. A subconscious need to endow representational practices with the gravity (and gravidity) of medical procedures becomes evident. No matter how powerful the cultural myths about the transcendent superiority of artistic creativity, they fail to attenuate, given the prestige of medical authority, a sense of deficiency when it comes to the art of reproduction.

The book of Genesis, more powerfully than any other text, has scripted the notion of creativity as a lofty, spiritual project and of procreation as an inferior, biological process.[40] Elevating the myth of cosmogony over the reality of parturition can be seen as part of a project designed to compensate for the exclusion of men and of some women from reproductive labor. But what is important for our purposes is that Dix's artistic production, from its conception to its delivery, seems in constant competition with parturition even as it is declared superior to it. I think here again of *Still Life in the Studio*, which juxtaposes a motheaten dummy with a pregnant women in order to make a point about mortality even as it foregrounds a sturdy easel that captures the two in its frame and confers on them the "immortality" of artworks.[41]

The notion of the artist as creator *and* progenitor comes alive in Dix's *Self-Portrait with My Son Jan* (*Selbstbildnis mit dem Sohn Jan*, 1930). Instead of Virgin and child, we have a father in the pose of Saint Christopher (a hagiographic subject painted often by Dix in later years), with his son on his shoulder and a paintbrush in place of a staff. This painting marks a rare moment in Dix's oeuvre—what we see are idealized figures devoid of the grotesque flaws and distorted features that characterize so many of his human figures.

18. Otto Dix, *Portrait of the Surgeon, Professor Dr. R. Andler, Singen, in the Operating Room* (1943). The serene gaze of the surgeon and gracefully draped bodies of surgeon, assistant, and patient form a strong contrast to the violence of the gash inflicted on the body by the scalpel.

In its pure celebration of artistic and paternal sovereignty, the portrait of father and son reveals how intensely Dix was driven by a need to assert male hegemony in the realm of human reproduction and artistic production.

Notwithstanding the artistic hubris expressed in this painting and others,

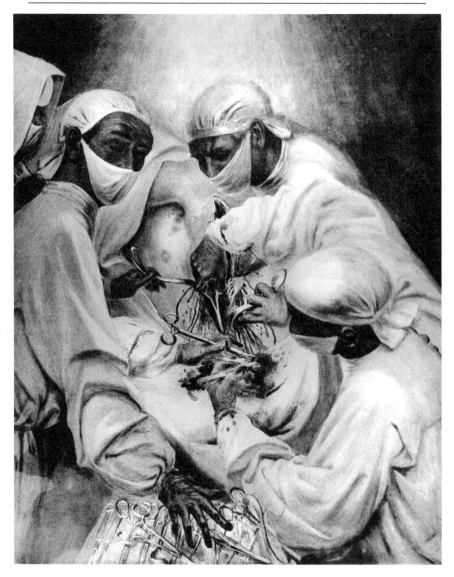

19. Otto Dix, *The Operation* (1943). The frenzied activity of the physicians has a menacing aspect to it. A self-portrait of 1942 shows Dix, palette and brush in hand, in precisely the same garb as the surgeons, but with paint rather than blood spattered on his gown.

there remains something undeniably admirable about the brutal honesty of Dix's oeuvre as a whole.[42] It may not be pleasant to see the mutilated corpse, castrated penis, and syphilitic torso that circulate, as figments of Dix's imagination, around the impeccably groomed artist, but these lurid represen-

20. Photograph of Otto Dix and his colleagues at the Dresden Art Academy (1930). With the outward look of medical interns, the students at the Academy labor to reproduce the corpulent female body situated in the background.

tations testify candidly to a glaring contrast between the scandals of male fantasies and the respectability of bourgeois appearances. While many contemporaries felt offended by Dix's scandalous images, they failed to register that the artist was moving in the realm of the confessional rather than in the arena of what the painter Conrad Felixmüller called "the pornographic."[43] Knowing that Dix felt the need to commit murders on his canvases in order to foreclose the possibility of doing so in real life is hardly reassuring, but it helps us face and understand some of the complexities of the war trauma and the cultural anxieties of the Weimar period. Dix's *Lustmorde*, the most virulent expression of his hostility toward women, are clearly linked to his four years on the brutalizing battlefields of World War I, for many of the women expire on his canvases in the way that he had seen comrades die before his eyes. But, as we have seen, these represented murders have a significance that goes beyond the war experience—beneath the replaying of war's brutalities lies a general reshuffling of cultural notions about creation and procreation, life and death, reproduction and ruination. Dix's obsession with the fallen soldier and with fallen women mark end points in the arc of his artistic

career, with the fantasmatic threat of a fertile Mother Earth at one extreme
and the equally fantasmatic threat of a female body associated with disease,
death, and decay at the other. "All art is mastery [*Bannung*]," Dix observed.
If it is, in his case the attempt to capture and to master anxieties through art
ended not only in aesthetic triumphs, but also in endless variations on symptoms that reveal a great deal about the need to conquer sexuality and mortality through the violence of representation.

Life in the Combat Zone: Military and Sexual Anxieties in the Work of George Grosz

At eighteen, this girl has already known the highest wealth, the lowest misery, men at all levels. She holds a magic wand with which she unleashes the brutish appetites so violently curbed in men who, while involved in politics or science, literature or art, are not without hearts. There is no woman in Paris who can so effectively say to the Animal: "Out! . . ." And the Animal leaves its cage to wallow in excesses.

Balzac, A Harlot High and Low

IN RECOLLECTIONS of life on Long Island with his father George Grosz, Marty Grosz described his astonishment at seeing friends from the family's Berlin days for the first time: "None of these men had ears missing, dog tongues, pig snouts, or fat rolls at the neck. Nor was I able, try as I might, to see through their wives' or daughters' dresses."[1] The son tells us what few observers of the father's drawings will fail to note: that George Grosz paints the faces of the ruling class (and of the working class, too, for that matter) in the most unflattering possible hues. But he also makes an important point about the strikingly different representational regimes—one reserved for men, the other for women—adopted by Grosz almost consistently throughout his artistic career. While the men are invariably attired in uniforms or suits, or are at least wearing pants, the women are naked, even when clothed, as a look at Grosz's *Greetings from Saxony* (*Gruß aus Sachsen,* 1920) (fig. 21) reveals. *Advertising* (*Werbung,* 1921) (fig. 22) goes a step further by suggesting that women, even when clothed, bare their breasts, flaunting their bodies with practiced nonchalance. In this case, however, the eye of the male artist seems to be disrobing the women for the viewer: it is not only the prostitutes in transparent dresses who expose and "advertise" their wares, but also a pubes-

21. George Grosz, *Greetings from Saxony* (1920). The naked breast of the woman gives the lie to the bourgeois propriety of her bearing. Note the leer on the face of the dachshund.

cent schoolgirl and a devout dowager with her hand on a Bible. One recent biographer sums up the artist's double standard in representational practices by observing that Grosz drew "men's faces but women's bodies, men with clothes and women naked."[2]

In many of Grosz's drawings and paintings, pictorial conventions and so-

22. George Grosz, *Advertising* (1921). The disapproving scowls of the three figures in the foreground are directed at the "seductive" women at work in the background. Schoolgirls, matrons, and prostitutes alike are all disrobed by the artist.

cial realism dictate the presence of unclothed female figures. Classic nude studies, street scenes showing prostitutes haggling with their clients over price, brothel settings, and domestic vignettes might seem artificially prudish without exposed bodies. But in leafing through Grosz's oeuvre, the regular-

ity with which the bare female body is presented in grotesque detail is astonishing. The heavy population of naked female bodies in every imaginable
context (street scenes, butcher shops, picnic sites, and so on) makes it virtually impossible to avoid questioning Grosz's passion for depicting women in
the flesh, especially when we come across one painting after another in
which asymmetrical representational practices for the two sexes become
glaringly evident, as in *Man and Woman* (*Mann und Frau*, 1926), where a
clothed man ogles a naked woman or in *Down with Liebknecht* (*Nieder mit
Liebknecht*, 1919), where a naked woman incongruously occupies the visual
center of a painting concerned with political matters.

Western artists of the last two centuries have, with some notable exceptions, so favored the nude female body over that of the male for representational purposes that it has become "natural" to associate the female nude
with art. "More than any other subject," Lynda Nead writes, the female nude
symbolizes "the transformation of the base matter of nature into the elevated
forms of culture and spirit," functioning as "an icon of western culture."[3] But
Grosz, rather than doing what the distinguished art historian Kenneth Clark
has described as "producing a figure that would conform to the ideals of his
time, that would be the kind of shape men liked to see," insisted on producing bodies marked by rough surfaces, undisciplined excesses, and crude irreg-
ularities. While Clark applauds artistic efforts to produce the "balanced, pros-
perous, and confident body" (what he dignifies with the name "nude"), he
recoils in embarrassment at the thought of reproducing the "huddled and
defenseless body" ("naked" is his term for the body before its aesthetic transformation into "pure form"). Instead of *re-forming* the unsightly material reality of naked female bodies and producing the idealized nudes of creative
artistry, Grosz pressed his talent into the service of further *de-forming* naked
bodies, until they became what Clark, in a critique of Rouault's paintings of
prostitutes, found particularly repulsive:

> All those delicate feelings which flow together in our joy at the sight of an
> idealized human body ... are shattered and profaned. The sublimation
> of desire is replaced by shame at its very existence.... From the point of
> view of form, all that was realised in the nude on its first creation, the sense
> of healthy structure, the clear, geometric shapes and their harmonious
> disposition, has been rejected in favour of lumps of matter, swollen and
> inert.[4]

Grosz's resistance to representational practices that construct idealized images of female plenitude and perfection seems entirely consonant with his
Dadaist irreverence toward conventional artistic ideologies. Much as the art-

ist, late in his life, affected admiration for the work of American illustrators like Norman Rockwell (for a time he even tried, with touching earnestness, to emulate them) and was perversely drawn to what he perceived to be the refreshingly healthy and normal American way of life ("saubere amerikanische Normalität"), he found himself constitutionally unable to produce comfortable and comforting images—his pen seemed to take on a life of its own to create images that distorted reality (*Zerrbilder*).[5] The naked bodies he draws are so unnatural and unstructured in their presentation that they begin to unsettle the boundaries between art and pornography, between disinterested aesthetic contemplation and engaged somatic arousal—one that, however, can take the form of revulsion as much as desire.

It will come, then, as no surprise that some cultural critics have celebrated Grosz's courage in trying to break down the barriers between the "secret" realm of pornography and the public realm of high art.[6] Grosz himself, in later years, anxiously tried to uphold the distinction between the two when he referred to his work of the 1920s as a "'filthy' period" and asserted a desire to return to "an ideal of beauty" and to "art."[7] In the "progressive" account of Grosz's artistic output while in Germany, images of sexual libertinage amount to sexual liberation, and the pornographer becomes the creative inventor of ever more daringly transgressive scenes. Note how Roland Barthes eulogized the Marquis de Sade as a figure who "invented" under the impetus of "imaginative" debauchery.[8] The pornographic imagination, Susan Sontag claims, turns the artist into "a freelance explorer of spiritual dangers" who charts forbidden territories in the realm of corporeal pleasures.[9]

The critical view that would align Grosz's images of bourgeois debauchery and urban pathologies with sexually and artistically liberating forces fails, however, to take note of the full significance of the social critique embedded in his pictorial excesses. It also misses a more important point about the way in which Grosz's work reinscribes prevailing ideologies and perpetuates the very notions on which the high art/pornography distinction is founded. By focusing on the repressed half of the binary opposition "naked/nude," Grosz does not, as might be expected, dismantle the opposition—instead he restabilizes it by displaying its scandalous side in yet another triumph of male artistic mastery of the female body. Rather than idealizing and thereby disciplining and controlling the threat of disruptive female flesh (those "lumps of matter, swollen and inert" that so revolt Kenneth Clark), Grosz deforms the female body, containing it, framing it, and disfiguring it in such a way that it often can no longer arouse physical desire. In this sense, Kenneth Clark's observation is quite correct: if artists who represent nudes have traditionally been invested in the "sublimation of desire," those who draw naked bodies express shame at the very existence of such a desire and triumph over it by deforming rather than idealizing the female body.

The emphasis in Grosz's art on women's bodies and the almost single-mindedly representation of women as dissipated prostitutes or slovenly house-wives presses home a point made in the correspondence. In the spring of 1918, Grosz took his brother-in-law Otto Schmalhausen into his confidence when he wrote:

> Between the two of us: I could give a shit about depth in women. Usually that means that they suffer from a repulsive excess of male characteristics—angularity and thighlessness; in this matter I am in agreement with Kerr (the critic): "I'm the only one with a mind."[10]

Like many contemporaries who believed that the female body, as the site of procreation, is axiomatically more overpoweringly sensual than the male, Grosz linked women with fleshy earthiness, convinced that they were nothing more than skin-deep. He enthusiastically embraced Weininger's relegation of women to the sphere of the biological, sexual, and reproductive. "We worshiped Zola, Strindberg, Weininger, Wedekind—naturalistic enlighteners, anarchistic self-tormenters, devotees of death, and erotomaniacs," he wrote.[11] Since women are associated exclusively with the carnal in the calculus of Grosz's gender politics and lack the transcendent spirituality of "male" existence, their essence can easily be revealed simply by putting their flesh on display. But Grosz flagrantly violates artistic conventions by presenting what he perceives to lie beneath the cosmetic polish of the fetishized female body of traditional cultural representations. The women that populate Grosz's canvases—at times massively porcine, as in an oil of 1928 depicting the artist and his model—are designed less to stir erotic thoughts than to repel the viewer and to fortify the notion of the female body as a disruptive figure, the site of corruption, dissolution, and the biologically grotesque aspects of sexuality and death.

There are, to be sure, not many attractive figures, male or female, in Grosz's drawings or paintings. From the artist's correspondence we know the intensity with which he flew into misanthropic rages, particularly in times of high anxiety—for example, when the threat of induction into the army loomed large once again, but even during less stressful periods, as on holidays, when he found himself gloomily absorbed in thoughts about the banality and bad taste of the German petit-bourgeoisie.[12] To Schmalhausen he confessed in 1917 that his misanthropy had taken on colossal proportions and that he frequently fell into states where he found himself consumed by loathing for everyone. But his most telling statement comes a year later when he tells Schmalhausen that he is guided always by the maxim "People are swine" [Menschen sind Schweine] and recommends the phrase as wisdom to live by from the cradle to the grave.[13] These are strong words but not particularly shocking in the context of similar maxims bandied about by Expressionist poets when they lapsed into moments of cynical despair and by virtually everyone who rallied around the banner of Dada. Yet the phrase does take on a special resonance when read along with what Grosz himself referred to as "swinish" letters to his wife Eva, letters that habitually refer to his wife as a "swinishly voluptuous and sweet maid" and as a "sweet, swinish mare" even as they express delight in the couple's "swinish games" and the way in which they behave like "swine" when together. Throughout Grosz's correspondence, anything sexually titillating is described as "swinish"; pornographic films are described as "swinish movies" just as a female stripper sings a "swinish song" to accompany her disrobing.[14]

Woman, being at the furthest remove from "mind" (*Geist*), not only becomes affiliated with flesh and matter but also with crude animal instinct, above all, "swinish" lust. While Grosz's male figures are seldom depicted as spiritual beings and respond in kind to sexual overtures, they become caricatures of their real-life models through exaggerated emphasis on their personal vices and social failings. The faces of the ruling class, in the volume of that title, are, for example, unbearably smug and supercilious; generals rattle their sabers and bare their teeth; preachers foam at the mouth as they fulminate from the pulpit; schoolteachers strut pedantically with volumes of poetry tucked under their arms. Grosz's female figures, by contrast, require neither costumes nor props; when they appear naked, often with a lascivious expression, they reveal their "swinish" essence. Figured and refigured as naked prostitutes in lewd poses, as aging housewives with sagging breasts, or as naked female icons towering over cityscapes, they repeat a single message about the female body, turning it into the bleak site of a grotesque corporality that represses all associations with birth and life to conjoin sexuality with corruption and death. Can it be accidental that of the multitude of women in Grosz's oeuvre only a few are mothers (an occasional figure pushing a carriage in a street scene or a figure in a family portrait done in a naturalist style), the rest streetwalkers, trollops, and harridans? Or that even when a woman is finally shown as *mater* as well as *materia*, as in Delivery (*Niederkunft*, 1917) (fig. 23), she lies across the canvas in spread-eagle fashion, giving birth to a snout-faced monster?

A painting of 1920, a year that marked a turning point in Grosz's life as the date of his marriage to Eva Peter, is especially revealing about the "true nature" of female sexuality. *Daum Marries Her Pedantic Automaton George* (the

23. George Grosz, *Delivery* (1917). Woman's reproductive power becomes the center of this otherwise garish look at urban night life. The grim expression on the woman's face suggests that there is little pleasure in giving birth to the snout-faced monster between her legs.

caption was in English) (fig. 24) remains somewhat cryptic without Wieland Herzfelde's gloss on it:

> Grosz is getting married! For him, however, marriage is not just a personal, but first and foremost a social event. To some extent a concession to a society resembling a machine which unfailingly makes man into one of its components, into a little cog in its wheel mechanism, so that marriage really signifies a moving away from the bride in favor of the community. At the same time a moving away from eroticism and sexuality. It is different for the woman. For her, marriage stands everything on its head. If the symbol of the young girl is a naked figure who is concealing her private parts with her hand or some sort of tassel, then in marriage this denial of sexual needs is removed, is indeed emphasized. And yet from the first hour of the marriage there falls like a shadow between man and wife the fact that, at the moment when the woman gives vent to all her secret desire and can freely reveal her body, the man turns his attentions to other, sober and pedantic problems of calculation.[15]

Herzfelde's commentary is remarkable in a number of ways, but what makes it particularly noteworthy in this context is its emphasis on woman's "secret" sexual desires and the way in which those desires finally surface in the privacy of marriage. The painting itself makes the bride's face in profile (the fantasy preserved by the prospective groom in "the furthest recesses of his consciousness") far more attractive than the bride's hefty body, clad in grotesquely revealing undergarments. Once woman reveals her "true nature," once she lets down her guard to put her body on display in a gesture of uninhibited sexuality, she arouses little more than revulsion.

No document sheds more light on Grosz's obsession with the naked female body and his personal stake in its representation than a chapter of his autobiography, *A Little Yes and a Big No.* In it Grosz describes in arresting detail a scene that he allegedly witnessed as a fourteen-year-old boy. Arriving at a friend's house to pick up an adventure story, he "innocently" took a peek into the boy's room from outdoors, and—startled by the sight of the thirty-eight-year-old aunt living with the family—realized that he had gotten the wrong window. The young Grosz was, however, riveted to the spot: "Something powerful seized hold of me and made me feel weak. . . . A mysterious craving to see had me in its devilish grip. . . . As if pricked by tiny burning needles and driven by a passion I had never before experienced, I stood there and watched the woman."[16] Grosz is not himself; he is wholly disempowered by the woman and engulfed by feelings entirely alien to his being ("a mysterious craving" and a passion he has "never before experienced"). In this retrospective account of the childhood event, the adult Grosz portrays himself as

24. George Grosz, *Daum Marries Her Pedantic Automaton George in May 1920. John Heartfield Is Very Glad of It* (1920). The belief that women can turn men into animals becomes evident in Grosz's Circe-drawings. Marriage, by contrast, figures as an institution that tames men, turning them into smoothly functioning parts of the social and economic machinery.

the overwhelmed victim of a power beyond his control, a force that issues from the site of the female body and is at once sexual ("driven by a passion") and satanic ("had me in its devilish grip"). In later years, Grosz would draw on numerous mythological sources to strengthen his visual arguments that women are so sexually powerful and robustly superior that they reduce men to debasing servility. *Circe* (1912–13) (fig. 25), for example, shows exactly how abjectly men have to grovel once they fall under the spell of a woman.[17] In his artistic production as in his personal life, Grosz never ceased to link sexual desire with demonic powers that transform, paralyze, or otherwise overwhelm men. His autobiography, for example, describes his disciplined efforts to resist the desires aroused by the seductively voluptuous daughters of a landlord. When he looks at their breasts, he feels possessed by a "sensual devil" and bemoans the "devil of sensuality" pursuing him.[18]

Grosz himself was astonished by the fullness of detail in his adolescent recollection. He could remember exactly the night table of his friend's aunt, right down to the position of the coffee cup and the color of the ribbons that were placed on it. What had taken place many decades ago remained vivid in his imagination; it had imprinted itself with photographic precision (*haargenau*) on his memory. Most readers of the autobiography can predict, from Grosz's description of his arousal, subjugation, and immobilization, that the spectacle had just begun when the fourteen-year-old positioned himself at the window. Indeed, what follows leaves the young Grosz literally panting for breath (*atemlos*)—the aunt completely disrobes in a process that takes the adult Grosz a good five pages to describe. The lengthy description stems not merely from the extraordinary number of undergarments she is wearing or from the youthful voyeur's deep fascination with the spectacle; the lavishness of Grosz's account is driven by the recognition that this childhood experience was, in artistic terms, more formative than almost any other.

The young Grosz is enthralled by what he sees. As the product of a milieu in which, as he himself observes, women were not even allowed to expose their ankles, he is captivated by the sheer corporality of what is before him and harps repeatedly on the massive proportions of the breasts and buttocks. What emerges from Grosz's description is, on the one hand, a passionately idealized, sentimentalized, and eroticized vision of woman in the flesh. We are treated to similes comparing the breasts to ripe fruits and to little mountains even as we hear incessantly about the heart-shaped pattern of the pubic hair. On the other hand, satanic elements enter the description in ways less obvious than the frequent references to the devilish power that has the young Grosz in its grip. Once the woman is fully disrobed, she loosens her hair, which uncoils "like serpents" [in Schlangen]. When Grosz tells us that he cannot turn his head from the image ("Ich konnte von dem Bild nicht

25. George Grosz, *Circe* (1912/13). A self-confident modern Circe adds another victim to her collection of beasts. Each of the victims remains arrested in a different state of abject subjection to the temptress.

loskommen"), it is difficult to avoid thinking of Medusa, that mythological figure whose locks Freud associated with female genitals, the sight of which petrify men.[19] Freud's Medusa, we may recall, arouses both dread and desire: she frightens the observer by displaying "the terrifying genitals of the Mother" at the same time that her snakey locks "replace the penis, the absence of which is the cause of horror."[20] The implied mythological allusion is complemented by an explicit theological reference—one that is, on the surface of things, more positively charged: the aunt, in her naked state, is utterly "transformed" and turns into an "image of Eve"—an image that bears no resemblance whatsoever to the fully clothed earthly aunt. She not only becomes sexuality incarnate ("das reine Geschlechtswesen") but also a symbol: "woman as the eternal source and sustainer of the human race." That the noun used to render the term "human race" is also the word for sex (*Geschlecht*) makes the text's linkage of women, sexuality, and reproduction all the more emphatic.

As the "image of Eve," the unclothed aunt is all flesh. She has been transformed into pure corporal surface: "Everywhere there were curves with rose-colored, white, and brownish shades of flesh and with light-blue veins that occasionally showed through the skin."[21] This first encounter with female flesh immediately triggers associations with animals. Grosz spontaneously free-associates to horses and to the striking resemblance between the posteriors of women and animals, thereby unwittingly revealing part of the personal pathology that led him to the belief that women turn men into beasts. It is the resemblance to horses that sweeps the boy away ("It was overwhelming [*ungeheuerlich*]") and transforms him into a sexual being ("I felt myself being awakened to manhood.").

When Grosz hears noise and voices, he flees, but not without taking along a mental snapshot: "the image of the naked, Rubenesque woman." The phrase is particularly weighty because it reveals the process by which the feelings of anxiety aroused by the sight of female corporality can be brought under control and contained. The young Grosz, under the pressure of the moment, pulls himself together by translating the dizzying excesses of real female flesh into a cultural representation of the female body. He frames the body—transfiguring it in such a way that it turns from human flesh into a transcendent cultural symbol—"something eternal," as he describes it. Woman remains affiliated with pure carnality, but the male artist can contain and master both the flesh and the sexual delirium it causes by reconceptualizing the female body as a work of art, as the object of disinterested contemplation. That Rubens' art comes to Grosz's mind has a special bearing on this context, for Rubens happens to be an artist singled out by Kenneth Clark as exerting indisputable stylistic and formal control over his subject matter: "[Rubens] learnt what a severe formal discipline the naked body must undergo if it is to survive as art. Rubens' nudes seem at first sight to have been tumbled out of a cornucopia of abundance; the more we study them the more we discover them to be under control."[22] As pivotal an experience as the encounter with the naked aunt appears to be in Grosz's autobiographical account, it is less the aunt than the image of the aunt as cultural artifact that shapes Grosz's subsequent artistic production. The mental picture "hanging up in his brain" displaces the woman of flesh and blood to become what could be taken to be both the source of artistic inspiration and of erotic pleasure: "[The image] is still hanging up there and later I was to make it come alive."[23]

Grosz's text seems at war with itself, with one faction of verbal troops constructing an idealized, seductive vision of woman, another sabotaging the work of the first by affiliating woman with sinful horror. Yet these warring tendencies have comfortably coexisted whenever positioned at the site of cultural constructions of the feminine. The image of Eve comes closest to capturing the conflicting tendencies articulated in Grosz's concept of femininity, for Eve stands at our origins, as both mother of the human race and as agent of sexuality, sin, and death.[24] In the end, however, no matter how alluring female flesh may be, its affiliation with evil gives it an edge so dangerous that the effect is ultimately sobering. In the chapter of his autobiography that follows the scene of voyeurism, Grosz describes the moral reproaches of a much-admired mentor, who, for no explicit reason, berated him for his "sinful" ways and admonished him to walk the straight and narrow. What the adolescent boy does to expunge his feelings of guilt is telling. After witnessing a woman "in the flesh" for the first time, he destroys his collection of magazine photographs of half-naked women, then becomes a vegetarian, refusing to eat meat (*Fleisch*), which is described as "the source of all evil."[25] It is worth noting here that the German term *Fleisch* means both "meat" and "flesh," for the boy's abstinence in culinary matters is surely little more than a mask for his perceived need to practice celibacy, to stay away from the female flesh he has just described in such glowing terms. These observations linking the evils of the female body with indulgence in *Fleisch* seem to be made without the slightest awareness of their misogynist implications.

What makes Grosz's text especially remarkable, beyond its relentless demonization of sexual desire and its containment of the seductions of female flesh through aestheticizing strategies, is the way in which it so unmistakably makes the object of desire a maternal body. (Grosz even explicitly contrasts the "undesirable" and "undeveloped" bodies of his female contemporaries with the voluptuous fullness of the aunt, who is about the right age to be his mother.) This explains in part just why the idea of transgression permeates the entire chapter devoted to describing the vision. "A Look into the Thirteenth Chamber"—this title, with its transparent reference to the forbidden, intensifies the felt sense of furtive, voyeuristic sexuality. Along with the profuse references to the devil, it marks the scene of the awakening of sexual desire as the locus of prohibition and evil, moving against the grain of all the explicit references to the female body as the source of sensual vitality and nurturing care. That the "thirteenth chamber" is mentioned again in Grosz's autobiography—this second time in connection with World War I—reveals how deeply the war experience was imbricated with female sexuality. The mystifying conflation of the horrors of war with the horrors of (female) flesh becomes evident from Grosz's use of the phrase "bloody thirteenth chamber" to signify the psychic space to which he had banished his memories of the war. That Grosz, like Dix, viewed women as anxious conspirators in a plot to lure men into the frenzied brutality of military bloodbaths will become evident as we chart his artistic development.

"A Look into the Thirteenth Chamber" goes far toward expanding our understanding of Grosz's lifelong obsession with the unclad female body, but more important, its subterranean demonization of woman begins to tell us just why Grosz so often sketched that body in revoltingly ugly strokes and positioned it as the target of murderous assaults. The aunt in Grosz's autobiographical account has all the characteristics of the phallic mother, the woman whose omnipotence and activity arouse in the child a sense of helpless dependency. One recent model of psychosexual male development emphasizes that boys, in order to establish a masculine identity, begin by denying their dependence on the mother and end by devaluing her, a process that culminates in a generalized tendency to avoid relational networks and to demean women.[26] Susan Gubar succinctly formulates the process that lets the male artist "master" the trauma of separation from the mother and at the same time indulge in a fantasy of re-union with her:

> By re-creating in his own image the woman who created him, by repossessing through fantasy the woman who had to be relinquished, by punishing the woman whose separateness was itself experienced as a punishment, and by eroticizing the woman whose eroticism was taboo, the pornographer converts his greatest trauma into his greatest thrill, a fact that explains why the perusal of pulp magazines and the communal showing of stag films function like *rites de passage* for so many adolescent boys.[27]

"A Look into the Thirteenth Chamber" recounts one of two powerfully formative experiences in the artist's youth. The other, which appears in the very first chapter of his autobiography, has less to do with the artist's awakening sexuality than with his attraction to violence. Unable to resist the seductions of popular literature, particularly penny-dreadfuls that sensationalized crimes of passion, Grosz dwells in detail on the "titillating sensations" he felt whenever he passed by stores that carried such titles as *Red-Handed Hugo, or the Dancing Corpses on the Raven's Rock, Count Steinfels, or the Lady-Killer,* and the immensely popular *Victims of the Lady-Killer.*[28] It may come as something of a shock, however, to know that Grosz considered this fiction, with its depiction of savage violence, to be something "quite appropriate and ideal in its own way." What Grosz saw in this literature was a form of popular culture (*Volkskunst*) relatively untainted by institutionalized forms of censorship. For him, the colporteur novels purveyed popular culture in much the same way that folktales like "Bluebeard" and "The Robber Groom" (which also contained scenes of female carnage) carried the voice of the people through refreshingly direct and uncensored narratives.

Grosz divides high art from popular culture in an unusual fashion: the one he sees as "anemic," the other as marked by "blood." Until the Second World War and its aftermath, he argues in his autobiography, the brutality of everyday life was not a legitimate subject for high art and remained confined to the sphere of popular cultural representations. But the protective veneer of noble humanism marking high culture was forever removed by the full revelation of the destructive horrors of mass slayings. Elite art could no longer affect an attitude of aristocratic indifference to the realities of life, to the violent bloodshed at both military and domestic battle sites. What is particularly interesting about Grosz's remarks is the extent of their fixation on blood as the marker distinguishing "high" from "low," particularly in light of the artist's pivotal role in legitimizing scenes of gore as the subject of high art. The ambivalent feelings Grosz harbors toward blood—it is a sign of attractive vitality yet also of revolting carnality—are exactly replicated in his conflicted attitude toward female flesh. Reading the two chapters of Grosz's autobiography together, the one on female flesh and its seductive pleasures and evils, the other on blood and violence, makes the artist's fascination with sexual murder and mutilation an almost too obvious consequence of the two seminal experiences retrospectively narrated in his autobiography.

When faced with the sheer number of female slayings represented on Grosz's canvases, most critics reveal a curious unwillingness to question their explicit, referential dimension and do not move beyond the most superficial sorts of observations. Uwe M. Schneede, an authority on Grosz, notes that the subject of sex murders became a prominent theme in Grosz's work and explains it as reflecting "Grosz's inner rebellion against the Prussian mentality of law and order."[29] Other critics reveal their squeamishness about what Grosz depicts by seeking refuge in a flurry of speculative questions. A recent biographer, Hans Hess, notes that crime, murder, suicide, and rape had "a strange attraction" for Grosz, then asks: "Was it because there man could be depicted at his rawest? ... Maybe there was something far deeper and stronger in his own make-up that drew him to the scene of crime? Or was he so modern that he thought of murder as a form of art, its accomplishment equalling the difficulty of a tightrope act? Did Grosz see the potential for murder in every face, or was the murderer and his victim one of the realized situations of human possibilities? There is no simple answer."[30] To be sure, Grosz's obsession with rape and murder must be overdetermined and there is no direct, simple explanation for its source. But Hess, like many critics, muddies the waters with his whirlwind questions about individual pathology, the human condition, and artistic license.

The Weimar cultural critic Eduard Fuchs seemed to be on the right track when he heralded Grosz's many drawings of female murder victims as symptomatic records of what happens in a society as sexually repressive as that of Wilhelmine Germany.[31] If nothing else, Grosz reveals himself to be what Angela Carter has called the "pornographer as terrorist," the artist who paints the psychosexual realities of a regime marked by tyrannical sexual relations. Grosz's "pornographic" representations of *Lustmord* become subversive not because he intended them to incite murder but because, once analyzed and dismembered themselves, they show just how forcefully a work of art can reveal and reinscribe prevailing forms of sexual oppression.

26. George Grosz, *Sexual Murder* (1912/13). The female figure reclines in a position that is closer to an erotic pose than a horrified reaction to the armed assailant pointing his rifle at a sexual rival.

By ignoring the basic issue of the gender of murderer and victim, critics make Grosz's seeming obsession with sexual murder more mystifying than it really is. While Grosz may have produced some drawings that show female killers as well as male perpetrators, these proved to be the exceptions to the rule of portraying crimes of heterosexual passion, with female victims and male slayers.[32] More important, the extravagant anatomical detail of Grosz's mutilated and murdered female corpses becomes especially striking when compared with combat drawings from World War I. The bodies of the dead soldiers in, say, *Battlefield with Dead Soldiers* (*Schlachtfeld mit toten Soldaten*, 1915) or *The Grenade* (*Die Granate*, 1915) remain clothed and physically intact despite explosive assaults on the battlefield. It is almost as if Grosz establishes a contrast between what Margaret Miles, drawing on the work of the Russian critic Bakhtin, has called the "permeable" female body and the "closed, smooth, and impenetrable" male body. Unlike its female counterpart, the male body remains invulnerable to physical assault and becomes emblematic of "individual, autonomous, and 'perfect' existence."[33]

In the prewar period, Grosz's representations of *Lustmord* place far greater emphasis on *Lust* than on *Mord*. The female victims are fleshy nudes, often

27. George Grosz, *The Mielzynski Affair* (1912/13). The female nude in the foreground remains singularly unaffected by the sexual hostilities played out behind her. Her body, on display as an erotic object, remains frozen in its function as the motive for violence between men.

reclining in sexually suggestive poses reminiscent of the voluptuous figure in Grosz's *Erotic Scene* (*Erotische Szene*) of 1912 and *Couple in a Room* (*Paar im Zimmer*) of 1915. In some cases, only a title alerts us to the fact that a murder has taken place or is about to take place. *Sexual Murder* (*Lustmord*, 1912–13) (fig. 26), for example, could be seen as a conventionally posed female nude were it not for the presence of an armed assailant, who has stormed the room and aims his rifle at an off-canvas sexual rival. The female nude in *Sexual Murder* is replicated almost exactly in a watercolor and pencil drawing entitled *The Mielzynski Affair* (*L'Affaire Mielzynski*, 1912–13) (fig. 27), where again only the presence of male sexual rivals transforms the canvas into the depiction of a motivated event rather than the presentation of a naked body. Even the macabre *End of the Road* (*Das Ende der Straße*, 1913), the scene of a triple death, foregrounds the female body as erotic object in a setting cluttered

28. George Grosz, *The Double Murder in the Rue Morgue* (1913). This scene of the crime is charged with erotic energy. The female corpse in the foreground lacks the morbidity of most victims of sexual murder, while the couple in the background seems locked in an embrace rather than in mortal combat.

with corpses and domestic belongings. Erase everything but the woman's body from the neck down and you have an unsensationalized nude. *The Double Murder in the Rue Morgue (Der Doppelmord in der Rue Morgue,* 1913) (fig. 28), without its title, would look more like an example of erotic art than the representation of a murder scene from Poe's story. All of these prewar works

29. George Grosz, *When It Was All Over, They Played Cards* (1917). The leering card player sits on a crate into which the hacked-up body of a woman has been stuffed. Note the presence of the murder weapon in the foreground.

link murder with conventional motivations ranging from sexual jealousy to existential desperation and emphasize the voluptuous sensuality of the female body (the qualities that make it "Rubenesque") rather than the grotesque carnality we see in works from a later period.

Grosz's wartime and postwar drawings and paintings of female nudes are devoted to little more than the unattractive side of human anatomy. Time and again the focus is on the repulsive side of corporality—folds of fat, legs scarred by varicose veins, bloated bellies, and sagging pouches of flesh, as in *Papa and Mama* (*Pappi und Mammi*, 1922). With the exception of occasional vignettes à la Rubens or well-turned-out prostitutes, Grosz portrays naked female bodies which, despite the sexual context in which they appear, are designed to arouse little more than horror and revulsion in the mind of the viewer. Bloated corpses, hacked body parts, and cut throats are put on display with whimsical artistic touches that blunt the notion of seeing the drawings as weapons in Grosz's arsenal of social criticism. Consider the caption for one particularly grisly scene that shows a grinning cardplayer seated on a box into which a female corpse has been stuffed: *When It Was All Over, They Played Cards* (*Als alles vorbei war, spielten Sie Karten*, 1917) (fig. 29). Or, note the

30. George Grosz, *Murder on Acker Street* (1916). A murderer furtively washes his hands after decapitating a woman. On the room divider hangs Grosz's trademark reed cane.

presence of Grosz's trademark reed cane in a drawing of 1916 entitled *Murder on Acker Street* (*Mord in der Ackerstraße*) (fig. 30) showing a murderer furtively washing his hands behind a daybed on which the body of a decapitated woman reclines.[34]

As we have seen, the representational practices of German writers and artists who lived through the First World War were profoundly affected by the experience of trench warfare. However brief his actual military experience, Grosz, like other veterans of the war, found himself haunted by nightmarish recollections of disease, death, and decay. In his autobiography, he recounts in detail the slow, painful death of a soldier whose body had been reduced to a "misshapen mass."[35] Few experiences were more central to soldiers than those moments in which they came face-to-face with the sheer physical horror of death. Ernst Toller eloquently captured the feelings of revulsion that engulfed him and his comrades at the moment when death on the battlefield lost its heroic appeal and manifested itself as nothing more than the biological reality of torn flesh, dried blood, and decaying body organs. As a boy, Toller had thrilled to the same scenes of murder and mutilation that Grosz had seen in graphic, pictorial exhibits displayed at local fairs. Like Grosz, he felt that these scenes had, to some extent, steeled him for the combat experience and prepared him for the explosive violence of the battlefields. But one particular moment in the trenches resisted "naturalization" as one of the dreary realities of military life and stood as a turning point in his life:

> I'm standing in a trench, probing the earth with my bayonet. Its steel point gets caught. I start twisting and pull it out with one heave. A slimy knot is hanging on it, and when I bend over to look at it, I realize that it is the intestine of a human being. A dead man is buried here.[36]

Toller's encounter with human innards seems tame by comparison to what August Stramm experienced in combat. His conversion to pacifism was even more radical than either Toller's or Grosz's. In the fall of 1914 Stramm railed on about how killing was "duty, heaven, and god." "I'm not writing any more poems," he declared at the front, "because everything around me is a poem."[37] But by the winter of 1915 his militaristic tune had changed dramatically, modulating into a call for pacifism. In a letter to Herwarth and Nell Walden, he draws upon the increasingly prevalent association of the battlefield with the slaughterhouse to strengthen his condemnation of war:

> Have you ever seen a butcher's shop where slaughtered people are laid out for sale, with machines making a terrific racket as they slaughter more and more people with their ingenious mechanism? And you lie there mute, thank God you are mute, at once the butcher and the beast. And suddenly black devils are everywhere as they make their way up from the depths— the butchers, the grenades . . . bustle about. . . . Yesterday one of those butchers smashed the person next to me into pieces with one blow and mockingly covered me with blood and flesh and guts.[38]

Trench warfare confronted virtually every combatant with death in its most grisly bodily manifestation. Grosz too perceived the First World War as one gigantic human slaughterhouse, in which soldiers were led to sacrifice by their generals. In a letter to Otto Schmalhausen written in April 1917 while recuperating in a sanatorium, Grosz trained his attention on the horrors of war, in particular its terrifying display of the human body in mangled or decomposed form:

Where have the nights gone, Pierrot . . . ? Where are the women? Adventurers?—And our friends have been mutilated, dispersed, duped, bewitched and turned into grey uniformed butcher's boys!! . . . What a finale to this hell, to this brutal murdering on all sides—to this witches' sabbath, to this horrifying castration, butchering, one cadaver after another, a decaying, green corpse of privates is gaping!—If there would just be an end to this soon!!—[39]

Interestingly, the conflation of eros and death—the way in which erotic adventures abruptly reconfigure themselves as fatal escapades—comes to be played out, in the postwar years, on domestic rather than on military battlegrounds. Once Grosz returns to civilian life and refocuses his attention on scenes from everyday life, the mutilated corpses represented on paper are nearly always female, not male. Instead of remaining fixated on the horrors of war (as did many other artist-veterans), Grosz responded to the war experience by drawing urban/domestic scenes of violence along with satirical barbs aimed at capitalist industry and at the military, theological, and educational establishments. Rather than offering up scenes from the bloody historical battles of World War I, he begins to specialize in snapshots capturing the eternal battle of the sexes. Here *he* is in charge, delighted at the opportunity to assume the role of general in orchestrating the scenes of slaughter. In June 1917, two months after his discharge, he writes with exhilaration to Otto Schmalhausen about his sense of a new mission in life:

Work is the way to formulate powerful ideas and to organize gigantic tableaus, to layer an array of colors, to organize lines like a general, entire battlefields full of bleeding reds and black verticle lines—*for me this means* the thousand things that happen at the same time in one banal day—how hard it is to represent the movement of the turbulent streets, the curious movements of the types there: people, their machines, animals, the flowering of trees . . . .[40]

In practice this meant that Grosz took upon himself the role of leading his civilian troops of pen-and-ink figures into powerful domestic conflicts. Take, for example, the lively drawing entitled *"Sports and Love"* (*"Sport und Liebe,"* 1921) (fig. 31), which is a crude, graphic picture of the relations between men and women. Once the instinct that draws the couple in the foreground together has vanished, nothing is left but the raw aggression trained on the partner of the opposite sex as revealed by the couple in the background.

More important, Grosz's sense of desperation about the war expresses itself in a curious form of radically sexualized politics. What one would expect in this context from the rabble-rousing, if shell-shocked, twenty-four-

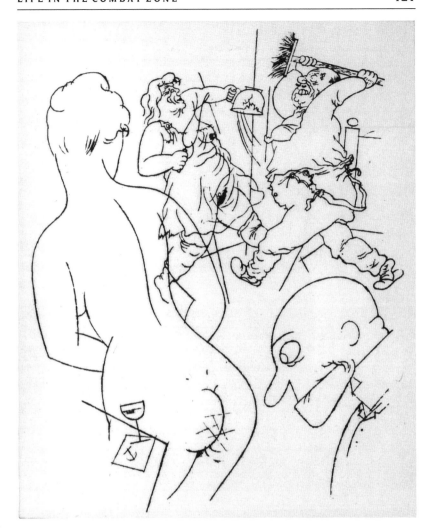

31. George Grosz, *"Sports and Love"* (1920/21). The battle of the sexes that keeps the elderly couple locked in combat forms a contrast to the erotic attraction that bonds the male observer to the female body.

year old would be a denunciation of the belligerents responsible for the carnage—something along the lines of *For the Fatherland—To the Slaughterhouse (Zur Schlachtbank fürs Vaterland . . .,* 1924) (fig. 32), which shows blindfolded men led to war by an officer beneath the drawing of a heavily decorated general (with Hitler on his lap) and a smug, obese capitalist. While such images remain part of Grosz's artistic repertoire, they are shadowed by even

32. George Grosz, *For the Fatherland—To the Slaughterhouse* (1924). Blindfolded men are led off to military service. Above them a general holds a little Hitler on his lap, while a top-hatted capitalist "ape" wields a knout as he squats among the cannon.

more powerful indictments of the female body. Recall how, in the letter to Otto Schmalhausen, Grosz's nostalgia was trained on "the good old days" when he and his friend were sexual adventurers. All that changed with the war; his friends were "bewitched" and their adventure was turned into a "witches' sabbath" marked by castration and death to become what Grosz described in his autobiography as a "sado-masochistic orgy."[41] It is not hard to detect in these observations that Grosz had somehow managed to turn World War I into a hair-raising conspiracy of castrating women. The sexual orgies of the prewar era have suddenly been transformed by the agents of pleasure into hellish nightmares of unmatched corporal devastation—hence perhaps Grosz's need to master the experience by turning himself into a militant artist who mobilizes his resources to ravage and despoil the female body until it is deprived of both erotic and reproductive power.

That Grosz's sexual fears shaded into and became colored by combat anxieties, and vice versa, becomes evident from a look at his sketchbooks from the years before and during the war. The early sketchbooks reveal an extraordinary, and for the later Grosz atypical, fixation on male genitals. Disembodied penises, mechanical penises, penises so long that they need to be wound up like hoses—all consume page after page. Two years later, after his military discharge, the same types of images appear, but this time interwoven with others. Beth Irwin Lewis summarizes the contents:

> The notebook concentrates on two subjects: females and penises. Distorted nudes, ugly hags with clawlike hands, cadaverous sirens, and stylish fat women in transparent dresses are interleaved on these pages with smiling penises running on legs, smoking cigars, transformed into cannons, attached to miniscule bodies, serving as barbells, sprouting wings, and spraying semen.[42]

The castration and performance anxiety manifest in the early images from the sketchbooks could only have been intensified by the war, which Grosz experienced as the threat of physical and mental disintegration. While Grosz writes occasionally of the terrors of combat, his representational energies are channeled into defining the real agent of sexual threat and bodily harm as the calculatingly seductive and often physically repulsive women of all types and ages that grace his sketchbooks. They come to occupy center stage as the years pass, even as the signs of sexual and military anxieties—disembodied male genitals and scenes of war carnage—are suppressed from the pictorial repertoire.

Mutilation and dismemberment stand as the fate of the female victims of Grosz's wartime and postwar depictions of *Lustmord*. But it would be a stunning oversimplification to attribute to the war experience alone the violation of the female body in Grosz's artistic production. The savage act of dismemberment has, for example, a legion of mythological sources and Grosz—uneducated but reasonably well read—knew at least one of them: Ovid's story of Diana and Actaeon.[43] Mutilation appears not infrequently in classical sources, but the extent of its enmeshment in sexual politics is expressed nowhere more forcefully than in Ovid's story of Actaeon. Actaeon has the misfortune of stumbling upon the bathing Diana, who, furious that a mortal has seen her in a state of undress, splashes water in the witness's face and turns him into a stag. As Actaeon runs through the forest, the scent of his body attracts his dogs, and he is torn by them limb from limb. Susan Griffin's proposal that this myth reflects the fear that the sight of a woman's body "calls a man back to his animal nature, and that this animal nature soon destroys him" has more than the ring of truth to it, especially if we consider it in light of Grosz's childhood experience and the subsequent refashioning of the childhood vision in his art.[44] In Grosz's drawings, however, the "enchanted" male often preempts the murderous hostility of the female and dismembers her body before he can become its victim. The Actaeon complex informs both Grosz's childhood vision and adult perception of female sexuality (not only does he draw modern Circes turning men into animals, he also addresses his wife as "Circe" in letters), just as its abridged and inverted form (in which the man is turned into an animal and dismembers the woman) can be seen as one ideological matrix for his representations of *Lustmord*. In a sense, the myth of Actaeon—by staking the female body as the motivation for bringing out the beast in man—also repeats the myth of military combat enunciated in Grosz's pronouncements on war as a witches' sabbath that turns sexual orgies into a nightmare of butchering and castration.

But more may be implicated in Grosz's staging of gender conflicts than what is enacted in combat anxieties and dramatized in the myth of Actaeon. The number of creation myths in which a male hero slays a woman, then forms the world from her dismembered body, points to a fierce need for destroying and appropriating the powers of the body implicated in the production of life. Yet Grosz's works never show what René Girard has called the "transformation of maleficent violence into beneficent violence"—the point at which ritual dismemberment triumphs over death by restoring and rejuvenating its victim.[45] It is only the perpetrators who, as in *When It Was All over They Played Cards*, calmly return to business as usual after committing murder. For Grosz there is neither rejuvenation nor salvation. What we see in one drawing after another is the female body, debilitated by its own daily rituals and desires (from the culinary to the sexual), fragmented through destructive human assaults.

A work dating from the prewar period points to one possible explanation for the ravaging of the female body in Grosz's oeuvre. *Homunculus* (*Homunkulus*, 1912) (fig. 33) sets the stage, in many ways, for the carnal savagery that marks the depiction of female nudes from 1916 on. The drawing shows a corpulent male figure engaged in the act of creating human life in the laboratory. But the secret to life does not reside in the art of mixing ingredients properly (as it did for Goethe's Wagner in the play *Faust*)—Grosz's "scientist" appears to be creating life from life through a process of dismemberment and reconstitution of bodily parts. Or, since the term "homunculus" can refer to the tiny, fully-formed human body once believed to be contained in the

33. George Grosz, *Homunculus* (1912). The scientist seated at the right seems to have failed miserably in his efforts to create human life in the laboratory. The mutilation of the female corpses seems to be less for the purpose of appropriating their reproductive organs than for eliminating the conventional source of procreative power.

spermatozoon as well as to a diminutive human being and to the human fetus, it may be that the scientist hacks the bodies of women to pieces (note the presence of an ax) because they are superfluous creatures once he has discovered the secret to male autogeny. That the dismembered corpses are female becomes evident from the upper part of a torso hanging from a ceiling hook. It is as if the "creator" must mutilate and destroy the biological source of life in order to usurp and control the means of re-production. Only the death of woman can open up the possibility of pure male autogeny and autonomy, however unsuccessful that project may be. The creature perched on the scientist's knee is, in the final analysis, as lifeless and dreary as the drawing created by Grosz.

To some extent it seems plausible to speculate that here too, as was the case with Otto Dix, woman's ability to produce palpable, biological bodies rather than "mere" artistic representations of them may have fueled some of Grosz's anxieties about the female body.[46] What greater rival could there be for the male painter of the human figure than a woman, and how else but through transcendent artistic creativity could the male surpass procreation to produce works of art that triumph over biological decay and death? In the work of both Dix and Grosz, the initial obsession with female corporality and sensuality turns, after the war experience, into a fixation with women as carriers of corruption and death. It is not wholly implausible that the gender antagonisms created between the reproductive labor of women's bodies and the compensatory productive work of men's hands were intensified by the war experience and magnified Grosz's hostility toward the female body.

Reading between the lines of Grosz's reminiscences about his childhood reveals that his fascination with the female body is charged with ambivalent feelings. His drawings, by contrast, openly enact this ambivalence. *John, the Lady-Killer (John, der Frauenmörder*, 1918) (fig. 34), in one of its variants, paints a decapitated female victim with the murderer in flight. The fleshy nude sprawled across the canvas, like the eclipse depicted in the painting's background, marks the site where opposites converge and merge. The voluptuous, pink roundedness of belly, breasts, and thighs contrasts markedly with the cuts at the shoulder, neck, and elbow of the corpse. In the pubic region, the contours of the flesh are "cut" once again, this time by the labial line. What we see is, on the one hand, a figure of feminine plenitude and unity, yet, on the other, a body signifying deficiency through the disfiguring marks of bleeding gashes and slits. This double encoding of the feminine image as marked by plenitude and emptiness turns the female body into the target of what Laura Mulvey, in a seminal article of feminist criticism, has called the fetishistic/scopophilic gaze and the sadistic/voyeuristic gaze.[47] While the two "gazes" may not be completely separate and distinct, rarely are they so clearly coupled as in Grosz's *John, the Lady-Killer*, whose title already traffics in ambiguity by presenting the central male figure as a man who both courts the favor of women (note the presence of a bouquet) and slays them.

The war experience—or at least the war as lived experience—more than anything else, seems to have given Grosz the license to magnify the murderous aggression trained on the female body. As the trauma of war deepened and the attendant crisis of male subjectivity and bodily integrity intensified, the mask of sexual desire for women fell to reveal little more than murderous aggression toward women. We have seen the extent to which frenzied desire and slavish reverence masked a dread of women in Grosz's account of his youthful voyeuristic adventure. With the exception of the brutally grotesque *Homunculus,* the early murders committed on paper mingle eroticism with aggression to produce a *Lustmord* in which the initial term of the compound noun has not yet been effaced. In *Homunculus*, as in the post–World War I drawings and paintings, eroticism vanishes from the scene of the crime to leave behind a bleak display of mutilated female flesh. The extent to which the war experience somehow legitimized for Grosz the ravaging of the female body, or at least allowed his hostility to escape further artistic repression, is something that can never be determined with certainty. That the sources of war were feminized by Grosz and that the war experience came

34. George Grosz, *John, the Lady-Killer* (1918). The torso of the slain woman remains intact as a sign of female plenitude and voluptuous sexuality, but the disfiguring cuts on the limbs and at the throat signify fragmentation and depletion. "John" is a lady-killer in both the figurative and literal senses of the term: he courts women with bouquets and slays them as well.

to serve as a conduit for much of his anxiety about bodily integrity and sexual performance becomes clear from his writings and drawings. What is endlessly astonishing, however, is the degree to which Grosz as artist invested his paintings and drawings with a crudely misogynist view of the world, yet as a person remained trapped in oblivion and repression, never once interrogating his motives for drawing one female corpse after another.

35. George Grosz, *Pimps of Death* (1919). The trio of military officers in the foreground traffics in death by exposing soldiers to the perils of warfare. Soldier and prostitute are linked by their affiliation with death. The drawing covertly reveals the connections between female sexuality, disease, and dissolution.

Given the close association between women and carnality, it is not surprising that the bodily devastation inflicted in combat could be repressed and displaced onto female rather than male bodies. *Pimps of Death* (*Zuhälter des Todes*) (fig. 35), drawn immediately after the war in 1919, is particularly enlightening with regard to Grosz's gendering of death. The male generals may be the pimps of death, but the soldiers, who appear feminized as prostitutes, are the ones with skulls in place of faces, with bodies encoded as both victims and carriers of death. In this drawing, Grosz is not only preaching about the relationship of generals to soldiers and about the evils of war, but also unmasking the trade of prostitution as a form of traffic in death. The glamorous coats and sensual bodies are so overpowered by the gaping death's head that the consequences of succumbing to the allure of the fetishized body becomes self-evident. Here it is the completely sexualized and commodified women, not the cold-blooded officers, who elicit the grim affiliation with death.

Though Grosz saw the war as a gigantic slaughterhouse run by generals who blindly lead soldiers to their deaths, he only once drew a sketch enacting this metaphor. That single drawing remains remarkably restrained, giving no physical details about the butchering that is to take place once the blindfolded men have reached their destination. This restraint stands in stark contrast to *"Just a Half Pound!"* (*"Ein halbes Pfund, bitte!"* 1928) (fig. 36), a postwar drawing of a "real" butcher shop that specializes in carving up and selling female carcasses. The detail in this drawing is nothing short of excessive: the scene is littered with a wealth of individual body parts and internal organs, along with a chopping block in which an ax is lodged, a saw for cutting bones, and two butcher knives. The self-censorship that seems to have prevented Grosz from representing fragmented male bodies does not seem to have been activated when the artist turned his attention to carved-up female bodies. What disturbs here is not only the focus on the female body as the target of grotesquely explicit mutilations but also the tongue-in-cheek mood of the drawing—note how the butcher eyes the ample bosom of the matronly client with his knife poised for a cut. Here Grosz seems to be doing little more than reflecting, distorting, and reinscribing male violence against women. His drawing not only fails to incorporate a critique of its subject matter, it also suggests that the dead seriousness of the earlier images of sexual murder had a pleasurable side as represented in the "humorous" sketch of one butcher's business.

What makes this image all the more disturbing is its link to contemporary discursive practices for figuring the relationship between victim and agent. Consider, for example, Grosz's own citation of the words used by an anonymous Nazi caller harrassing him: "Listen, you Jewish swine, tomorrow night we are coming to slaughter you and your whole brood."[48] Grosz could hardly have failed to register the frequent allusions to slaughterhouse imagery in Nazi anti-Semitic rhetoric, whether it left its traces in chants, songs, or propaganda. Yet in reminiscing about a conversation with Thomas Mann in the summer of 1933, Grosz recalled the way in which he had always be-

36. George Grosz, *"Just a Half Pound!"* (1928). This butcher shop scene offers the perfect site for exhibiting murder weapons. Though the *Hausfrau* offers a defiant gaze, the butcher seems to leer at her in a way that suggests she may be his next victim.

lieved the masses to be nothing more than "swine" and "calves," who "gladly chose their own butchers." The image is particularly telling in the context of another autobiographical observation in which Grosz refers to his drawing board as a "battlefield" (the German term *Schlachtfeld* is literally a "field of slaughter") or as a "place of execution," thus turning him once again into the general or into an executioner who dispatches his victims. These wholly unself-conscious rhetorical practices reveal the degree to which women's bodies are positioned in *"Just a Half Pound!"* as pure victims, as nothing more than *Fleisch* (both "flesh" and "meat") that has been slaughtered and put out for display both by the butcher represented in the drawing and by the artist who represents the image. It no longer seems like an accident that Grosz interspersed his sketchbook drawings of dead mice (sixteen in all) with a nude female torso. There, as in *"Just a Half Pound!,"* the context has erased any trace of erotic interest, leaving behind nothing more than flesh—a grotesquely naked image of the pure carnality that is woman.

The Corpse Vanishes: Gender, Violence, and Agency in Alfred Döblin's *Berlin Alexanderplatz*

I had a date with a girl that I had met at the lake, but I wasn't
in the mood to see her. Soon love would no longer be love,
and sex no longer sex. Wasn't Picasso just then cutting
women to pieces in his cubist pictures, as if they were just
pieces of a toy for children?

Richard Huelsenbeck, Journey to the End of Freedom

OTTO DIX AND GEORGE GROSZ produce astonishingly uninhibited displays of
gore on military and domestic battlefields. While it is not always easy to
determine the extent to which the savage violence depicted in their artistic
production is symptomatic of personal fears or cultural anxieties, the battle
scenes themselves tell transparent stories about mortal combat and sexual
conflict. As artists who remain wedded to referentiality and who veer away
from modernist abstraction, Dix and Grosz can be seen as critical realists
whose art is openly ideological. Their modernist cousins, many of whom
proclaim the emancipation of form from content, seem less personally implicated in the scandals of what is displayed on their canvases. We need only
look at Picasso's cubist *Demoiselles d'Avignon* (1907), with its fragmented and
disfigured prostitutes that have been turned by critics into modernist icons of
transcendental purity, or Giacometti's abstract *Woman with Her Throat Cut*
(1932) to recognize that few twentieth-century artists have portrayed the
dread and desire evoked by female sexuality as directly as Dix and Grosz. It
is telling, however, that the Dadaist Richard Huelsenbeck, quoted in the
epigraph to this chapter, had no trouble at all understanding what was at
stake in Picasso's work. He recognized the referential dimension at once and
realized that even an "abstract" canvas could both validate and shape gender
relations in real life.

If we turn from the canvases of Dix and Grosz to a fictional work that has become a central site for understanding literary modernism and Weimar culture, sexual violence again appears in the foreground. Yet readers of Alfred Döblin's *Berlin Alexanderplatz* have, until recently, found their critical imaginations engaged by thematic and formal issues that have little bearing on the gender conflicts permeating the novel. Those issues have obscured not only our understanding, but even our awareness, that this technically innovative work binds the modernist project of fragmentation with a disfiguring violence trained on the female body.

The extraordinarily comfortable and seemingly natural conjunction of modernism with sexual violence is not easy to explain, but a look at any number of works from the 1920s reveals that a policy of fragmentation and disfiguration can be applied both to the body of a "text" as well as to the women represented in it. Charles Bernheimer has much to say about how the theme of prostitution "simultaneously activates fears of decomposition and decay and stimulates the creation of new artistic strategies, which display that very disintegration and proclaim their modernity."[1] Bernheimer's brilliant analysis, with its heavy investment in the cultural construction of female sexuality as castrated and diseased, fails to address fully the aggressive edge to the "new artistic strategies" and to reveal that they aim for more than a display of "disintegration." Also at stake is, as I have noted, a defensive move against the sexually aggressive Judiths and Salomés that are legion in turn-of-the-century cultural representations. What we see again and again in modernist works is a policy of fragmentation—one that in its often savage intensity makes the writer or artist less a chronicler of decay and disintegration than an agent of violent disfiguration.

That women figure as the targets of sexually charged violence—even before the war—becomes evident from a short story published by Döblin in 1910. In "The Murder of a Buttercup," the actual target of violent assault is not a woman's body, but a flower. Yet the murder is depicted in such a way that it quickly becomes evident that Mr. Michael Fischer, the story's stuffy protagonist, has vented his anger on the body of a woman, not on a buttercup. The flower "attracts" his attention, is "beheaded" by his walking stick, loses "blood," and turns into a cadaver that must be made to disappear. Fischer even entertains the following mental description of the crime: "Grown buttercup murdered on the path from Immental to St. Ottilie, between seven and nine at night." Neither a hardened criminal nor a crazed psychotic, Fischer is instead the quintessential German businessman, punctilious in his outer habits, but benighted about his inner life. Like Franz Biberkopf, he never reflects on the degree to which his aggressive violence is motivated by a profound need to punish women, to strike out at "nature," and to revel secretly at the sight of its vulnerability to his destructive force.

The narrator lavishes his greatest attention on the description of the flower's "torso." "White blood" flows from the buttercup's neck to form a "stream of slime" with "yellow foam," and an entire paragraph is devoted to the crushed head that becomes a "stinking, yellow mass" resembling "vomit."[2]

Before exploring the confluence of literary modernism and sexual violence in Döblin's work, I want to examine why readers have adopted two complementary interpretive strategies for coming to terms with *Berlin Alexanderplatz*. On the one hand, critics have strained their resources to find totalizing possibilities in the novel's fragmented narrative style; on the other hand, they have resisted analyzing or trying to make sense of the novel's shocking mutilation of bodies even as they construct a protagonist who emerges in the end as a unified self with stable ego boundaries.

The double title of *Berlin Alexanderplatz: The Story of Franz Biberkopf* has served as the point of departure for absorbing debates about the novel's central focus—debates that dominate the critical literature. Was Döblin writing about a city or about a man? Had he produced the prototype of the German urban novel or was he mobilizing parody, stylization, and ironic inversion to give a unique twist to the venerable novel of education (Bildungsroman)?[3] Those who promoted the work as an urban novel focused on the ways in which modern city life had changed the conditions for representation and had led Döblin to resort to a range of innovative narrative techniques (foremost among them, montage) to write about Berlin. Those guided by the generic terms of the Bildungsroman (or the Entwicklungsroman) found the indeterminate conclusion to be the novel's most compelling feature, since it was decisive in evaluating whether any development had really taken place. These critics may have avoided the term *Bildung* (which they perceived as wholly inappropriate for a figure like Biberkopf) and substituted for it the paired concepts of "breakthrough" and "transformation," but they ended by drawing on the legacy of humanistic discourse to explain the novel's conclusion.[4]

We might for a moment stop short in this attempt to differentiate the two camps and to identify where the battle lines were drawn to ask first what was at stake in this debate. To be sure, both positions produced ever more sophisticated analyses at the micro- and macro-textual levels, with formalists and narratologists drawing attention to the novel's stylistic nuances, and genre historians and psychoanalytically oriented critics refining our understanding of Biberkopf's presumed move from dependence to autonomy. We can see on the one hand a strong tendency to redeem the novel from its surface messiness by imposing order on the "seeming" chaos through formalist and narratological interventions.[5] On the other hand, we find an attempt to recuperate the work and stabilize its meaning by negotiating parallels to a historical genre or to historical lives. Both interpretive moves not only gloss over the novel's inherent disorder and indeterminacy but also erase, through their exclusive focus on a man and the milieu in which his story unfolds, a matter that did not become visible to many readers until Rainer Werner Fassbinder translated the novel's words into images. I refer here, as every viewer of Fassbinder's film will know, to issues that turn on violence against women and on sexuality—to the way in which the novel's drive to erase its promis- cuously suffering real women and to construct images of licentious, murder- ous females (the Whore of Babylon, Clytemnestra) can be seen as part of a cultural project that binds women to the role of sacrificial victim even as it propagates the myth of female agency.

When Robert Minder proclaimed some years ago that Döblin had written "books without women," no one thought to raise a voice in protest or even to raise an eyebrow.[6] While it is true that Biberkopf hardly ever makes a move that is not in some way colored by his relationship with the opposite sex, the women he encounters are habitually presented as the victims of rape or murder and are disempowered or effaced from the written page with a frequency that is nothing short of alarming. In addition, the foregrounding of Biberkopf's story deflects attention from the parade of women in his life, who by their sheer number begin to seem like what one critic (in an analysis of Fassbinder's film) calls "a series of gross, silly, and pathetic trollops."[7] Because Biberkopf is presented to us as the victim of repeated "blows of fate," as a man deprived of agency ("he must must"), he gradually becomes the target of our sympathetic identification. That the narrator encourages this kind of empathy becomes clear in the repeated claims about Biberkopf's determination to remain "decent" or the assertion that "Step by step, we could have done what he did and experienced what he did" (237), a statement whose patent absurdity becomes evident when we reflect on the class and gender gap separating most empirical readers from Franz Biberkopf.[8]

Paying attention to the women in *Berlin Alexanderplatz* means, in many cases, reading against the grain of the narrator's glosses on the action.[9] But more important, it draws us into a subversive interpretive enterprise, one that, in focusing on those who become the victims of brute physical violence, challenges the notions of mastery and autonomy put forth by those who wish to enshrine the novel as a modern twist on the Bildungsroman. This same enterprise obliges us to rethink the way in which a rage for order creates blind spots in our interpretive ventures. Acknowledging the messy, disruptive, and unsightly presence of women in the novel essentially requires us to turn from the lofty humanistic discourse that has dominated discussions of the Bildungsroman and from the dispassionate, quasi-scientific discourse generated by narratological and formalist models to look squarely at the brutal "flesh-and-blood" conflicts of a novel that plays a powerful role in our understanding of an important epoch in German history and that haunts the present as a source of cultural self-understanding. It is doubly significant in this context to hear Fassbinder's voice asserting the continuities he finds between fictional text and the organization of daily life and consciousness: "My life, to be sure not as a whole, but still in a few moments more decisive than I can judge today, would have run a very different course from the one it ran with Döblin's 'Berlin Alexanderplatz' in my head, under my skin, in my body as a whole, and in my soul."[10] The nearly palpable presence of the novel in the body and soul of the filmmaker—the way that his statement calls attention to the interpenetration of literature and life, while also preserving the distinction between the two—lends a special sense of urgency to analyzing the sexual politics of violence and agency in *Berlin Alexanderplatz*.

To do so, I must first dismantle some of the developmental paradigms borrowed from the Bildungsroman and drawn into interpretive service for Döblin's novel. Rather than acknowledging anxiety and instability as markers of the protagonist's inner life, critics are often so eager to see psychic integrity and social integration in the novel's resolution that, in one reading after another, we are faced with implausibly upbeat predictions about what lies ahead for Biberkopf. He becomes a figure who has established a new, positive masculine identity in the wake of one assault after another on the female body. "He gives up his old ego, along with his anxiety about life and sense of fatalism. In its place is installed a new sense of responsibility," one critic confidently declares. We hear about the *"progress* of a man from naive arrogance and willful pride to the acceptance of his role as sacrificial victim and his *rebirth* into the community of men" (my emphasis) and about the way in which recognition of guilt "eradicates the old, benighted Franz Biberkopf; a new man arises in his place."[11] Exploring Biberkopf's relationship to women and to sexuality curbs the impulse to veer off into the optimistic mode dictated by resorting to interpretive traditions that willfully place sexuality in a peripheral role and valorize fundamentally linear models that move a protagonist from blindness to insight, dependence to autonomy, and defiance to assimilation.

In a second interpretive move, I challenge the notion that the discordant clamor of Döblin's novel can be reorchestrated to produce a carefully composed symphony of meaning.[12] For several decades now, critics have been straining their interpretive resources to build connections between disparate elements, to assimilate deviant narrative moments, to colonize the alien, and to smooth the rough edges of the text—all the while unaware that they are transposing what they perceive to be a symphonic theme onto the piano keyboard (to use Bakhtin's memorable metaphor).[13] Nowhere is this more evident than in the insistent construction of parallels between Biberkopf's life and the biblical stories woven into its telling, and for this reason I will give special attention to them in an effort to affirm a destabilizing policy of contradiction, fragmentation, heterogeneity, and multiplicity at work in the novel.

Our cultural discomfort with thematic messiness and stylistic anarchy becomes evident in critical efforts to construct an ending that positions the protagonist as a triumphantly autonomous male subject and to detect a hidden transcendent order and unity in the narrative design. The massive denial of the fragmentation and disfiguration that is to be found at the level of narrative technique and theme seems largely driven by the negation of the sexuality, powerlessness, and instability aligned in the novel with the feminine.

My reading of *Berlin Alexanderplatz* seeks to shift the terms of debate about Döblin's novel not only by looking at women in the social configuration of gender relationships, but also by attending to the ways in which the feminine comes to figure as an attribute of the city, itself a symbol of disorder. The Berlin of Döblin's novel is presented in a master trope as the Whore of Babylon, the incarnation of destructive sexuality, but that city is also populated by real-life prostitutes—women whose bodies, as Alain Corbin has convincingly demonstrated, are linked with the notions of desire, disease, and decay.[14] Recognizing the degree to which the corrupt carnality and sexual threat of women works into the urban pathology of Döblin's Berlin can further our understanding of the novel's many dimensions and allows us to escape the limited and limiting vision of the novel as the study of a man and a city.

The very first page of *Berlin Alexanderplatz* announces the fate of its protagonist. Biberkopf will suffer, but he will be a better man for it. More than that, we are told that he will reach a certain degree of self-understanding ("It will be made perfectly clear to him how everything came about"), and that his life will acquire meaning. The clipped style and dispassionate language of the novel's prefatory passages are calculated to inspire confidence in the narrator's judgments and to quell suspicions about this narrator's authenticity or reliability. Yet this teller of Biberkopf's story does more than give us the facts: he both reports events and makes sense of them, thrilling his audience with melodramatic accounts (both sentimental and sordid) even as he purports to be imparting lessons by framing his story as a cautionary tale.

The narrator goes even beyond the role of reporting and commenting: he also constructs the events in such a way that they produce a referential network to other genres, most notably to classic Greek tragedy, which, as Theodore Ziolkowski has pointed out, structures the plot. Although the novel is "a conscious travesty of tragedy with all its most characteristic elements," it

still, according to Ziolkowski, pays homage to the travestied model by chart-
ing the course of a man from blindness to insight and ends by showing us a
protagonist armed with a "new objectivity" and with "an attitude of critical
detachment toward reality."[15] The narrator tells his story in such a way that
it also invites parallels with the classical Bildungsroman, which moves its
protagonist from youthful irresponsibility and contestation of social expecta-
tions to quiet domestication and social integration. Thus there is a double
pressure on the reader to adopt the narrator's perspective and to read *Berlin
Alexanderplatz* as a tragic, yet enlightening, drama of human life and as an
instructive fable of human development. We do not, however, have to read
between the lines to find that contradictions and inconsistencies emerge as
we collaborate in the narrator's project of establishing parallels to canonical
genres. As soon as we consider the positions women occupy in the micro-
politics of everyday life as represented in the novel, it becomes impossible to
sustain the literary parallels (which offer models of cognitive breakthroughs
or psychological progress) or to share the narrator's expressed confidence in
human decency, social solidarity, and the superiority of reason over instinct.
When women enter the novel, the notion of self-determination is undermined by the presence of drives and desires beyond control, even as sexuality
becomes the site of power, violence, and a form of self-assertion that subverts
the policy of enlightened rationality championed by the narrator.

Let us begin by looking at the three major scenes of Biberkopf's defeat, the
three setbacks that precede his "conversion experience" at Buch. Shifting
attention from Biberkopf's noble but failed efforts to remain "decent," and
from his sense of betrayal, to the sheer physicality of what happens to
women in Döblin's novel blocks access to the rhetoric of pathos so often
mobilized to discuss these three episodes. Not surprisingly, it has always
been easier to write with enthusiasm about Franz Biberkopf's sense of elation
and liberation when he finds his potency restored after his release from
prison than to turn the spotlight on Minna, the victim of his rape, who is left
in a state of abject disarray, with a black eye and torn apron.[16] And it has
proved virtually irresistible to elide passages that describe the way in which
Reinhold beats up Trude, tears out her hair, breaks a mirror on her head, and
boxes her on the mouth. It is nothing short of astonishing to witness the way
in which Biberkopf, who may be the prisoner of certain passions and subjected to certain socioeconomic arrangements but who still remains something of a free agent in his relations with women, becomes for many critics
"a victim of circumstances."[17] Biberkopf is presented as the recipient of triple
hardships and betrayals, all of which engage and absorb our attention far
more than the misfortunes of his female intimates.

It is not long after his release from prison that Franz, a "decent" and "well-intentioned" man, is dealt a "blow" in the form of a "betrayal" by his friend Lüders. Yet Franz is not at all a victim: he sets himself up for betrayal by boasting about his sexual exploits to his friend Lüders, an arch-opportunist. One critic, following the narrator's revised line of reasoning, states: "Who besides Biberkopf will be surprised that the 'miserable' Lüders is seized by envy at the big boaster and that he too wants to try his luck?"[18] The terms of the debate can thus shift from Franz's victimization and betrayal by Lüders to the arrogance and naïveté displayed by Franz in his relationship with Lüders, but they do so in a way that erases the figure of the widow across whose body the entire exchange takes place.

In much the same way that the trouble between Lüders and Franz is so sharply foregrounded that the widow becomes virtually invisible, the conflict between Reinhold and Franz overshadows the bodies of the women who circulate between them. For a time, the two had engaged in a form of "girl-trading" (Mädchenhandel), with Franz taking in the women that Reinhold discarded. When Franz gleefully sets out to reform his friend, Reinhold, that most sinister and enigmatic of all the novel's characters, responds to Franz's intervention in his romantic affairs with violent rage, dealing a second "hammer blow" to Franz by shoving him out of a getaway car. Franz's attention remains riveted solely on Reinhold's betrayal of him. He never once stops to reflect on the interests that bind him to Reinhold or on Reinhold's multiple betrayals of women and his own collaboration in those betrayals. The narrator, even after he abandons a stance of empathetic identification with Franz, remains fixed on the dynamics of the man-to-man struggle and abandons the women as objects of narrative interest as quickly as Franz jilts them.

This valorization of what goes on between men and concomitant depreciation of the female partner in heterosexual relationships marks the description of the third and final blow of fate inflicted on the protagonist. A woman is killed, but her murder is regarded less as a personal tragedy for her than as a calamity for Franz. The seventh book of the novel, which describes Mieze's murder, commences with a story about the pilot Beese-Arnim. As it turns out, the "tragedy" of this man's life hinges on his murder of Pussi Uhl, an over-the-hill prostitute whose existence does not seem to count for much. In both cases the murder victims lose their claim on our empathy as soon as they are dead; it is the surviving male, even when he commits the murder, whose sufferings target him as the recipient of narrative interest or sympathy.

These three "blows of fate" may be understood as three variants on a scenario that enacts a Freudian drama in which two men—one associated with "the reaper" (the German term der Schnitter also means "the cutter"), the other repeatedly assailed for his passivity—encounter each other over the body of a woman. Their conflict gradually escalates from the desire to possess that body, to a wish to turn it into a source of profit through economic and social exchanges (note that Reinhold's women always arrive with a "gift" and that Franz lives off Mieze's wages as a prostitute), to a need finally to destroy it.[19] In a revealing study concerned with representations of women in Döblin's novels, David Dollenmayer points out that "beneath the consciously sublimated homoeroticism of the metaphysical battle between two males, the battle of the sexes continues, only superficially resolved by the recurring figure of redemptive prostitutes."[20] But what rages in *Berlin Alexanderplatz* seems to be both more and less than a battle of the sexes, more because it is so charged with lethal desire directed at both sexes, less because it seems so unilaterally fought. Women's bodies become the sites of conflict and of power struggles where male combatants collide as they struggle with the consequences of a "triangulation of desire" that conjoins eros with aggression.[21] As Eve Kosovsky Sedgwick has pointed out, some forms of male homosocial desire do not take the form of "brotherhood," but of "extreme, compulsory, and intensely volatile mastery and subordination."[22]

The young Döblin recognized the degree to which social and economic conditions made it impossible for women to function as the equals of men, and he wrote about the subject with passion. "As long as women do not *feel* themselves the equals of men," he declared in an essay penned in 1896, "they will remain subordinate to them and will let themselves be demeaned and humiliated by them."[23] It was only a matter of time before he represented the sexual consequences of this degradation in what must figure as one of the most notorious literary examples of male desire figured as a form of wanton sadism. Johannes, the protagonist of "The Black Curtain," triumphantly rails on about his beloved in words that seem shaped by a reading of Otto Weininger's notorious *Sex and Character*: "You must serve and let me savor my solitude as I rule over you. I didn't want to suck her into me but to spit her out, to force her to her knees. . . . I never [loved] my despising little angel more than . . . now that I have completely turned her into a whore." Irene accepts the humiliating role scripted for her in a series of stylized self-denunciations: "Oh, how ashamed I feel to be a woman. . . . Let me atone for being a woman. . . . You can destroy me completely, for it was only for you that I blossomed."[24] Johannes obliges, putting an end to her power to arouse sexual desire and to divert him from loftier matters, when he kills her by biting her in the throat. The coda to the novel makes the meaning explicit: "Our arms are not for embracing each other in ecstasy, but for defending ourselves and for fighting against the other and for murdering."[25] Death triumphs over love as the male partner channels erotic drives into destructive, martial aims to eliminate the degraded and degrading object of his desire.[26]

Klaus Theweleit's study of the mental world of Freikorps soldiers has shown us the ease with which a culture can legislate that sexual desire be placed in the service of destruction.[27] Like Johannes, the Freikorps-man ceaselessly wages war against pleasure by repudiating his own body and forging an ethics of self-denial and brutal violence. Theweleit's analysis of the psychological conflicts of Freikorps-men turns from the Oedipal model of a punishing father and tyrannized son and attaches primary significance to the pre-Oedipal dynamics of mother and child. For the soldiering men of *Male Fantasies*, women in general figure as a source of fear and dread precisely because of their association with softness, fluidity, sensuality, and pleasure. To protect themselves against a simultaneous longing for pre-Oedipal fusion and terror at the implied dissolution of the self (the two extremes of our being that are invariably associated with women as the bearers of life and death), the soldiering man develops a notion of his own body as a hard, organized dam against the streams, torrents, and floods of femininity in general and of female sexuality in particular.

Theweleit's disquisition seems particularly pertinent to *Berlin Alexanderplatz*, for Döblin's novel is not only littered with the bodies of raped and murdered women but also ends with the triumph of Death (in personified form) over Sexuality (incarnated in the figure of the Whore of Babylon). The protagonist seems to emerge triumphant in the end, sealed off against female sexuality, immune to wayward passion, and endowed with a new capacity for agency. He may be awake, with eyes open, but his life is emphatically devoid of affect—almost pathologically so—and of action. The final pages of the novel present a desexualized Franz, a Franz who has lost all interest in Eva and in the child that she had been carrying as a result of their sexual union. The description of the couple is stylized into the dreary picture of two people who may be at peace with each other and the world, but who have little to say or do as they contemplate their past and engage in eating pastries, the only form of pleasure left to them.

That a settled existence is a corollary of desexualization is powerfully suggested by the reflections on sexuality in "The Black Curtain." What never ceases to astonish the protagonist of that novella is the way in which the division of the human race into two sexes ruptures the notion of a stable, autonomous self and leads to a relentless drive for union with the other sex.[28] So unsettling is this subversion of autonomy through desire that it can lead to murderous rage. Like Johannes, Franz assaults the objects of his desire— once battering Ida until she is dead, a second time beating Mieze within an inch of her life. After Reinhold murders Mieze, Franz may manifest deep remorse but he has also posted a certain psychological gain in slaying the demon of sexuality. Yet by freeing himself of his "bestial" side, he also seems doomed to lead something of a bovine existence, one that can hardly be what it is cracked up to be by the narrator and by some commentators.

We have seen how the novel deliberately diverts attention from the victimization of women and channels it toward male agents of violence, making them passive sufferers rather than the initiators of action. Biberkopf himself is first presented as a casualty, a man more sinned against than sinning. His attempts to exonerate himself may ring false: his trivialization of Ida's murder ("manslaughter, nothing more . . . it wasn't that bad") (18) and his rationalization of it as a "mere" accident will fail to prove convincing to most readers, though they seem to have persuaded at least one critic that the protagonist can be described as "strong as an ox, impulsive, hot-tempered, but *basically good-natured* [my emphasis]."[29] It is ironically the women in the novel who are forever extolling Franz's virtues, in particular his self-effacing goodwill, and who thus become complicitous in building the case for his helpless innocence. Cilly finds him naive; Eva refers to him as "a good-natured lamb"; and Mieze sees in him a sweet, gullible man. The narrator concedes Franz's flaws—above all his failure to come to terms with his deeds—but his relentless insistence on Franz's good intentions and basic decency diverts us from facing the full consequences of his murderous violence.

All this seemingly changes in the scene that stages Franz's death and rebirth. Lying in his hospital bed at the asylum Buch, Franz hallucinates his own merciless slaughter at the hands of an ax-wielding death figure that makes mincemeat of him. Ironically it is in this very scene, when Franz falls victim to Death's hatchet, that the three major episodes marking his life are rescripted to reveal him as the real agent behind each "blow of fate." Death's relentless patter as it slices him to pieces demolishes the myth of his life as a sequence of betrayals and mishaps. Biberkopf created his own destiny, which Death replays for him in vivid, painful detail. Yet these words are embedded in a context that presents Biberkopf as the supremely abject victim of a ritual sacrifice that may be hallucinatory, but seems very real nonetheless.

The scene of Biberkopf's death and rebirth has been read, thanks to Döblin's own gloss on it, as the moment in which the protagonist magically works his way to autonomous selfhood through sacrifice. As Döblin observed about his book: "The real theme is: You must sacrifice. You must make of yourself a sacrifice [*Opfer*]."[30] Here, it is important to emphasize once again that the German term *Opfer* collapses the notion of victim and sacrifice, hence providing strong continuity between Biberkopf's self-styled role as victim and his sacrificial capitulation to Death. In a sense, one could argue (as many have done) that the surrender to Death is nothing more than an extension and intensification of the tenor of his entire life.

Only after the encounter with Death is Biberkopf positioned as a conscious and self-conscious initiator of action. To be sure, some things remain beyond his control, but these seem to be nothing more than elemental, natural forces:

> The air can hail and rain. You can't do anything about that, but you can do a lot about other things. I'll never again bellow as I did before: It was fate, it was fate. You can't stand in awe of fate. You have to look it in the face, grab it, and destroy it. (501)

That cultural traditions, social institutions, or economic conditions might impinge on this originary self and constrain its agency seems omitted from the final account of Biberkopf's position. No longer perceiving himself as a victim, as the effect of social and historical processes, he embraces a post-enlightenment notion of the subject as rational ("Reason is given to every man; oxen make it up with a clan,") (500), discerning ("When he fell, he opened up his eyes,") (499), and part of a collective humanity ("Much unhappiness comes from going it alone,") (500). This conclusion shores up a version of the victim/agent relationship that places the two terms in an emphatically static binary opposition, with Biberkopf elevated to the status of pure agent after undergoing a searing process of victimization and sacrifice. The bulk of the novel, however, moves against the simplistic notion of victimization and agency as clear-cut antitheses and complicates the relationship between the two by perpetually writing and rewriting stories about their determining role.

The biblical quotations and paraphrases in *Berlin Alexanderplatz* are the site of the novel's most intense preoccupation with the problem of agency, though one could argue that virtually every story in the text is implicated in the issue. Take, for example, the chilling determinism put on display as the narrator reveals what lies ahead for Max Rüst (including the precise wording of his obituary and the notice taken out by his family to thank friends for their condolences), whom we see as a fourteen-year-old boy descending from the street car on his way to speech therapy. Or think of the opportunistic license taken by Stefan Zannowich, swindler, manipulator, and con man par excellence, who asserts his status as a free agent and curbs intervention in his life up to the bitter end by committing suicide. It is in the biblical intertexts, however, that we have the novel's most complex and nuanced presentation of agency and causality.

The first of the biblical episodes woven into the novel—the betrayal in the Garden of Eden—is spliced into the story of Lüders, thus ostensibly giving credibility to Franz's sense of victimization.[31] The presence of the biblical paraphrase implies that the "innocent" Franz, who has struggled to remain decent, has been betrayed by that snake in the grass Lüders. But we must pause at this point to ask if this is a legitimate interpretive maneuver. The biblical paraphrase, after all, has a function beyond being a tip-off to the reader: it is part of a dense cultural code—one that also includes advertising slogans, newspaper stories, weather reports, and street signs—that determines Biberkopf's self-understanding, motivating and constraining his every move. That it shapes Biberkopf's consciousness goes without saying. That it also motivates and constrains us in making certain interpretive moves is a point that needs to be stated: here is a moment at which the consciousness of both character and reader are constituted by the same cultural text.

The snatches of text from Genesis are powerfully evocative. Although there are only five passages quoting from or paraphrasing the story of Adam and Eve, most readers are under the impression that many more exist simply because only a few words are required to produce the entire story. What becomes evident as we examine those passages is that there is no clear correlation between Biberkopf, the widow, and Lüders on the one hand, and Adam, Eve, and the snake on the other. Although conventional critical wisdom sees in Lüders the snake in the grass, Biberkopf has also (as his own worst enemy) been identified with that creature, and the widow, as the agent of sexual desire, can also be seen, like Eve, to be allied with the snake. Instead of smooth continuities from intertext to text, we find overlapping, contradiction, disjunction, and fragmentation—devices that lead the reader to become aware of the ways in which cultural texts like the story of Adam and Eve limit our interpretive capacities as much as they expand them, and interfere with our ability to understand motivation and agency as much as they facilitate it.[32]

The temptation to equate Biberkopf with figures in the two other principal biblical intertexts is best illustrated by the voice of a critic who has devoted an entire book to the religious dimension of Döblin's life and work. "Biberkopf is compared with Job, with Abraham and with Isaac," Monique Weyembergh-Boussart declares.[33] To be sure, there are certain moments of consonace with Biberkopf's life in the stories of Job and of Isaac. Since Job represents overweening pride as much as he symbolizes the depths of victimization, Biberkopf can remain affiliated with him even as his perceived status gradually shifts from victim to agent. Yet the incongruities are startling. Job loses his family and his possessions: God takes his sevens sons and his three daughters, his seven thousand sheep, three thousand camels, five hundred yoke of oxen, and five hundred she-asses. Biberkopf may be devastated by Lüders' betrayal of his confidence, but the calamity that befalls him is trivial by comparison with Job's lot. To refer to Biberkopf as "a creature tested by torment"—to place a hyphen between his name and Job's—seems almost ludicrous when set against the context of the biblical story.[34]

The story of Abraham and Isaac, often paired with the slaying of Mieze by Reinhold (the third "blow of fate" inflicted on Franz) sounds fuller thematic chords than its two predecessors. Sacrifice and slaughter not only imply victims and agents, but also touch on the entire range of issues raised by the novel's slaughterhouse scenes, which in turn are evoked at critical points in the lives of both Franz and the women in the novel. The slaughterhouse scenes prepare the way for an entire range of parallels and contrasts between man and beast (e.g., "girl-trading" / "cattle-trading"; "Reason is given to every man; oxen make it up with a clan," and so on), at the same time that they create the opportunity for presenting uncensored versions of violent deaths with all their gory details. The biblical text, in portraying sacrifice at its most emotionally charged and self-abnegating extreme, stands in sharp contrast to the episodes describing the mechanical, instrumentalized business of butchering. The description of Mieze's murder is both interwoven with references to the slaughterhouse killings and juxtaposed to the story of Abraham and Isaac, setting up two competing texts for interpreting her murder. Predictably, Mieze has been perceived either as a wholly innocent and unsuspecting victim *or* as an agent of redemption through her self-sacrifice.[35] The two interpretations may not be entirely incompatible, but they illustrate the way in which critics arbitrarily seize on one or another isolated intertext, interpolated story, or montage element as guides for reading a character.

Rather than offering interpretive clues for Franz Biberkopf's third major setback, the story of Abraham and Isaac destabilizes the relationship between life story and biblical gloss. If anything, it reveals that sacrifice can turn into self-sacrifice, that the agent can become the victim, and, as important, that even the most notoriously scandalous event does not necessarily lend itself to easy interpretation. The repeated framing of sacrificial stories ranging from slaughterhouse scenes and sexual murders to mythological accounts and biblical tales shows the extent to which the issue of victim and agent resists general definition and can be captured only in the specificity of single events.

Franz Biberkopf slays Ida, rapes Minna, and brutalizes Mieze. Yet although he is referred to as a cobra, he is also labeled a helpless calf—the term "ox" when applied to him implies something of his borderline state of rugged vulnerability. Biberkopf, who falls under Reinhold's lethal influence and comes under Death's hatchet, applies deadly force but also becomes its recipient. Anxieties about his vulnerability surface perhaps most tellingly when he chants a contemporary rhyme (cited at the beginning of this book's first

chapter) about a real-life "butcher": the homosexual serial killer Fritz Haarmann, who uses his "chopper" to make "mincemeat" of his victims.

Inserting the Haarmann verse into the text of *Berlin Alexanderplatz* not only
evokes one aspect of the social realities of Weimar Germany and the attendant tragi-comic strategy for managing the anxieties aroused by it, but also
reveals how those realities play their role in constructing the psyche. The
Haarmann verse, like the voices of the streetvendors and streetcar conduc-
tors that sound throughout the novel, is of special significance because it
vividly illustrates how the world of *Berlin Alexanderplatz* vibrates with social
energy through the interchange between self and world.[36] More important,
by evoking the historical figure of Fritz Haarmann, the narrator, in formal
terms, welds the double threat incarnated in the figures of Reinhold and
Death.[37] Reinhold, with his powerful homoerotic hold on Franz, exerts an
influence as lethal as that of death. Throughout *Berlin Alexanderplatz*, his
entry into the narrative is marked by words from a popular folksong about
the grim reaper. Beyond fusing the murderous aspects of Reinhold's homosexuality with the slaughterhouse tactics of the Death figure at Buch, the
Haarmann verse that runs through Franz's mind positions the protagonist as
potential victim, one as helpless as the stockyard animals whose murders are
so graphically depicted in the novel. Reinhold affirms his alliance with the
slaughterhouse violence of Death when he refers in the same breath to Franz
as an "ox" and to Mieze as a "sow." Franz's encounter with Death in the
asylum at Buch is staged as a meeting between butcher and victim, with
Death swinging its hatchet and slicing Franz into pieces. Here, it is important
to bear in mind, however, that Franz's death is no more than a hallucination
(notwithstanding the narrator's insistence on his extinction in all but name)
and that, unlike Mieze, he is pieced back together and rejuvenated.

Much as the story of Franz Biberkopf introduces an element of unruly
complexity into the victim/agent problem, the real-life women in that story
reinscribe the notion of "pure" roles: they are all passive victims who seem
to take a kind of masochistic pleasure in their helplessness. A seemingly
endless supply of female bodies is made available to the protagonist, who,
like nearly every other character in the novel, builds to those bodies a relationship both monetary and murderous.[38] While the corpses found in this
"Bildungsroman" are almost invariably female, it took Fassbinder's film,
with its insistent foregrounding of Ida's and Mieze's murders, to draw our
attention to the way in which violence toward women permeates the novel
from start to finish.[39]

How could critics find it so easy to suppress the polarization of the text's
social energy into male violence and female victimization?[40] The narrator
uses a number of techniques that go beyond the problematization of Bi-

berkopf's agency to obscure and mystify what is happening in the novel. At the same time that every effort is made to promote the traditional identification between "hero" and reader, a wedge is driven between the reader and the female figures. Let us begin with a look at the retrospective narration of Ida's murder. In a flashback some eighty pages after the description of Franz's release, Ida's murder is related in dry, matter-of-fact prose culminating in the translation of the homicidal event into mathematical formulas describing the movement of "bodies" in space. The effect of the dispassionate scientific language ("loss of a vertical position on Ida's part, transition to a horizontal one,") (105) is to suppress the agent of the assault and to dehumanize the victim. By contrast, an account of the murder of Agamemnon, which follows hard on the account of Ida's killing, is narrated in language charged with pathos:

> When the woman gets him home, she puts him in the bath. She shows then and there that she is a monster beyond compare. While he's in the water, she throws a fishing net over him so that he can't make a move. And she has brought along a hatchet used to chop wood. He moans: "Woe is me, I've been struck!" Outside they wonder: "Who can be wailing so loudly?" "Woe is me, woe is me!" The Hellenic beast finishes him off without batting an eye. Outside she even has the nerve to bellow: "I did it. I threw a fishing net over him and struck him twice. At the second groan, he was laid out, and then, with a third blow, I sent him to Hades." (107)

This account of murder both sensationalizes the event and takes a stand on it. Clytemnestra is designated as "a monster beyond compare" and "a Hellenic beast." She not only commits the murder in cold blood ("without batting an eye") but publicly trumpets the efficiency with which she carries out the deed. The helpless Agamemnon mobilizes all our sympathy when we hear his cries of anguish. While it is true that Agamemnon's murder is premeditated and Ida's is not, the contrast in the description of the two events is telling. On the one hand we have an act that seems nothing more than a "natural" event governed by the Newtonian laws of motion, on the other a vicious crime committed by a demented woman.

While the murders and violations of the women who inhabit Döblin's fictional Berlin are (with one exception) described without rhetorical passion, the description of murders by women all move in the mode of the melodramatic and sensational. But just who are these bloodthirsty women? Ida, Minna, Lina, Fränze, Cilly, Trude, Eva, Mieze? Not one of these women comes under the slightest suspicion. Instead we have one mythical figure, Clytemnestra, and one biblical figure, the Whore of Babylon. The latter, who makes repeated appearances in the novel until her conquest by Death, inserts herself, through her designation as a whore, into the series of "real-life" prostitutes that enter Franz's life. It is she who, through the powerful intensity of her evil, contaminates the others. Here is one of numerous variant descriptions mounted into the novel:

> There sits upon the many waters Babylon the Great, the mother of harlots and of all abominations on earth. She sits upon a scarlet-colored beast, with seven heads and ten horns, for all to behold, for all to see. Every step you take delights her. She is drunk with the blood of the saints she has torn to pieces. Behold the horns with which she gores. She rises from the depths and goes into perdition. Behold her, the pearls, the scarlet, the purple, the teeth she bares, the thick, plump lips over which blood has flowed and with which she has drunk. (320)

It is interesting to observe how a novel that repeatedly enacts male violence against women genders the incarnation of murderous evil as a feminine entity. There may be a masculine counterpart to the Whore of Babylon in the figure of Death, who functions as her antagonist and conquerer, but it is the Whore of Babylon who comes to represent the real principle of death, for her seductive bloodthirstiness is linked with the unreproductive sexuality of the prostitute. Death, by contrast, becomes allied with the principle of life: "I am life and true strength. Now at last, at long last, you will stop trying to preserve yourself" (475). In a process that replicates the notion of rejuvenation through dismemberment found in myths and fairy tales, Death slices Franz Biberkopf into pieces to make a "new man" out of him. Thus Death, gendered masculine, becomes the site of procreation and the source of redemptive life, while the Whore of Babylon is linked with the series of bloody deaths inaugurated by the slaughterhouse scenes.

The myth constructed by Döblin in *Berlin Alexanderplatz* pits a masculine Death figure against a bloodthirsty and bloodstained feminine principle associated with the city and with prostitution. It is difficult to avoid seeing Death as the principal actor in an Oedipal scenario that positions Franz as the son who, through the anxiety created by the castration threat, submits at last to the law of the father. Turning from the Whore of Babylon, who represents lasciviousness ("the mother of harlots"), excess ("seven heads and ten horns"), and the threat of engulfment and cannibalistic incorporation ("she is drunken with the blood of the saints she has torn to pieces"), Franz begins a new regime in which allegiance to the feminized principle of sexuality has been banished.

The degree to which the configuration of gender relationships and the presentation of female sexuality purveyed in *Berlin Alexanderplatz* can take on a mythical dimension transcending political and social realities is vividly illustrated by the portrait of Rosa Luxemburg in the fourth volume of Döblin's tetralogy *November 1918* (1937–43). Here we see an aging, physically frail woman, wasting away in prison as she is driven to hysteria by the death of her lover Hannes Düsterberg (based on the historical figure Hans Diefenbach). Döblin's Rosa Luxemburg devotes her days of incarceration to deranged fantasies in which her deceased lover returns to "consummate" their marriage and to invade her body so that he can return to life. After Rosa's release, Hannes returns in the form of a demon lover—or rather, Satan disguises himself as Hannes to seduce Rosa:

> These were her nuptials, this time her real wedding, and how different it was from that first one in prison with that icy shadow who wanted to draw warmth from her, that poor, broken warrior. The man who was here was warm, hot, and magically handsome. He exhausted himself, and she did not hold back. She fainted from the ecstasy and intoxication.[41]

By presenting Rosa Luxemburg as the victim of sexual hysteria and even placing the devil to whom she becomes a sexual slave at the site of her shooting, Döblin's narrator turns her assassination into a murder motivated by more than political considerations. David Dollenmayer has observed that Rosa's violent death is connected to her sensuality and, in Döblin's rewriting of her life, she becomes more or less a victim of unrestrained sexual desires.[42] It is especially telling that the figure with whom she becomes linked in her death is not the stalwart Liebknecht but rather a homosexual schoolmaster whose fatal beating is placed in a direct causal relationship with a life ruled by sexual desire. This man is described as getting exactly what he deserves: "What did he know of himself in the end? What did he, in the final analysis, identify with, if not with eros, with sweet desire and lust, to which he submitted? They proceeded with him according to their laws."[43]

Rosa Luxemburg is presented as a figure who, like women in general, is perversely attached to the notion of self-sacrifice. "What are we without love? How sweet it can be to sacrifice oneself,"[44] she reflects in one of her many effusive monologues. Female sexuality is invariably coupled with masochistic self-effacement; note how Düsterberg takes over Rosa's body at the height of their passion. Thus it is no surprise that Rosa not only deeply empathizes with the suffering of slaughtered animals, but becomes identified with such creatures at the site of her murder. The novel introduces the assassin Runge in its first pages through a letter in which Rosa bemoans the wanton torture to which oxen are subjected by the very man who will murder her in the last pages of the novel. But rather than expressing outrage at the torturer, she empathizes with the animals as models of stoic suffering. And indeed, when she herself is felled by a blow from Runge's rifle butt, she "moans," throws "mute glances" at her murderer, and collapses like a slaugh-tered animal ("wie ein gefälltes Tier").[45] If Rosa Luxemburg is nothing more than a "waddling duck" to her assassin and "bloody Rosa, the red sow" to her political enemies, she constructs herself as a suffering creature who mutely endures the tortures inflicted on her.[46]

Now it is true that Rosa Luxemburg, in a letter to Sophie Liebknecht, revealed that she felt a sense of empathetic identification with tortured crea-tures.[47] Margarethe von Trotta's 1985 film *Rosa Luxemburg* enacts the scene described in the letter, with the helpless heroine witnessing the brutal beat-ing of two buffaloes. As the camera focuses on Luxemburg with tears in her eyes, a voice-over reveals her thoughts:

> The animals stood perfectly still and the one that was bleeding stared straight ahead with an expression on its black face like that of a tear-stained child. . . . I stood in front of it and the animal looked at me; tears ran down my face—they were *its* tears. One cannot tremble more painfully for one's most beloved brother than I did in my powerlessless in the face of this quiet suffering. Oh, my poor buffalo, my poor beloved brother, we are both standing here so silently and are joined only in pain, in impotence, in longing.

But while the film mobilizes this particular moment to demonstrate Luxem-burg's deep emotional (as well as intellectual) commitment to socialism, Döblin's book turns the empathy into a sign of masochistic self-indulgence and suggests that the identification goes so far as to shape the terms of her murder.[48]

Like the prostitutes of *Berlin Alexanderplatz*, Döblin's Rosa Luxemburg falls victim to violence motivated as much by male contempt for women as by sociopolitical considerations. As we are subjected to page after page of Lux-emburg's deranged erotic hallucinations, we begin to understand the source of the contempt. In her jail cell, Rosa Luxemburg is less a political captive than the prisoner of her own wanton sensuality and masochistic hysteria. Döblin devotes far more attention to the fictional fantasies than to the histor-ical facts of Luxemburg's life.[49] While it would be reassuring to emphasize the ideological differences separating Döblin's narrator from, say, an Otto Weininger, it would be misleading to suggest that the two are worlds apart in their views on women. For both, women's consuming interest in sexual matters separates them from men and imperils them. Friedrich Becker, the central figure of *November 1918*, laments the way in which it is virtually impos-sible to remain immune to female sexuality: "These women have infected me with their sordid doings."[50] Like Rosa Luxemburg, women, through their greater absorption in sexuality, become the sufferers, those willing to make any sacrifice for the sake of love. Thus they endure coercive male violence with the passive stoicism of the slaughtered beast.[51]

There is more, however, to this myth of female suffering and male violence than meets the eye. (I pointedly use the term "myth" here, for Döblin himself validated the notion that his books worked out masochistic and sadistic experiences foreign to his own state of mind.)[52] The narrators of *Berlin Alexanderplatz* and of *Karl and Rosa* propagate a concept that constructs women as creatures who derive a measure of pleasure from their suffering, just as males achieve some kind of release through their assaults. Implicit in this sociosexual argument about the organization of pain and pleasure is the principle of male physical and intellectual superiority. Yet what we also find in *Berlin Alexanderplatz* is a radical undermining of this belief in male superiority, an underlying subversive myth about the powerful Whore of Babylon and a story about the bloodthirsty Clytemnestra. It is these "subversive" narratives that, in a sense, produce the condition for establishing and securing a coercive set of beliefs about female suffering and male aggression. The myths and interpolated stories offer an account of female depravity that mitigates and authorizes the violence that we find at the level of the "real" events in the book. They explain just why it is that "blood must flow" at a speed and degree that will astonish nearly every reader who begins to reflect on its presence in Döblin's novel. Franz and Reinhold may be indicted by the narrator and by the law for their murderous impulses and actions toward women, but the stories of the Whore of Babylon and Clytemnestra lift the burden of guilt from their shoulders. These two "timeless" and "universal" fables of female violence transcend the timebound, cultural specificity of the novel's account of male violence, producing a work in which agency is relentlessly projected onto the victims even as suffering becomes the declared project of the agent.

"Blood must flow, blood must flow, rain right down in thick red currents." These words from a Nazi song are intoned at various intervals throughout the novel. While their actual source is not clear (is Biberkopf reciting them or is the narrator simply giving us another cultural citation?), the words themselves invariably appear in the context of politically charged social conflicts—when, for example, Franz decides to sell Nazi newspapers and is confronted by communist comrades. If we recall that, in this particular novel, blood flows most freely whenever the Whore of Babylon makes an appearance, then it becomes evident that political conflict and sexualized violence are in many ways of one piece, or at least shade easily into one another. The story of the Whore of Babylon, a mosaic of biblical quotations and cultural citations, constructs a bloodthirsty female demon as the real villain, and it is this villain who, in the moral calculus of the work, contaminates the female victims of male violence with her savage lust even as she exonerates the male agents of sexual violence.

What is especially disturbing about this myth of female bloodthirstiness and the way in which it is pressed into service to blame the victims is its congruence with Nazi ideological constructions of the Jews. Recall the verses cited in an earlier chapter:

> They slaughter animals, slaughter people,
> Their bloodthirstiness knows no bounds!
> The world will return to health
> If we save it from the Jews.

I am, of course, not trying to establish a direct link between Döblin's novel and Nazi racial propaganda, only a parallel that has its roots in the psychological dynamics of projection. The sexual demonization of women in *Berlin Alexanderplatz* has a function not very different from the racial demonization of Jews in the Third Reich. In both cases, repression and projection operate in such a way as to turn the target of murderous violence into a peril of monstrous proportions, one that threatens to sap the lifeblood of the "victims" and thereby authorizes a form of unrestrained retaliatory violence marked by frenzied excess. Döblin, along with others, recognized the structure of the pathology (if not its exact content) long before it made its most frightening appearance on the stage of German history.

The Killer as Victim:
Fritz Lang's M

> I am the wound and the knife!
> I am the blow and the cheek!
> I am the limbs and the wheel—
> The victim and the executioner.
>
> *Baudelaire,* L'Héautontimoroumenos

NEARLY TWENTY years after the making of *M* (1931), Fritz Lang recalled how he and his wife Thea von Harbou had set out to make a movie about the worst imaginable crime—the crime most likely to arouse feelings of personal repulsion and public indignation. "Originally, it was not the story of a child-murderer," Lang recalls. "We discussed the most heinous crime, and we came [upon] the writing of anonymous poison letters. . . . We started to work on it and one day . . . I don't know what made me do it, I said wait a moment, I think I have another thing: a child-murderer, a man who is forced by some urge, by some perverted urge . . . a sick man . . . to kill."[1]

   M never specifies the "perverted urge" that drives Beckert to kill school-children. Just as Lang's syntax breaks down as he attempts to talk about that urge, so too the film makes only halting and hesitant moves in the direction of explaining its central scandal. Beckert's confession refers to "fire," to a "voice," and to the "pain" that haunt him and impel him to seek out new victims, but it never moves much beyond naming symptoms to reveal the psychic trauma or physiological defect that determines his need to murder. In this sense, the cinematic narrative appears to deepen the enigma posed by Lang in his retrospective reflections. "Who is the murderer?" This is instead the question repeatedly enunciated, circulated, and addressed in the opening scenes of the film. Placards and newspaper headlines demand to know the identity of the murderer; the police and the citizenry are frantic for an arrest. Instead of foregrounding the enigma of motive, the film immediately declares its investment in the process of detection.[2] The criminals and the police may eventually succeed in identifying the murderer, but neither ever penetrates the mystery of the crime, which seems to remain as vaguely formulated in the end as Lang's reference to "some perverted urge."

According to Siegfried Kracauer, Fritz Lang had revealed to him that "the Düsseldorf child-murderer Kürten" was the inspiration for his portrait of the killer in *M*.[3] In later years, Lang claimed that there was no single historical model for the serial murderer Beckert—furthermore, the screenplay for *M* was complete even before Kürten was apprehended. "I am more than an attentive reader of newspapers. I read the papers of *more* than just one country and try above all else to read between the lines. . . . At the time that I had decided on the theme of *M*, a number of serial murderers were on the rampage—Haarmann, Grossmann, Kürten, Denke—and so, naturally enough, I asked myself: What led these people to commit these deeds? . . . Not a single one of these men was a murderer of children, but at about that time children became the victims of terrible crimes in the city of Breslau, and the perpetrator was never caught."[4]

M is very much in the mode of the "Whodunit?" despite the fact that it immediately lets the audience in on the secret of the murderer's identity. But it also focuses almost consistently on the disturbing effects rather than the causes of crime. Those effects were precisely what contemporary newspaper accounts of the still-unsolved Kürten case found so fascinating. The press, as noted in chapter 3, was less interested in the murderer's pathology ("What makes him tick!" as Lang put it) than in the nervous anxiety aroused by the socially disruptive act of murder. Kürten may not have stood as model for Franz Beckert, but the press reports on the wave of terror he spread in Düsseldorf and other parts of Germany could not have failed to capture the imagination of a filmmaker who specialized in representing faces etched with fear and in scenes of mass hysteria.

Although Lang harped repeatedly on *M* as a film with a social message about the importance of taking good care of children and as a film that stages a debate about the death penalty, he made one particularly telling offhand observation about just what it was that fascinated him about the serial murders of the 1920s. In following various cases in the newspapers, Lang was struck by the way in which the unsolved murders seemed almost automatically to foster what he described as a psychosis of fear (*Angstpsychose*)—for him, a revolting mentality that mingled misanthropy with overzealousness to produce the kind of behavior that led to the denunciation of neighbors and other associates. *M* mounts a number of scenes immediately following the news of Elsie Beckmann's murder in which the usual suspects are rounded up, both by police officials and by the mob mentality. This is very much in keeping with the facts of the Kürten case: the *Frankfurter Zeitung* reported that one police raid had resulted in the arrest of sixty citizens and that several dozen men had been charged by neighbors with the Kürten murders. Press reports consistently focused on the hysterical state of the public. The *Frankfurter Zeitung* wrote of the collective psychosis of fear ("Angstpsychose der Bevölkerung") in Düsseldorf, using the very term that Lang was later to adopt to describe rampant paranoia and hysteria. *Fury*, Lang's first American film, was based on a screenplay entitled *Mob Rule* and showed how mass hysteria can destroy an innocent man, a theme that was to play a prominent role in Lang's American films.

Murder marks a moment of uncanny disruption in the social order. Even the arch-criminal Schränker, in a moment of high comic irony, declares his desire for a return to normal conditions ("geordnete Verhältnisse")—otherwise the hysteria of the police, which manifests itself in stepped-up surveillance, will put him and his colleagues out of business. His concern, too, lies less with the criminal deeds and with their victims than with the effect of the murders on his "trade." While his preoccupation with effects is real, it also serves to camouflage some of his anxiety about the murder of children. Why else would this suave safecracker, who is otherwise never at a loss for words, find himself groping for the term *Kindermörder* and then stuttering over it? Like the shadow cast over the placard at the film's beginning, a shadow that makes the names of the victims virtually illegible, Schränker has successfully suppressed the nature of the crime and focused on its immediate effects for business.

M stands in an interesting relation of contrast to the work of Dix and Grosz in that it resolutely conceals the body of the victim, and, once the deed is done, deflects attention from the victim to the investigative process used to apprehend the perpetrator and to the social consequences of his crime. Rather than displaying the mutilated corpse of the child, Lang represents the girl's death as a spatial and acoustical absence. The vacant stairwell and empty attic, along with the untouched place setting, are counterpointed by Frau Beckmann's increasingly frantic cries, to which there is no response. The cinematic aversion to representing the murder of a child is not at all surprising, but the taboo on showing the act of murder and displaying its effects on the body operate with a logic entirely different from the one we have seen applied to the adult female corpses drawn and painted by Dix and Grosz.

Some might argue that Lang's cinematic narration of Elsie Beckmann's murder is more visually arresting and emotionally charged than a direct representation of the deed. In *M*, both the homicide and the corpse are indirectly rendered. Once we see the balloon—bought by the murderer for his victim—trapped in overhead wires, we know Elsie's fate. The balloon-puppet reappears in the trial scene to haunt Beckert when the blind street vendor testifies and releases a similar balloon in the "courtroom." "El . . . El . . . Elsie . . . El . . . Elsie. . . ," Beckert cries out as the dancing balloon drifts heavenward. His shrill cry at the sight of this whimsical object certifies the murder of the child and simultaneously disavows it by morbidly displacing the death onto a marker of buoyant spirits.

The anxious disavowal of the child's corpse in the film's representational regime has, to my mind, just the opposite effect of what Lang intended. Failing to realize that the cinematic images might be far preferable to subjective recreations of the crime, Lang insisted that each viewer would mentally fill in the blanks left by the omission of the act of murder:

> Because of the loathsome nature of the crime M dealt with, there was a problem of how to present such a crime so that it would not sicken the audience, yet would have full emotional impact. That is why I only gave hints—the rolling ball, the balloon caught in the wires, after being released from a little hand. Thus I make the audience an integral part in the creation of this special scene by forcing each individual member of the audience to create the gruesome details of the murder according to his personal imagination.[5]

Lang's "hints" are, however, so visually riveting and absorbing that any viewer moderately resistant to the notion of mentally constructing the murder of a child will go with the flow of the cinematic images, which, despite their emotional power, give us a sanitized and aestheticized version of the murder.

The most obvious of Lang's "hints" that the child has been murdered comes in the image of the balloon-puppet struggling to free itself from utility wires. But we also see various aspects of the abduction and murder covertly and overtly dramatized, with potential victims standing in for the murdered Elsie Beckmann. The most arresting of these reenactments occurs in the courtroom scene, when we witness the killer in the actual throes of the passion that compels him to kill. As Beckert tries to explain his powerlessness to defy the voices directing him to kill, he descends into a state of homicidal frenzy, mimicking before the eyes of his "judge" and "jury" a murder scene that reveals the degree to which killing provides him with a release normally affiliated with a sexual act. The confessional scene stages a cliché that is familiar enough from slasher films of recent vintage: the compulsion to murder is homologous with the sexual drive. The serial murderer commits his crimes in the heat of sexual arousal, both to punish his victims for the sexuality that he witnesses or projects onto them and to discharge sexual urges that he can neither contain nor channel into normal outlets. Here, as Carol Clover has shown, sex and violence are "not concomitants but alternatives," with one substituting for the other.[6] Beckert's crimes may be sexually motivated, but the sexual intent turns upon itself to produce a result that is destructive rather than procreative. Violence becomes not an adjunct but a substitute for sex, turning Beckert's crime into that peculiar blend of destructive desire known as *Lustmord*—in this case a *Lustmord* that resists representation because it violates the body of a child.

If Lohmann and Schränker, the two principals in the investigative process, remain singularly unattuned to and uninterested in the psychological complexities of a figure who is a prisoner of the irrational, Lang himself tried on at least one occasion to move beyond the nebulous idea of "some urge" and to address the question of the killer's pathology: "The desire to hurt, the desire to kill is closely joined to the sexual urge, under whose dictate no man acts reasonably."[7] Lang's pronouncement on the relation between homicidal and sexual drives still does not move us closer to an understanding of the "voice" that drives Beckert to kill, a voice that, according to the murderer, can be silenced only by the victim's screams. In this context it is important to remember that in the film's logic Beckert's crimes always have at least two victims: the child and the child's mother. When a murder is committed, the child-victim screams with horror; when the child's death is represented on screen by silences and empty spaces, the mother-victim screams in despair. In a sense, both the terrified murder victim and the horror-stricken mother become the sources of voices that override the voice directing the murderer to kill—but only once it is too late.

Although Beckert is clearly the agent who inflicts suffering on his victims and their mothers, when he is finally hunted down and confesses his deeds to the criminals assembled to try him, he appropriates for himself the role of a victim haunted by avenging spirits: "And behind me race the ghosts of mothers . . . of children. . . . They won't go away. . . . They're always there. Always! Always!"[8] The strength of the maternal outrage and rage provoked by Beckert's murders becomes fully apparent only in the film's final scene when a plea on behalf of the maternal victims unleashes the full fury of the assembled law breakers. "You've never had children, have you?" one woman defiantly asks Beckert's "attorney." "Well, then, you haven't lost any either. But if you want to know what it's like to have one of your kids taken from you, then go ask the parents of the children he took away" (119). To these angry accusations another woman adds: "Ask them about the days and nights when they didn't know for sure what had happened . . . and about the ones later on when they finally knew what happened. Ask the mothers!" (119–20). The crowd of criminals, which has remained indignantly angry yet controlled and composed throughout the proceedings, turns into a furious mob just at the point when voices cry out: "You should ask the mothers . . . the mothers . . . ask them . . . Do you think you'll get mercy from the mothers for the man who murdered their children?" (120). The presence of mothers and of those who can identify with their rage foments opposition to the counterfeit logic and reason of the mock judicial proceedings and gives rise to a wave of vengeful savagery. That the scene takes place in a cavernous underground space, a space often cinematically linked to the womb, strengthens the suspicion that it is the mothers above all who are implicated in wreaking vengeance on Beckert.[9]

In this final scene, Beckert has fully succeeded in positioning himself as helpless victim, as the target of lethal maternal fury that threatens to engulf and destroy him. The revenge scene, more clearly than any other, provides the tip-off for what makes Beckert tick: a self-destructive need to provoke a form of maternal rage that will be turned on his trapped body. Lang, unlike Hitchcock, leaves us in the dark about such crucial matters as the killer's family history. Not a word on the matter. Beckert's whistling, however, turns out to be worth many words, if not a thousand. To my knowledge, no critic has stopped to ponder the reasons for Beckert's obsession with the haunting bars from Edvard Grieg's *In the Hall of the Mountain King*, in part perhaps because the music seems so aptly to intensify the sinister atmosphere established in the film and therefore does not cry out for commentary. That Beckert whistles the notes with particular vehemence right before he murders alerts us to their significance. If we move for a moment into the royal hall of the old man of the Dovrë, as he is known in Ibsen's *Peer Gynt*, we find the protagonist in the realm of trolls and goblins. It is in this place that Peer Gynt, on the brink of marriage, is nearly turned into a monster. Before marrying, he is to be endowed with a tail, and he reacts to the proposal with astonishment:

> PEER GYNT: No, you don't! Are you making a beast out of me?
> OLD MAN: Don't come courting my girl with no tail on your rump!
> PEER GYNT: Turning men into beasts!
> OLD MAN: No, my son, you're mistaken; it simply makes you a courtly wooer.[10]

This scene from Ibsen's drama comes close to enacting the time-honored cliché that women, by inspiring sexual desire, turn men into beasts. Admittedly, Lang's murderer kills only children, and children of both sexes at that.

But *we* see him in the grip of a passion that obliges him to pursue young girls alone and that subsequently abandons him to the power of a fury that is emphatically gendered female and designated as maternal. We are very much in the realm of Norman Bates, who, in one formulation, is driven to kill by the "'mother half of his mind' . . . when he (the Norman half) found himself aroused. . . ."[11] Whatever the age and gender of the victim, in any case, the killer is driven by the need to commit acts that will end by unleashing maternal rage to punish him for his craven sexual desires.

Sade's *Philosophy in the Boudoir*, as Angela Carter has demonstrated, shows us an extreme case in which murderous aggression is turned directly on a "Holy Mother" who is perceived as the "shrine of reproductive sexuality" and who embodies the "repression of sexual pleasure."[12] For Carter, Sade's novel of transgressive desire run amok has wide-reaching implications for understanding the psychosexual dynamics between mother and child. By seemingly placing their sexuality solely in the service of reproduction and thus implying the prohibition of sexual pleasure, mothers tacitly become agents of moral prohibition and arouse powerful feelings of hostility in their sexually adventurous offspring. Beckert could be seen as channeling this kind of rage into aggression directed at children, at the products of the mother's instrumental form of sexuality. In an act of morbid defiance that operates within a double libidinal economy, he derives sexual pleasure from the act of destroying the "products" of her "labor" and turning his own sexuality into an unproductive form of expenditure, one that takes him to the very limits of pleasure and of anguish, as we so clearly see in his reenactment of the murders.[13]

The opening shots of M establish the terms of an opposition that is fully developed in the film's initial sequence and becomes the dominant component of the contrast between mother and murderer—that between labor and play and between suffering and pleasure. The children's game that introduces the action stands in sharp contrast to the activities of the two mothers, Frau Beckmann and her pregnant colleague. Playful repetition of the little girl's rhyme ("Just you wait 'til it's your time") represents a form of mastering the fear of the bogeyman invoked in the chant, and it also results in a process of serial elimination (each repetition ends with the words "You're out!") that eerily forecasts the disappearance of children. It is this chant that provokes the ire of the pregnant laundress, whose chief daily activity consists of a form of labor marked also by repetition, but a repetitive activity totally devoid of pleasure or mastery. From the start, the film sets up a barrier between women ("mostly haggard," as one critic puts it) and children— between labor and play, between an oppressive regime of hard work and one

37. In *M*, Beckert gazes with evident delight at the items on display in a toy shop window. Note the similarities between his profile and that of the potential victim.

of liberating pleasures—just as it will establish the mothers as the murderer's antagonists (this despite the existence of affinities, signalled in the syllable that joins Beckert's name with that of Frau Beckmann).[14]

Beckert's physical appearance, along with his name, keeps him closely identified with his victims. Critics from Kracauer on have casually connected Beckert with the world of children and of women. Kracauer described the child murderer as "a somewhat infantile petty bourgeois" who looks "effeminate rather than resolute."[15] *M* repeatedly draws attention to Beckert's regressive traits, marking him as a creature of emphatic orality. We listen to Beckert's compulsive whistling and rarely see him without a cigarette, a sweet, or a hand at his mouth. One shot of Beckert is particularly revealing, for it must have been staged with the thought of drawing special attention to the childlike side of his personality (fig. 37). He and a prospective victim stand at the window of a toy shop, gazing with obvious pleasure at the items on display. The features and expressions on the two faces, while separated by age and gender, are remarkable in their physical resemblance. While the childish element in the killer seems a deliberate part of the film's representational strategies—Lorre's face must have seemed particularly "right" because of its soft, rounded features—the feminine aspect of the murderer seems less visually pronounced and possibly more a product of our cultural habit of connecting nature, passion, and unruly desire with the feminine.[16]

The murder weapon, presumably a knife, links Beckert's regressive orality and his murderous sadism with powerful cinematic effectiveness. Consider the scene in which Beckert snaps open his pocket knife to reveal a blade that will be used to penetrate the skin of an orange he peels for a potential child victim. The culinary function of the knife, which belongs to the semantic order of cutlery, is entirely effaced by the spectator's knowledge that it will become a murder weapon. But the very object that most emphatically indicts Beckert and points to the repugnant sadism of his pathology is also harnessed into service to exonerate him. One of the key shots in *M* shows Beckert staring with evident fascination into a shop window, his face framed by a rhomboid reflection of the knives on display. That shot, as Kracauer declares, is one of three moments that define Beckert as "a prisoner of his evil urges," that is, as victim rather than menacing agent. The others occur when Beckert is shown hidden behind an ivy-covered trellis and trapped in the lumber room of an office building. "Evil urges," Kracauer comments, "overwhelm him in exactly the same manner in which multiple objects close in on his screen image."[17]

Lang begins, early in the film, to mobilize sympathy for the man who has committed the "most heinous" crime possible. By the end, it is something of a relief when Lohmann intervenes in the mock judicial proceedings to save Beckert from the mothers. Spirited from an office building to the "courtroom" in a rolled-up rug from which he struggles to escape in vain, Beckert emerges as an abjectly pathetic figure who must face a line of stony-faced prosecutors and persecutors. Yet even these unsympathetic judges find themselves nodding with empathetic understanding when Beckert describes the urges that take over before he kills. One interpretive cue after another compels us to see Beckert as a victim—the victim of "evil urges," of "pain," of a "voice" that all prevent him from acting as a free agent. Even the arguments marshaled by Schränker to prove the killer's criminal intention have little power to erase the pathos of Beckert's dramatic enactment of how he must submit to the voice that relentlessly dictates his deeds. Almost imperceptibly, Beckert moves from the role of terrorist to terrorized, from cold-blooded murderer to abject victim. Few shots are more arresting than the one captur-

38. Terror is written on Beckert's face when he discovers the "M" chalked on his coat.

ing the face of Franz Beckert frozen with terror when he discovers the letter "M" chalked on his overcoat (fig. 38) or the one in which he is hunted down by the criminals while trapped in a storage room (fig. 39).

Just as Beckert slides into the role of stalked prey, the potential targets of his homicidal urges come to be positioned as complicitous in their victimization. The suggestion of collusion on the part of Beckert's victims is nowhere more evident than in the scene when the girl for whom Beckert has peeled an orange picks up the knife he has dropped and returns it to him (fig. 40). To read the girl's gesture as anything more than innocent benevolence may seem far-fetched, but M couples children and women with the murderer in countless subtle and not so subtle ways. The film establishes, in the very opening scenes, that Beckert and his victims are linked by mutual needs and affinities even as they are locked in agonistic, mortal combat. As noted, the film opens with a children's game that takes on ominous overtones in its symbolic foreshadowing of the murderer's elimination of one child after another. But the leader girl's chant about the "evil black man" who will come with his "chopper" to make "mincemeat" of the children does more than

39. Trapped in a storage room like a caged animal, Beckert is frozen with fear.

prefigure what is to come. Much as the game of elimination enjoys the status of an activity designed to dispel fears—exorcising evil by invoking it in a playful way—it also reveals the powerful lure of danger for the children and points more generally to the pleasures of the terrors that the film itself will represent. Hardly has the chant of the child faded when we see Frau Beckmann succumb to the same need for spine-chilling horrors as she purchases the latest installment of a dime novel: "A thrilling new chapter . . ." the vendor announces as Frau Beckmann receives the goods, "passionate, moving, sensational" (13). In the cinematic context, Beckert produces in real life the fictitious sensations conjured up by the children in their play and the fictional delectations consumed by Frau Beckmann in her reading. It goes without saying that he also answers the needs of the filmgoer, whose appetite for lurid sensationalism (for the worst crimes imaginable) is every bit as prodigious as that of the children and women represented in the film.

Beckert realizes, with a vengeance, the spectator's desire for the kinds of spine-tingling effects generated by children's games and by penny dreadfuls. Like the villain Mabuse in Lang's brilliant film *Dr. Mabuse the Gambler*, who turns his gaze on the spectators to illustrate the riveting power of both his

40. A girl who could be Beckert's next victim hands him the knife he has dropped while peeling an orange.

own personal evil and more generally of the compelling magic of the cinema, Beckert provides (through the "latent fascination in murder," as Lang put it) a vivid example of the power of cinematic representations of killers to engage the emotions of viewers through terror.[18]

It is nothing short of astonishing that Lang succeeds in turning a man who commits "the most heinous crime" into a sympathetic, if also pathetic, character. By suppressing the corpus delicti and by aestheticizing the representation of Elsie Beckmann's death, Lang gets Beckert off the hook. By the end of the film, Beckert's pathology begins to take a back seat to the hysteria of the mothers, who are prepared to rush him and to tear him limb from limb. Lang stages a finale that not only shows the killer escaping the clutches of the mothers and their allies, but which also marks the mothers as guilty in Frau Beckmann's final pronouncement decreeing that mothers must be more vigilant of their children.

The very first image in the film (an image that also appeared on posters advertising the movie) sets the stage for a problematization of the victim/agent relationship and for the effacement of the barrier separating the one from the other.[19] What we see before anything else (even before the credits begin to run) is the palm of a hand marked by the letter "M"—a red "M" as the screenplay emphasizes, although the movie was filmed in black and white (fig. 41). This "M" is not to be confused with the white "M" chalked on

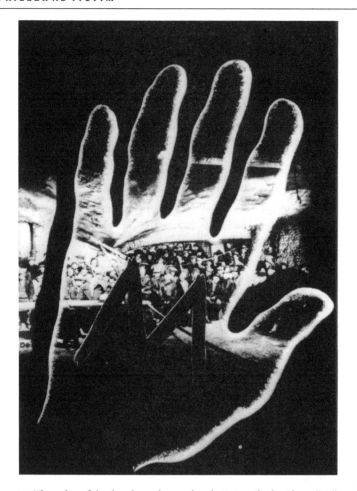

41. The palm of this hand—and every hand—is inscribed with an "M."

the hand of Beckert's pursuer. Instead, it seems to engrave the cinematic hand with the letter "M" that becomes visible in the creases of every hand when the palm is cupped. Here is the first hint that the "murderer among us" (as the film was originally to be called) may not be alien to us. The "M" inscribed on every palm marks us all as both predators and prey, as those who mark others and those who are marked.

After the credits run across the hand, the screen goes blank, and we hear the voice of the leader girl chanting her rhyme as she stands at the center of a circle of children. Each time she finishes the verse, she singles out the child positioned in the place where her finger stops and cries, "You're out!" The gesture of randomly pointing at, then targeting a person for elimination ominously foreshadows both the murderer's game and the protocols of his pursuers. If the children's play, with its strong element of arbitrary selection, seemingly deviates from the adult pastimes, it still accents the role of random selection, not only in the murderer's procedures, but also in the criminals' "legal" proceedings. In revealing how players are selected haphazardly for elimination at the level of childhood games, Lang seems to suggest that that mechanism must operate at a universal level, putting everyone at a certain risk for becoming the victim *or* agent of random violence. ("Everybody is potentially a murderer," Lang asserted in an effort to emphasize the way in which killers are victims of circumstance.) The children's rhyme is repeated three times, but the ritual itself is evoked visually on several occasions, most notably when we see in a shop window a sexually suggestive display of swirling concentric circles and an arrow perpetually moving up and down.[20]

The Law Enforcers (headed by Lohmann) and the Law Breakers (headed by Schränker) mobilize their forces to identify, confine, and eliminate the "alien" whose presence is giving them a bad name and who reminds them of just how ineffectual (in the case of the law enforcers) and vulnerable (in the case of the law breakers) their own organizations are in the face of the irrational. These two competing regimes are foregrounded in such a way as to further efface the crimes of Beckert and to train our attention on the process of detection. What is at stake for both the police and the criminals is not loss of life but loss of face. Elsie and the other victims recede into the background as we observe the riveting (and at times comic) drama in which the police and the criminals pursue their quarry in a manner so maniacally impassioned that we soon find ourselves rooting for the villain.[21] The "net" of surveillance cast over the city by the criminals and the concentric circles drawn on city maps by the the police further underscore the way in which official organizational practices double the children's and the murderer's rituals of elimination, creating a wave of terror—in the one case directed against the murderer, in the other against the criminals in general.[22]

Much has been made of the film's central scene in which shots recording a police conference alternate with shots capturing a meeting of criminals. What is especially striking about these shots is the way in which they seemingly dismantle the opposition between the representatives of law and order on the one hand and the exponents of crime and transgression on the other. As the camera shifts from one site to the other, it begins to dawn on the spectator that there is no real difference between the two factions. A sentence begun by a police inspector is finished by a safecracker. This explicit collapsing of two social categories is paralleled by the implicit blurring of the boundaries between victim and perpetrator. Yet while the link between the police and the criminals is ideologically authorized through its representation, the notion that the killer can be a victim never receives full, official articulation.

Both the law breakers and the law enforcers form hierarchically structured, autonomous organizations that depend on stability and predictability
for their survival. Schränker, ringleader of the criminals, is not a whit less
methodical and punctilious (perhaps even more so) than his police counterpart, Inspector Lohmann. The similarities between the two are underscored
early in the sequence of parallel scenes when Schränker concludes his speech
with a sentence and gesture that, as the film cuts to police headquarters, are
completed by Lohmann. (At the end of the conference sequence it becomes
virtually impossible to distinguish the smoke-filled meeting room of the police from that of the criminals.)[23]

The cinematic virtuosity of these scenes diverts our attention not only
from the victims of Beckert's crimes and from Beckert's criminality, but also
from the parallels that exist between the two principals heading the investigations and the criminal they both pursue with such energetic dutifulness. Who
can fail to notice that Lohmann, like Beckert, first makes his appearance as
a shadow and as a disembodied voice? Only as the criminals chant "Lohmann, Loh-mann, Loh-mann!" (33) does he emerge from the shadows to
reveal himself in the light. It is telling that Lohmann addresses the assembled
thieves and whores as "children" and that they call him "Pop Lohmann,"
thus creating a mock kinship structure reminiscent of "Uncle" Beckert and
the child who picks up his knife. Once again, the film rewrites the relationship between adult and child as one in which the "children" are singled out
for persecution and eliminated. As Lohmann interrogates the parade of criminals arrested during the police raid, we see one after another singled out for
further "investigation" and spirited off to headquarters.

"A murder story . . . ," Lang once declared, "is a puzzle against which to
match the sharpness of the mind."[24] Lang shows his Inspector Lohmann in a
double contest, matching wits not only with the murderer but with the criminals who race him to the finish line to solve the crime. Lohmann's interest
in the crime seems, at first blush, not to extend much beyond intellectual
engagement. The energies he applies to solving the crime lie in the realm of
what Poe called ratiocination: he searches for evidence, sifts clues, interrogates those implicated, and puts together the pieces of the puzzle in a rigor-
ously systematic exercise of logic. But we see just how closely this rage for
order borders on a mania when it is manifested in his indignation at the
discovery of a typographical error in a police report. Whenever he finds
himself sliding into a state of agitation, Lohmann resolutely steers clear of
passion and asserts control. On the brink of discovering the murderer's
whereabouts from one of the criminals, he vanishes into a washroom to
suppress his excitement by dousing himself with cold water and returns as
cool, calm, and collected as ever. Still, when we hear the chief of police
rehearse the tactics used to catch the criminal and see shots of officers comb-

ing the woods, of bloodhounds following trails, and of police interrogations, we know just how much power Beckert exerts over his adversaries, turning them into creatures whose regimented, mechanical style becomes contaminated by his own obsessively maniacal passion.[25]

While the connections linking Lohmann to Beckert can be constructed through a careful reading of the film's visual clues, the affiliations between Schränker and Beckert appear right on the surface. It is the very strength of the criminal kinship binding the two that drives Schränker to distance himself frantically from Beckert and to pathologize his behavior. Vocally and visually, Schränker asserts a clear line of demarcation between the "normal" criminals under his command and the "deviant" killer. Though he himself has murdered many times in cold blood, he resists recognizing in Beckert a kindred spirit and insists on branding him an "outsider," an alien being that must be uprooted and exterminated.

Lang made a point of drawing out both sides of the killer—first the shockingly repulsive side that stalks innocent children, then the hopelessly pathetic side that is the victim of "evil urges." In the film and in his pronouncements on it, Lang repeatedly emphasized the human side of the killer, the side that makes him a victim and engages our sympathies, leading us to feel relief that we escaped his fate but also understanding the degree to which we are all vulnerable to the same dark impulses.[26] "I have tried to approach the murderer imaginatively," Lang emphasized, "to show him as a human being possessed of some demon that has driven him beyond the ordinary borderlines of human behavior, and not the least part of whose tragedy is that by murder he never resolves his conflicts."[27] That Beckert is a tragic hero who succumbs to a demon that could prey on anyone of us becomes evident from the notes to Lang's screenplay of 1934 entitled *The Man behind You*. There we learn, with a melodramatic flourish informed by vulgarized forms of Nietzschean philosophy, that atavistic urges repressed through centuries of civilization lurk in the soul of every human being. Occasionally, these drives take over, turning a person into a criminal who commits deeds that society must not only try to understand, but also judge using standards different from those applied to "ordinary" crimes.[28] Years later, speaking to a reporter for the *Los Angeles Herald Express*, Lang declared that he had "reluctantly" come to the conclusion that "every human mind harbors a latent compulsion to murder."[29] In *M*, Beckert begins as a singular case, a horrifying example of aberrant behavior, but develops into a character connected through his passions and manias with those around him. The assembled criminals, at the least, can mobilize some understanding for him, but others also betray latent sympathy through their own pathologies.

Because Beckert moves so effortlessly from the role of villain to that of victim, it is no surprise that Lohmann's appearance at "court" is perceived more as a pardoning of Beckert than as an arrest. Lohmann's arrival and his announcement (once again as a disembodied voice) of Beckert's apprehension "in the name of the law" is followed by a shot of three mothers in mourning, one of whom—Frau Beckmann—declares that all mothers must "keep much better watch over our children" (122). This self-indictment sends a powerful message that deepens maternal guilt even as it further exonerates the killer. Lang himself found that message to be the film's central concern:

> In *M* I was not only interested in finding out why someone is driven to a crime as horrible as child murder, but also to discuss the pros and cons of capital punishment. But the film's message is *not* the conviction of the murderer but the warning to all mothers, "You should keep better watch over your children." This human message was felt particularly strongly by my wife at the time, Thea von Harbou.[30]

The conclusion to the film not only shows Beckert "rescued" by the police, it also shifts the burden of blame from his shoulders to those of the mothers who have failed to provide round-the-clock monitoring of their children.

The mothers, who are anointed as the guardians charged with the protection of children from psychopaths, are themselves deeply implicated in the mental lives of the psychopaths who imperil children. Beckert's pathology, as we have seen, is linked to a need for maternal punishment embedded in a fear of maternal surveillance. What could be more ironic, then, that the film should anoint mothers as the solution to the very problem they have created? And, as if to introduce a further ironic contradiction between its surface message about maternal vigilance and its latent meanings, the film repeatedly invalidates the efficacy of vision—of "keeping watch" over children—and endorses sound as a privileged medium for detecting evil. Shortly before she is murdered, Elsie Beckmann is escorted across the street by a policeman and virtually delivered into Beckert's hands. There is no way of distinguishing the murderer from any other person, of *seeing* his singularity. Sound, on the other hand, not only creates and haunts the killer, it also betrays him by revealing his hiding place to the crooks. Moreover, it is Beckert's whistling that discloses the identity of the killer to a man who is, in a further ironic twist, blind. Lang's message about the importance of maternal vigilance is undermined by the underwriting of sound (in his very first talkie) as the more reliable channel for knowledge.

M is something of a shocker not only because of its open treatment of the worst crime imaginable, but also because it reveals the ineffectuality and collapse of the visible power structure in the face of the irrational, of the foreign body that resists assimilation, taming, or expulsion. Yet even as the film deflates that power structure and seemingly empowers a subterranean "female" regime of surveillance, it stops short of shifting the site of punishment from the law to the mothers. In this sense, Lang is correct in his assessment of the film as the purveyor of social lessons about the protection of children and about the issue of punishment. M is a film designed to get the attention of mothers, to impress upon them that it is their lot to keep watch over children. More important, it charges mothers with an impossible task, with a vigilance so constant and attentive as to leave no room for the "chance," split-second meeting between child and stranger.[31]

M endorses the image of a vigilant mother who is engaged in unending bodily monitoring of her child. In sharp contrast to the mother stands the figure of the father, "Papa Lohmann"—distant, remote, and dispassionate. However much he may fail as protector, it is he who takes upon himself the role of judge and who is authorized to mete out punishments to transgressors. Beckert may momentarily disarm the law and nearly fall prey to the mothers, but his story turns into a cautionary tale that upholds the notion of both maternal surveillance and paternal legislation. In this sense, the coda, while grossly oversimplifying what the film conveys, is also not so far from the mark. The maternal figures gazing out at the spectator and the disembodied paternal punisher give us a condensed version of a scene that is enacted, in all its psychological intricacies, throughout the film.

The end of M gives us an image of the mother in triplicate: the three women fill the screen with their corporeal presence to create a somber barrier facing the viewer (fig. 42). What Roger Dadoun says of Psycho also applies to the impact of this final scene: "The most horrific moment of the film, the scene that is the fantasmatic and emotional pivot of the whole story, is the one where the mother is everywhere, occupying the whole screen from one edge of the frame to the other."[32] The admonition to watch more carefully over the children receives its supreme invalidation through the bleak image of these three women. The film's visual message, which lets the triply represented mother follow hard on an image of the cowering Beckert—redeemed from maternal fury by paternal benevolence—tells us far more about who is figured as the real victim in this drama than any of the various pronouncements made by Fritz Lang.

◆ ◆ ◆

The Nazi film The Eternal Jew contains a film clip of Peter Lorre enacting the panicked response of the murderer Franz Beckert to his capture. This cinematic moment, transplanted to a document of virulent anti-Semitic propaganda, is intended to assert the identity of the foreign-born Jewish actor with his role: the Jew who plays at being a criminal also is the criminal. It was no

42. The three mothers occupy the screen to form a somber barrier facing the viewer.

accident that this particular segment from Fritz Lang's film was spliced into a piece of Nazi propaganda. Like the real-life serial killers who were apprehended during the years of the Weimar era, the criminal Franz Beckert and the actor-criminal-alien-Jew Peter Lorre are cast as pathogens—as sources of fatal contamination that must be eliminated before infecting the general population. Jews, positioned as arch-criminals in Nazi ideological constructions, took on all the characteristics of the criminal "monsters" whose murders had been so carefully documented by the press.

Criminals were invested with lethal powers far beyond their individual agency, but, as *M* reveals, they could also slip with ease into the role of victims, hostage to circumstances or impulses beyond human control. The voice commentary in *The Eternal Jew* to the scene of Lorre's confessional effort to exonerate himself indicts not only the actor but also the message conveyed by his performance: "In line with the saying 'The victim, not the murderer, is guilty,' an attempt is made to twist our normal sense of justice, to put a good face on a crime, and to excuse it with a performance designed to arouse compassion."[33] While Nazi ideology may have resisted the notion of criminals as social casualties, the Nazis, in practice, had no trouble positioning themselves as victims whenever one in their numbers committed murder. The Nazi novel *Sin against Blood* reveals just how short a step it was from perpetrator to victim. Recall the words of Hermann Kämpfer, as he defends his murder of a Jewish officer: "I committed this deed only in order to sound a warning from my heart, from this very place out into the world. With firm resolve I shall sacrifice my life for the fatherland, and I hope I shall not have done this in vain."[34] The murderous agent takes on the role of a victim, who has sacrificed his life by killing. Weimar's criminals led a strange double life that allowed them to occupy the extreme positions of murderous monster and self-sacrificing innocent—the two roles that Yvan Goll saw exemplified in the figures of the serial killer Fritz Haarmann and the classical poet Friedrich Hölderlin. For the Nazis, it was easy enough to take advantage of the demonizing discursive strategies surrounding criminality, just as it was possible to tap into notions of bloodletting (in this case, not their own blood but the blood of the Jews) as a kind of purifying ritual that turned the murderer into a paragon of heroic self-sacrifice.

Reinventions: Murder
in the Name of Art

There, where the mark was, I plunged my knife in to the hilt.
The blood welled out over her delicate white skin. . . . With a
shudder I stared at the stony brow and the stark hair and the
cool pale shimmer of the ear. The cold that streamed from
them was deathly and yet it was beautiful, it rang, it vibrated.
It was music! Hadn't I felt this shudder before and found it at
the same time a joy? Hadn't I once caught this music before?
Yes, with Mozart and the Immortals.

Hermann Hesse, Steppenwolf

IN THE REPRESENTATIONAL practices of Weimar Germany's "high" culture,
victims of sexual murder far outnumber victims of racial or political murders.
What we have seen repeatedly is a positioning of women as targets of disfiguring violence. Cut, mutilated, fragmented, dismembered, and maimed, the
female body is put on display as an icon of cultural crisis and as the site of
transcendent artistic experience. Alternatively, the corpus delicti is suppressed in order to salvage the reputation of the perpetrator and create a
credible fable about his victimization. Rarely are the bodies of the victims so
fragmented and disfigured as to defy recognition, and often the corpses are
presented in frighteningly realistic detail. Yet however graphic the carnage,
it is still possible to disavow what is out in the open by focusing on the
representational energies channeled into the project of disfiguration, on the
aesthetic qualities of the desexualized, spiritualized body, or on the transfiguring power of feminine death.

In 1915, Ernst Ludwig Kirchner painted *Self-Portrait as Soldier* (*Selbstbildnis
als Soldat*) (fig. 43), a visually arresting picture of the artist wearing the full
uniform of the 75th Artillery Regiment in which he had enlisted. The right
hand of this artist-soldier is severed at the wrist, rendering him inadequate

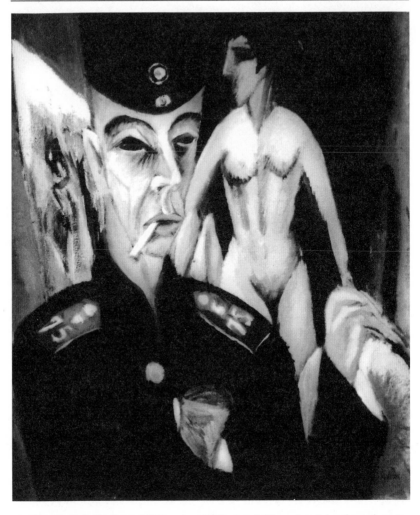

43. Ernst Ludwig Kirchner, *Self-Portrait as Soldier* (1915). The painter's hand may be missing, but he is still figured as an artist who has produced the painting within the painting.

both to the tasks of painting and military service. That the missing hand is read by critics as a marker of sexual deficiency as well as artistic and military impotence becomes especially significant in light of the nude female body behind the soldier. Is she a model, a lover, a prostitute? There may be no clear answer to that question (she could be all three), but the woman herself seems figured as whole, as another sign of self-sufficient feminine plenitude—until we note that her right arm also ends at the wrist, cut off by the frontally positioned body of the artist-soldier.

Kirchner's self-portrait contains a paradox within its representational logic.

The artist without his right hand seems deprived of his creative power, yet he depicts himself in a self-portrait, thus undermining the critical view asserting that the painting makes a statement about the "'amputation' of his artistic talents during the period of the war."[1] Similarly, his appearance in uniform, though it may mark him as a veteran burdened by the lingering trauma of war, belies the view of physical paralysis, just as the presence of the nude woman challenges the notion that the missing hand signifies castration anxiety. The artist-soldier may have been mutilated in the war, but that has not stopped him from retaining a military posture, producing artistic images, and figuring himself in a sexually charged setting. The so-called crisis of male subjectivity occasioned by the war seems here to be articulated and endorsed even as it is contradicted and invalidated by the production of the painting.

What interests me about Kirchner's self-portrait is the way in which it functions as an exemplary pre-text for the artistic generation active in Germany during the post–World War I years. Kirchner's canvas validates the notion of the soldier as a war casualty, as a figure who presents himself as marked by a defect, yet who in turn recovers his full powers by marking the bodies of women with the sign of mutilation. What Kirchner's canvas only subtly hints at in 1915 reaches unprecedented fulsome expression in the postwar years on the canvases of Otto Dix and George Grosz, where artistic reputations are established over the maimed and murdered bodies of women.

Hugo Bettauer's novel *The Lady-Killer* (1924), although the literary product of an Austrian climate, deserves mention here. The notion of building a reputation on dead female bodies is transplanted in that particular work to the literary sphere and taken one step further.[2] The writer Thomas Hartwig is so desperate for acknowledgment of his literary talent that he carries out counterfeit murders of women to bring himself to the attention of the public. And succeed he does, for the "murders," his trial, and, finally, the revelation that it was all a hoax create such an uproar that Hartwig's novel becomes an overnight best-seller and his drama is finally put on stage. Hartwig's literary talent is deemed so sublime as to justify not only the deception but even the deeds. Reservations about his staging of the "murders" are dismissed as trivial, and the detective-hero of the novel proclaims—after reading Hartwig's work and without yet knowing for certain that the murders have been contrived for the sake of earning notoriety: "It may well be that your drama is worth more than the five girls you entrapped, murdered and robbed."[3] This particular "case" reveals the pragmatic edge to representing, or in this instance misrepresenting, murder. Even when the artist commits nothing more than a counterfeit murder, when he "produces" nothing more than the simulacrum of a corpse, his success is nearly guaranteed by the sensational subject matter.

The artists, writers, and filmmakers who committed—to canvases, books, and to the screen—the murders discussed in this volume were not out for mere notoriety. Yet they often staked their reputations or show us characters who stake their reputations on disfiguring bodies that represent a threat to the stability of male ego boundaries. Ironically, a crisis of male subjectivity stemming from sexual anxieties or from creative paralysis often proved to be the very condition (or at least the pretext) for securing sexual or artistic success. That the success stories are predicated on producing scenes of sexual revenge is not as astonishing as the way in which a crisis of artistic creativity is so easily resolved and reversed by creating images and narratives that train brutal violence on the female body.

In our own culture, the artistic production of images of violated female bodies has been linked frequently with male feelings of anxiety, rage, and aggression toward women. The notion that violent words and images constitute a socially acceptable alternative to committing violent acts has been succinctly expressed by the filmmaker John Waters. Reflecting on the advice he gives to boys at a hospital for "criminally insane" teenagers, he noted: "I teach them that everybody has the same rage you had when you committed these crimes, that they have to use their rage in a different way. Make a movie. Do a painting. Don't do the rape, do a painting of the rape."[4]

Waters underwrites the notion that creativity has a therapeutic value, providing the artist with a "harmless" outlet for murderous aggression and impulsive violence. It never occurs to him to question whether a culture that seems to breed rage and violence might feed off the images produced by angry young men and circulated as works of art. Just as important, his agenda, although seemingly gender-blind ("everybody" has "the same rage") becomes conspicuously gender-specific once subjected to closer scrutiny. That rage is immediately coupled with rape and linked causally to it not only implies, in the particular context of the remarks, that the enraged agent is a male and the victim a female, but also expresses the notion that rape figures as the spontaneous, "natural" expression of rage. Waters' belief that the represented rape will instantaneously defuse the rage of the representer may be appealing in its optimistic naïveté, but its logic remains stunningly reductive, creating gender trouble under the pretext of solving it.

In *book of kings*, Klaus Theweleit has argued that male artistic identity in Western culture has had a strong personal stake in the story of Orpheus and Eurydice, a tale that is for him more murder mystery than tragedy of star-crossed lovers. Orpheus, the singer/poet, descends into the underworld, sacrifices his wife by turning around to look at her despite the prohibition, and resurfaces to produce (as part of the work of mourning) artificial constructions of arresting beauty. For Theweleit, artistic creativity has been predicated on the notion of sacrificing women or of self-immolation, with sacrifice figuring as the dominant paradigm for the artist/survivor. As one critic has pointed out, Theweleit's assessment of how artistic energies come to be released and harnessed looks "rather bleak." "Art and History are either a snuff movie or the record of a suicide."[5] What becomes increasingly evident as one reviews with Theweleit the canonical and even many of the heretical "texts" of Western culture is the narrow determinism for foundational myths of artistic creativity, with its demand that one has "to sacrifice" or "be consumed."[6]

Both Waters and Theweleit insist, in somewhat overstated fashion, that artistic production is symptomatic of gender-based cultural and personal anxieties. As I have tried to show, the route from the work to the cultural context in which it is embedded and to the personal history in which it is implicated is rarely as direct and unimpeded as Waters and Theweleit would lead us to believe. What remains remarkable, however, is the tenacity of the trope linking artistic production with male anxieties about women and the casual acceptance of the idea that the violation or murder of the female body is a "natural" (or as Poe put it, "the most poetical") subject of art.[7] Once aware of the durability of this particular convention, however, it seems possible, through analysis and critique, to problematize its appearance in a work and thereby to demystify its power. Self-censorship and state-sponsored censorship can, on the other hand, lead only to the kinds of pious lies found in repressive regimes, with superficially comforting images of wholesome, radiant bodies and serene, untroubled faces.

The evidence that images of *Lustmord* figure as a defense against male fantasies about sexually seductive women is powerful. Wedekind's Lulu dies at the hands of Jack the Ripper in *Pandora's Box*, but she expires only after leaving a trail of male corpses—husbands, lovers, admirers who are depicted as slaves to sexual passion. *Professor Unrat*, Heinrich Mann's 1905 novel that served as the basis for Josef von Sternberg's *Blue Angel*, tells another story of abject personal and social humiliation at the hands of a femme fatale. Perhaps the quintessential German cultural fable of female dominance and male impotence can be found in a novel by the Dadaist Richard Huelsenbeck. *Dr. Billig's End*, written in the years immediately following World War I, is a portrait of a woman who drives men to distraction. "She is my liege, she is power, long may she live!" Billig declares after meeting Margot for the first time.[8] But when Billig discovers that the irresistibly attractive Margot murders men in the most coldblooded, brutal fashion—in the manner of the killers described in this book—he indulges in unbridled fantasies of revenge that include gunning down thousands of naked female bodies.

World War I, as I have tried to show, further escalated gender conflicts that had already become pitched battles as a result of emancipatory efforts. The soldiers who died on the battlefields may have been conceived as heroic martyrs to a noble cause, but those who witnessed their deaths could not always see beyond the flesh-and-blood realities of the mutilated bodies. Klaus Theweleit has suggested that patriarchal institutions such as the church, school, state, industry, and the military establishment had, over time, taken on the task of re-forming the imperfect child-born-of-woman to produce flawless "man-born-children."[9] But World War I gave the lie to the military fable (at the least) by revealing that the war machinery lacerated the soldier instead of turning his body into an impermeable mass of steel. Faith in the invigorating power of many institutions may have begun to crumble (Remarque's *All Quiet on the Western Front* documents the full depth of that crisis of confidence), yet the myth of art as the site of transcendent experience persisted even beyond the war years.

The belief that men might be able to reconstitute themselves through art and reassert their primacy as agents of creative energy becomes apparent in a 1918 watercolor by Paul Klee, entitled *Dogmatic Composition* (fig. 44). Klee, who regarded art as a divine act of creation (*Schöpfung*) as much as a release of creative energy, originally painted a work that represented the Virgin Mary (in German "Maria") giving birth to the Christ child in a symbolic landscape of church towers and crosses.[10] That composition became both more and less dogmatic when Klee cut the picture into two pieces, gluing the right side of the original watercolor onto the left side of the new work and the left on the right. Maria, whose name is inscribed above the head of the Virgin, is separated from her creation to become part of a composition that constructs an artistic reality even as it dismantles a theological icon. A new dogma has been conceived, this time by dissecting the old dogma of the Virgin birth, and literally piecing it together through the creative interventions of the artist. This "artistically staged murder of a woman" has been seen by one critic as a pretext for elevating the artist to the status of creator and lawmaker for mankind.[11]

That masculine identity and artistic identity come to be constituted over the bodies of women became an important tenet in the aesthetic dogma of Weimar Germany. That that dogma has by no means been put to rest becomes evident from a reading of Patrick Süskind's 1985 novel *Perfume: The Story of a Murderer* (*Das Parfum: Die Geschichte eines Mörders*), a text in which the legacy of Weimar Germany's *Lustmörder* is everywhere apparent. Reading this novel, a stunning commercial success on both sides of the Atlantic, makes it clear that the ideological issues raised by representations of *Lustmord* from the 1920s have a remarkable holding power, one that continues right into the 1980s. It may be true that Süskind's literary effort is something of a throwback to traditional narrative styles, but, as critics have also pointed out, the novel can be read as a postmodern parable of fascism and its enduring

44. Paul Klee, *Dogmatic Composition* (1918). Klee cut the original watercolor of the Virgin and child into two pieces, reversing the positions of the two sides. The "dogmatic composition" supplants theological dogma with a modernist aesthetic creed.

mystique or as a postmodern pastiche of Romantic and Aestheticist traditions.[12] While Süskind's novel is set in eighteenth-century Paris, it presents
the reader with a cultural story that has a familiar German ring to it. Jean-
Jacques Grenouille, the repulsive protagonist of *Perfume*, may be a murderer,
but all twenty-five of his victims are slain in the service of a transcendent
ideal, one that is divined by the father of one of the dead girls:

> For if one imagined—and so Richis imagined—all the victims not as single
> individuals, but as parts of some higher principle and thought of each one's
> characteristics as merged in some idealistic fashion into a unifying whole,
> then the picture assembled out of such mosaic pieces would be the picture
> of absolute beauty, and the magic that radiated from it would no longer be
> of human, but of divine origin.[13]

Richis's view is validated by the narrator, who notes that the father is "very
near the truth," though he makes the fatal error of thinking in visual rather
than olfactory categories.

"A murder had been the start of this splendor." These are the words of the
narrator as he describes Grenouille's artistic awakening—the liberation of his
creative energies—after taking a "master scent" from a girl he murders in the
rue des Marais. Contained within this scent is "the magic formula" for everything that can make a perfume great: "delicacy, power, stability, variety, and
terrifying, irresistible beauty" (44). The suspicion that Grenouille's life is
modeled on that of the creative genius rather than that of the charismatic
fascist leader grows as we read one passage after another describing the
works of the olfactory genius. "These were virtuoso odors," the narrator
writes of Grenouille's experiments, "executed as wonderful little trifles that
of course no one but he could admire. . . . He was enchanted by their meaningless perfection; and at no time in his life . . . were there moments of such
truly innocent happiness as in those days when he playfully and eagerly
set about creating fragrant landscapes, still lifes, and studies of individual
objects" (185).

The cultural story told in *Perfume* is not at all a new one. Grenouille the
artist captures spiritual essences by ransacking the bodies of virginal girls and
leaving behind their corpses, which for him have become empty shells, but
which others find "beautiful" and "awful" sights at the same time. Grenouille
is, of course, an imaginary toad laboring in imaginary gardens, but the story
of his artistic triumph, the constitution of his artistic identity through the
murder of women and the transformation of their physical being into a spiritual essence, can be read as a literalized account of modernist representational practices, with their underlying destructive impulse that manifests
itself as an eagerness to sacrifice life on the altar of transcendent art.[14] Gre-

nouille, who has nothing but contempt for his audiences, nevertheless earns the adoration of the masses through the essences that he captures from the bodies of the women he bludgeons.

The dead bodies of the twenty-five murdered virgins are, as noted, immaterial to Grenouille. After slaying his final victim, his gaze falls on the corpse: "Her form did not interest him. She no longer existed for him as a body, but only as a disembodied scent" (220). What is astonishing is that critics of the novel react to the corpses in a similar manner. Here is the voice of one, who proclaims that "it is a relief to be confronted with horrors that, unlike Auschwitz, genocide in Kampuchea or massacres in China, provide solely a source of diverting entertainment."[15] That the murders portrayed in *Perfume* are purely fictional seems to form the basis for this judgment, but it is curious that such murders in the name of art are regarded not only as wholly innocuous, but also wonderfully "entertaining." Like Brian De Palma and John Waters, this critic naturalizes the killings and sees in them nothing more than an intriguingly appealing convention of Western culture.

By distilling the olfactory essences of twenty-five virgins, Grenouille creates a new artistic identity, reinventing himself and defining his essence through his art, which is itself predicated on murder.[16] Süskind's novel could be said to make a mockery of the premises of modernist art, revealing its flagrant murderous intent and its need to sacrifice bodies (if only figuratively) for art produced by creative geniuses. In this sense, the novel can be said to offer an irreverent reprise of modernist aesthetic doctrines, offering a nostalgiac reinscription and a mordant critique of a dogma that required women's bodies to be sacrificed in the name of art.

But this is not the end of the story. Grenouille dies a victim, torn to pieces by a crowd of frenzied devotees who attack him "like hyenas" and devour his flesh and bones. It is this *Opfertod,* or sacrificial death, that forms a powerful link to the ideological nexus of murder, sexuality, and art in Weimar Germany. The scene of cannibalism is so fulsome in its graphic detail that it dwarfs all other accounts of savage assaults in the novel:

> The human body is tough and not easily dismembered, even horses have great difficulty accomplishing it. And so the flash of knives soon followed, thrusting and slicing, and then the swish of axes and cleavers aimed at the joints, hacking and crushing the bones. In very short order, the angel was divided into thirty pieces, and every animal in the pack snatched a piece for itself, and then, driven by voluptuous lust, dropped back to devour it. (254)

This spectacular *Lustmord* is driven in part by Grenouille's need for self-immolation, for sacrificing himself to his art in a final grandiose gesture that allows him to embrace the role of victim even after he has murdered repeatedly in cold blood, in a manner that is wholly devoid of the "voluptuous lust" felt by those who assault him. Grenouille's death allows him to partake at last of the *Lust*, or desire, missing in his own creative and destructive acts. In the final analysis, the act of self-sacrifice offers pleasures and triumphs that elude him in practicing his murderous art.

Time and again, we have seen how the status of victim has a remarkable appeal for agents of terror, an appeal so powerful as to produce behavior that is ultimately self-defeating, self-destructive, and suicidal. Consider how German soldiers marched off to war in 1914—invading foreign territory and engaging in combat, yet perceiving themselves as victims engaged in heroic acts of sacrifice. "Sacrificing oneself is a joy, the greatest joy" [Opfern ist eine Lust, die größte sogar], the sculptor and dramatist Ernst Barlach asserted in the context of reflections on war.[17] "Never before has a such a powerful desire for death [*Sterbelust*] and passion for sacrifice [*Opferdrang*] seized mankind," the painter Franz Marc declared in 1915, shortly before dying in combat.[18] The entire military mission was figured in terms of sacrifice, as the title of Fritz von Unruh's war novel, *Opfergang*, reveals.

The notion of the war effort as one great act of martyrdom was so pervasive that it easily effaced the reality of agency, turning the German soldier into a man prepared to sacrifice himself, but also a man who, in defeat, quickly slides into the role of victim—a victim of enemy forces, of incompetent military authorities, or of civilians at home. It is not surprising that the *Dolchstoßlegende*, the myth that the soldiers had been "stabbed in the back" by the military and by civilians, took such powerful hold in the 1920s. Nor is it accidental that Hitler could appeal to Germans by railing on endlessly about Germany's victimization, exploitation, and martyrdom. In the human slaughterhouse (*Menschenschlachthaus*) of World War I battlefields, the German soldier came to be figured initially as a man with *Opfermut*, the courage to sacrifice himself, but after the armistice as a martyr, Christlike in his helpless sufferings.

That the *Lust* in *Lustmord* had more to do with the retaliatory pleasures of an aggressor who perceives himself as victim than with sexual desire is a point worth emphasizing. We have seen how the war "sacrifices" were perceived as a painful tribute paid to those who had remained protected on the home front or as an obligation imposed on men by sexual and reproductive rivalries rather than by conflicts in national interests. The prewar Expressionist martyr complex reflected in plays such as Ernst Barlach's *Citizens of Calais* or Georg Kaiser's *From Morning until Midnight* was further strengthened by the war experience and persisted into the 1920s, where it was figured anew as a paranoid need to occupy the position of victim, without any regard to the real balance of power. Cultural representations of victims of *Lustmord* reveal the brutal realities of what happened to the victims, but they also cloud issues of agency through their aestheticizing strategies and their focus on women as provocative, complicitous, or deserving targets of violence. The murders discussed in this volume may have been committed in the name of art, but they have a relevance that transcends aesthetic concerns and calls out for analysis and demystification of far-reaching ideological issues.

Notes

CHAPTER ONE
MORBID CURIOSITY

1. The German version, as cited by Magnus Hirschfeld, reads: "Warte, warte nur ein Weilchen, / Bald kommt Haarmann auch zu Dir / Mit dem Hacke-Hacke Beilchen / Macht er Rinds-Gulasch aus Dir." *Zwischen zwei Katastrophen* (formerly, *Sittengeschichte der Nachkriegszeit*), rev. ed. (Hanau: Karl Schustek, 1966), p. 482.

2. The version recited in the film *M* appears in Fritz Lang, *M: Protokoll* (Hamburg: Marion von Schröder, 1963), p. 9. There it reads: "Warte, warte nur ein Weilchen, / Bald kommt der schwarze Mann zu dir, / Mit dem kleinen Hackebeilchen / Macht er Schabe-fleisch aus dir." An English translation of the screenplay appears in *Masterworks of the German Cinema*, ed. Roger Manvell (New York: Harper & Row, 1973), pp. 97–177.

3. Neither Peter Gay in *Weimar Culture: The Outsider as Insider* (New York: Harper & Row, 1968), nor Walter Laqueur in *Weimar: A Cultural History, 1918–1933* (New York: Putnam, 1974) takes note of Haarmann. Jost Hermand and Frank Trommler in *Die Kultur in der Weimarer Republik* (Munich: Nymphenburger Verlagsbuchhandlung, 1978) omit a discussion of the figure, as do most popular cultural histories, e.g. John Willet, *Art and Politics in the Weimar Period: The New Sobriety, 1917–1933* (New York: Pantheon, 1978); Bärbel Schrader and Jürgen Schebera, *The "Golden" Twenties: Art and Literature in the Weimar Republic* (New Haven: Yale University Press, 1988); and Frank Grube and Gerhard Richter, *Die Weimarer Republik* (Hamburg: Hoffmann und Campe, 1983). The exception that proves the rule is Alex de Jonge, who sees the Weimar period as "the age of the mass murderer," but devotes only a single page to documenting the notorious cases; see *The Weimar Chronicle: Prelude to Hitler* (New York: New American Library, 1978), p. 184. The Haarmann case does receive some attention from Richard Plant in *The Pink Triangle: The Nazi War against Homosexuals* (New York: Henry Holt, 1986).

4. *Frenzy*, dir. Alfred Hitchcock, Pinewood (London), 1972.

5. Alfred Hrdlicka, *Grafik* (Frankfurt a.M., 1973), p. 101. I owe this reference to Heinrich Theissing, who discusses Hrdlicka's plan in "George Grosz, die Morde und das Groteske," in *Festschrift für Eduard Trier zum 60. Geburtstag*, ed. Justus Müller Hofstede and Werner Spies (Berlin: Gebr. Mann, 1981), pp. 269–84.

6. "Un tableau est une chose qui exige autant de rouerie, de malice et de vice que la perpétration d'un crime." Cited by Paul André Lemoisne, *Degas et son oeuvre* (1946; reprint, New York: Garland, 1984), 1:119.

7. Günther Anders, *George Grosz* (Zürich: Verlag der Arche, 1961), pp. 16–17.

8. "On Murder Considered as One of the Fine Arts," in *The Collected Writings of Thomas De Quincey* (Edinburgh: Adam and Charles Black, 1890), 13:9–124.

9. See especially Patrice Petro, *Joyless Streets: Women and Melodramatic Representation in Weimar Germany* (Princeton: Princeton University Press, 1989); Beth Irwin Lewis, "*Lustmord*: Inside the Windows of the Metropolis," in *Berlin: Culture and Metropolis*, ed. Charles W. Haxthausen and Heidrun Suhr (Minneapolis: University of Minnesota Press, 1990), pp. 111–40; Carol Duncan, "Virility and Domination in Early Twentieth-Century

Vanguard Painting," in *Feminism and Art History: Questioning the Litany*, ed. Norma Broude and Mary D. Garrard (New York: Harper & Row, 1982), pp. 292–313; and Kathrin Hoffmann-Curtius, *George Grosz: "John, der Frauenmörder"* (Stuttgart: Gerd Hatje, 1993).

10. Louis A. Montrose, "Professing the Renaissance: The Poetics and Politics of Culture," in *The New Historicism*, ed. H. Aram Veeser (New York: Routledge, 1989), pp. 17 and 20.

11. Elisabeth Bronfen, *Over Her Dead Body: Death, Femininity and the Aesthetic* (New York: Routledge, 1992), p. 3.

12. Cited by Marcia Pally, "'Double' Trouble," *Film Comment*, October 1984, p. 17.

13. The "tidal wave of female aggression" is Leo Steinberg's phrase. It appears in his pathbreaking essay, "The Philosophical Brothel," which takes both art and sexuality to be the painting's central concerns. The essay appeared in two parts in the September and October 1972 issues of *Art News* (n.p.). Charles Bernheimer, who uses the phrase "savage, disfiguring sexual menace" to describe the work, emphasizes Steinberg's willful failure to perceive the connections linking prostitution, disease, and modernist art. See the concluding chapter of his *Figures of Ill Repute: Representing Prostitution in Nineteenth-Century France* (Cambridge: Harvard University Press, 1989), pp. 266–74.

14. Robert Musil, *The Man without Qualities*, trans. Eithne Wilkins and Ernst Kaiser (New York: Capricorn Books, 1965), 1:75.

15. Bram Dijkstra makes this point more fully and forcefully than other critics. See his *Idols of Perversity: Fantasies of Feminine Evil in Fin-de-Siècle Culture* (New York: Oxford University Press, 1986). For an attempt to differentiate among various ideological aspects of "icons of womanhood" in turn-of-the-century art, see Shearer West, *Fin de Siècle: Art and Society in an Age of Uncertainty* (Woodstock, N.Y.: Overlook Press, 1993), pp. 86–103. The Austrian context is elaborated by Alessandra Comini, "Vampires, Virgins and Voyeurs in Imperial Vienna," in *Woman as Sex Object: Studies in Erotic Art, 1730–1970*, ed. Thomas B. Hess and Linda Nochlin (London: Allen Lane, 1973). On the sexual threat of the femme fatale, see Gail Finney, *Women in Modern Drama: Freud, Feminism, and European Theater at the Turn of the Century* (Ithaca: Cornell University Press, 1989).

16. See the observations on the first performance of *Erdgeist* in Leipzig in Erhard Weidl, "Philologische Spurensicherung zur Erschließung der 'Lulu'-Tragödie Frank Wedekinds," *Wirkendes Wort* 35 (1985): 99–119.

17. Cited by Wilhelm Emrich, "Frank Wedekind—Die Lulu-Tragödie," in his *Protest und Verheißung: Studien zur klassischen und modernen Dichtung*, 3d ed. (Frankfurt a.M.: Athenäum, 1968), p. 211.

18. Georges Balandier, *Political Anthropology*, trans. A. M. Sheridan Smith (London: Allen Lane, 1970), p. 41.

19. Petro, *Joyless Streets*, p. 69. Renate Bridenthal and Claudia Koonz point out that the actual increases in the proportion of women working were not that dramatic (growing by only 5 percent from 1907 to 1925), but the move from farms and homes into factories made women "more visible as a work force and more likely to provoke resentment." See "Beyond *Kinder, Küche, Kirche*: Weimar Women in Politics and Work," in *Liberating Women's History: Theoretical and Critical Essays*, ed. Berenice A. Carroll (Urbana: University of Illinois Press, 1976), pp. 301–29. They also discuss the ways in which women blamed themselves for the low morale on the home front and took on some of the burden of blame for the military defeat (pp. 307–8).

20. Brigitte Reinhardt comments on the aesthetic features of Dix's *Lustmorde*; see "Dix—Maler der Tatsachen," in *Otto Dix. Bestandskatalog* (Stuttgart: Edition Cantz, n.d.),

p. 18. Otto Conzelmann reflects on the biographical elements in those works; see *Der andere Dix: Sein Bild vom Menschen und vom Krieg* (Stuttgart: Klett-Cotta, 1983), p. 23.

21. "Los haben wollt' ich's, sonst nichts!" Quoted by Conzelmann, *Der andere Dix*, p. 139.

22. Erich Wulffen, *Der Sexualverbrecher: Ein Handbuch für Juristen, Verwaltungsbeamte und Ärzte*, 4th ed. (Berlin: Langenscheidt, 1910), pp. 468–69. Beth Irwin Lewis finds a greater resemblance between Dix's "Lustmord" and the photographs on pages 459 and 476 of Wulffen's volume (*"Lustmord,"* p. 132) . On Dix's knowledge of Wulffen's work, see Lothar Fischer (who mistakenly refers to Wulffen as "Wulff"), *Otto Dix: Ein Malerleben in Deutschland* (Berlin: Nicolaische Verlagsbuchhandlung, 1981), pp. 81–82, and Paul Westheim, "Dix," *Das Kunstblatt* 10 (1926): 144.

23. Bronfen, *Over Her Dead Body*, p. 199.

24. Alexander and Margarete Mitscherlich, *The Inability to Mourn*, trans. Beverley R. Placzek (New York: Grove Press, 1975), p. 25.

25. Ibid., pp. 45–46.

26. Joyce Carol Oates, "'I Had No Other Thrill or Happiness,'" *New York Review of Books*, 24 March 1994, pp. 52–59.

CHAPTER TWO
"ASK MOTHER"

1. On the American Psychiatric Association's shifting position, see *Serial Murder: An Elusive Phenomenon*, ed. Stephen A. Egger et al. (New York: Praeger, 1990), p. 19.

2. Deborah Cameron and Elizabeth Frazer, *The Lust to Kill: A Feminist Investigation of Sexual Murder* (Cambridge: Polity Press, 1987), pp. 17–19.

3. Norman Mailer, *An American Dream* (New York: Henry Holt, 1964), p. 8.

4. Mailer, *An American Dream*, p. 31. It is difficult not to see in this passage a savage parody of Tom's words about Eva's death in *Uncle Tom's Cabin*: "When that ar' blessed child goes into the kingdom, they'll open the door so wide, we'll all get a look in at the glory." See Harriet Beecher Stowe, *Uncle Tom's Cabin or Life among the Lowly* (Harmondsworth: Penguin, 1981), p. 425.

5. Efforts to develop a typology of criminal homicide have usually misfired, though attempts to develop categories are legion. See, e.g., Katie A. Busch and James L. Cavanaugh, Jr., "The Study of Multiple Murder: Preliminary Examination of the Interface between Epistomology and Methodology," *Journal of Interpersonal Violence* 1 (1986): 5–23, and Robert K. Ressler et al., *Sexual Homicide: Patterns and Motives* (Lexington, Mass.: Lexington Books, 1988), pp. 1–14. Ronald M. Holmes and James DeBurger see lust killers as a subcategory of serial killers and outline a useful classification system. See *Serial Murder* (Newbury Park, Calif.: Sage, 1988), pp. 46–60, 97–111. For the FBI's attempt at defining certain types of homicide, see Robert R. Hazelwood and John E. Douglas, "The Lust Murderer," *FBI Law Enforcement Bulletin* (April 1980): 18–22.

6. Richard von Krafft-Ebing, *Psychopathia sexualis: A Medico-Forensic Study*, trans. Harry E. Wedeck (New York: Putnam's, 1965), p. 545.

7. Michel Foucault, *Madness and Civilization: A History of Insanity in the Age of Reason*, trans. Richard Howard (New York: Random House, 1965), p. 210.

8. Colin Wilson, introduction to *The Complete Jack the Ripper*, by Donald Rumbelow (Boston: New York Graphic Society, 1975), p. vii. Jane Caputi takes the phrase for the title

of her study of sexual murder: *The Age of Sex Crime* (Bowling Green, Ohio: Bowling Green State University Popular Press, 1987).

9. On the multiple identities of Jack the Ripper, see especially Sander L. Gilman, *Sexuality: An Illustrated History. Representing the Sexual in Medicine and Culture from the Middle Ages to the Age of AIDS* (New York: John Wiley, 1989), pp. 250–61, and Christopher Frayling, "The House That Jack Built: Some Stereotypes of the Rapist in the History of Popular Culture," in *Rape: An Historical and Social Enquiry*, ed. Sylvana Tomaselli and Roy Porter (Oxford: Blackwell, 1986), pp. 174–215.

10. Rumbelow, *The Complete Jack the Ripper*, p. 217.

11. Judith R. Walkowitz points out that the events of autumn 1888 bore an "'uncanny' resemblance to the literature of the fantastic; they incorporated the narrative themes and motifs of modern fantasy—social inversion, morbid psychological states, acts of violation and transgression, and descent into a social underworld" (p. 550). See her "Jack the Ripper and the Myth of Male Violence," *Feminist Studies* 8 (1982): 543–74.

12. Frayling, "The House That Jack Built," p. 206.

13. Cited in ibid., p. 211.

14. Cited by Caputi, *The Age of Sex Crime*, p. 23.

15. Numerous serial killers, among them Peter Kürten, Albert DeSalvo, and David Berkowitz, have either modeled themselves on Jack the Ripper or made a point of reading up on his crimes. See Caputi, *The Age of Sex Crime*, pp. 34–35.

16. Cited in Frayling, "The House That Jack Built," pp. 210–11.

17. As Foucault points out, sites of social control "radiate discourses aimed at sex, intensifying people's awareness of it as a constant danger, and this in turn create[s] a further incentive to talk about it." See *The History of Sexuality*, trans. Robert Hurley (New York: Random House, Vintage, 1978), 1:31.

18. Walkowitz, "Jack the Ripper and the Myth of Male Violence," p. 563.

19. *Basic Instinct*, dir. Paul Verhoeven, 1992; Fritz Lang, *M: Protokoll* (Hamburg: Marion von Schröder, 1963), p. 44.

20. Egger, *Serial Murder*, p. 17.

21. Donald Spoto, *The Dark Side of Genius: The Life of Alfred Hitchcock* (New York: Ballantine, 1984), p. 35.

22. Krafft-Ebing, *Psychopathia sexualis*, p. 119.

23. Michel Foucault, "About the Concept of the 'Dangerous Individual' in 19th-Century Legal Psychiatry," *International Journal of Law and Psychiatry* 1 (1978): 1–18.

24. Cited by Cameron and Frazer, *The Lust to Kill*, p. 43.

25. Tim Cahill, *Buried Dreams: Inside the Mind of a Serial Killer* (New York: Bantam, 1986), p. 6.

26. Cahill, *Buried Dreams*, p. 192. Gacy's thinking is not as clear-headed as it may appear, for the psychiatrists had some trouble convincing Gacy that he was the man who had killed the young men buried in the crawl space of his house.

27. See the examples cited by Caputi in *The Age of Sex Crime*, pp. 36–37.

28. Cameron and Frazer, *The Lust to Kill*, pp. 69–119.

29. Tania Modleski reverses the agency of this argument by stating that "men's fascination and identification with the feminine" is what engenders violence toward women. See *The Women Who Knew Too Much: Hitchcock and Feminist Theory* (New York: Routledge, 1989), p. 8. Jane Caputi identifies seven characteristic features of literary and cinematic serial murderers, one of which is: "The mother, or occasionally some other female member of the family, is blamed for the criminality of her son because of her psychological or

physical abuse of him." See her chapter "Crime Formulas," in *The Age of Sex Crime*, pp. 63–92.

30. Karl Menninger, *Love against Hate* (New York: Harcourt, Brace & World, 1942), p. 118.

31. On this point, see Alice Miller, *For Your Own Good: Hidden Cruelty in Child-rearing and the Roots of Violence*, trans. Hildegarde and Hunter Hannum (New York: Farrar Straus Giroux, 1983), p. 152.

32. Miller, *For Your Own Good*, p. 165.

33. Susan Brownmiller, *Against Our Will: Men, Women and Rape* (Harmondsworth, England: Penguin, 1976), p. 203.

34. Ibid., p. 204.

35. Lawrence D. Klausner, *Son of Sam* (New York: McGraw Hill, 1981), pp. 141–42.

36. Cahill, *Buried Dreams*, p. 188.

37. On the role of childhood abuse in the psychic development of sexual murderers, see Ann W. Burgess et al., "Sexual Homicide: A Motivational Model," *Journal of Interpersonal Violence* 1 (1986): 251–72, and Joel Norris, *Serial Killers: The Growing Menace* (New York: Doubleday, 1988).

38. As Tania Modleski puts it, "We might say . . . that the film *knows so well* who the culprit is and what motivates the crimes that it can dispense with the full articulation of the theme." See *The Women Who Knew Too Much*, p. 106.

39. *Psycho*, dir. Alfred Hitchcock, Paramount, 1960.

40. Thomas Harris, *The Silence of the Lambs* (New York: St. Martin's Press, 1988), p. 149.

41. Carol J. Clover, *Men, Women, and Chainsaws* (Princeton: Princeton University Press, 1992), p. 24.

42. Siegfried Kracauer, *From Caligari to Hitler: A Psychological History of the German Film* (Princeton: Princeton University Press, 1947), p. 220. Donald Spoto demonstrates the ways in which Peter Lorre's character in *Secret Agent* is "a logical continuation of his role as a child molester in Fritz Lang's *M*." See his *The Art of Alfred Hitchcock: Fifty Years of His Motion Pictures* (New York: Doubleday, 1976), p. 50. Note also, however, that Hitchcock claims not to remember *M* too well in interviews conducted in 1962. See François Truffaut, *Hitchcock*, rev. ed. (New York: Simon & Schuster, Touchstone, 1984), p. 91.

43. Julia Kristeva, *Powers of Horror: An Essay on Abjection*, trans. Leon S. Roudiez (New York: Columbia University Press, 1982), p. 76.

44. *While the City Sleeps*, dir. Fritz Lang, RKO Radio, 1955.

45. Robert J. Stoller, *Perversion: The Erotic Form of Hatred* (New York: Random House, Pantheon Books, 1975), pp. 135–62.

46. Klaus Theweleit, *Male Fantasies*, trans. Erica Carter and Chris Turner (Minneapolis: University of Minnesota Press, 1987), 1:196.

47. Bronfen, *Over Her Dead Body*, p. 67.

48. On the ways in which knowledge about "criminal man" was produced, see Marie-Christine Leps, *Apprehending the Criminal: The Production of Deviance in Nineteenth-Century Discourse* (Durham, N.C.: Duke University Press, 1992).

49. Karl Marx, "Abschweifung (über produktive Arbeit)," in Karl Marx and Friedrich Engels, *Werke* (Berlin: Dietz, 1965), 26:363–64.

50. Theodore Ziolkowski, *Dimensions of the Modern Novel: German Texts and European Contexts* (Princeton: Princeton University Press, 1969), p. 309.

51. Joel Black, *The Aesthetics of Murder: A Study in Romantic Literature and Contemporary Culture* (Baltimore: Johns Hopkins University Press, 1991), p. 81.

52. Cited in Clover, *Men, Women, and Chainsaws*, p. 52.

53. Clover, *Men, Women, and Chainsaws*, p. 53.

54. Walter Benjamin, *Denkbilder* (Frankfurt a.M.: Suhrkamp, 1974), p. 138.

55. Bronfen, *Over Her Dead Body*, p. 124.

56. Spoto, *The Dark Side of Genius*, p. 431.

57. The phrase has come into some prominence of late, with the publication of *The Violence of Representation: Literature and the History of Violence*, ed. Nancy Armstrong and Leonard Tennenhouse (London: Routledge, 1989) and Elisabeth Bronfen's *Over Her Dead Body*, which contains a chapter on the violence of representation and representation of violence (pp. 39–56). My own analysis is indebted to Bronfen's brilliant discussion of how pain located at the site of a female body comes to be effaced, through representation, and subordinated to the notion of artistic genius and aesthetic effect.

58. William Rothman, *Hitchcock: The Murderous Gaze* (Cambridge: Harvard University Press, 1982). See especially the analysis of *Psycho* (pp. 246–341).

59. Clover, *Men, Women, and Chainsaws*, pp. 166–230.

60. Ibid., pp. 211–12.

61. Spoto, *The Dark Side of Genius*, p. 522.

62. Many of the female leads in Hitchcock's films referred to his demand for total command over them. Joan Fontaine, for example, recalled: "He was a Svengali. He controlled me totally." See Theodore Price, *Hitchcock and Homosexuality: His 50-Year Obsession with Jack the Ripper and the Superbitch Prostitute—A Psychoanalytic View* (Metuchen, N.J.: Scarecrow, 1992), p. 156. The quotations are from Spoto, *The Dark Side of Genius*, pp. 173, 164, 462.

63. Susan Sontag, *On Photography* (New York: Farrar, Straus and Giroux, 1973), pp. 14–15, 24.

64. David Freeman, *The Last Days of Alfred Hitchcock: A Memoir Featuring the Screenplay of "Alfred Hitchcock's The Short Night"* (Woodstock, N.Y.: Overlook Press, 1984).

65. Truffaut, *Hitchcock*, p. 345.

66. Spoto, *The Art of Alfred Hitchcock*, pp. 392–93.

67. Truffaut makes the latter point in interviews with Hitchcock. See his *Hitchcock*, p. 121.

68. Slavoj Žižek, "'In His Bold Gaze My Ruin Is Writ Large,'" in *Everything You Always Wanted to Know about Lacan (But Were Afraid to Ask Hitchcock)*, ed. Slavoj Žižek (London: Verso, 1992), p. 237.

69. Spoto, *The Dark Side of Genius*, p. 483.

70. Cameron and Frazer, *The Lust to Kill*, pp. 23–26. As Ronald M. Holmes and James DeBurger point out, most known serial murderers are white males whose victims are white females. See *Serial Murder*, p. 21.

71. Clover, *Men, Women, and Chainsaws*, pp. 226–27.

CHAPTER THREE
CRIME, CONTAGION, AND CONTAINMENT

1. Yvan Goll, *Sodom Berlin*, trans. Hans Thill (Frankfurt a.M.: Fischer, 1988), p. 7.

2. *Frankfurter Zeitung*, 18 December 1924.

3. Magnus Hirschfeld, *Geschlecht und Verbrechen* (Leipzig: Verlag für Sexualwissenschaft, n.d.), pp. 209–11.

4. Noted by Erich Wulffen, *Kriminalpsychologie: Psychologie des Täters* (Berlin: Langenscheidt, 1926), p. 412.

5. For summaries of the Haarmann and Denke cases, see Magnus Hirschfeld's chapter, "Die berühmtesten Sexualprozesse der Nachkriegszeit," in *Zwischen zwei Katastrophen* (formerly *Sittengeschichte der Nachkriegszeit*), rev. ed. (Hanau: Karl Schustek, 1966), pp. 469–513. On the myriad tip-offs that went unnoticed by Denke's neighbors, see Kriminaldirektor Polke, "Der Massenmörder Denke und der Fall Trautmann: Ein Justizirrtum," *Archiv für Kriminologie* 95 (1934): 8–30.

6. Hirschfeld, *Zwischen zwei Katastrophen*, p. 49.

7. Ibid., p. 502.

8. *Frankfurter Zeitung*, 11 April 1931.

9. The *Berliner Illustrirte Zeitung* (30 November 1929), for example, which had never covered the Haarmann murders (it did print one captioned picture of Haarmann and his alleged accomplice Grans in the courtroom), had a full-page essay on the Düsseldorf murders with photographs of several victims, including two children.

10. For details on the trial, see Walther Kiaulehn, "Der Kürten-Prozeß," *Die Justiz* 6 (1930): 466–74. Kiaulehn's skepticism about Kürten's guilt offers an interesting angle on the case.

11. Walther Riese, "Probleme des Kürten-Prozesses," *Die Justiz* 7 (1931–32): 113–16.

12. Otto Rothbarth, "Zum Fall Kürten," *Die Justiz* 7 (1931–32): 117–23.

13. Writers for *Die Justiz* seemed particularly enamored of that phrase—one essay after another on the Kürten case refers to "das Rätsel Kürten," in part perhaps because Kürten's lawyer had referred to his client as "ein Rätsel."

14. *Frankfurter Zeitung* (Abendblatt), 30 December 1924, p. 2.

15. Margaret Seaton Wagner, *The Monster of Düsseldorf: The Life and Trial of Peter Kürten* (New York: Dutton, 1933), p. 21.

16. Polke, "Der Massenmörder Denke," p. 29.

17. The testimony of Kürten's father is included in the volume *Leben und Wirken des Peter Kürten, genannt der Vampir von Düsseldorf*, ed. Elisabeth Lenk and Roswitha Kaever (Munich: Rogner & Bernhard, 1974), pp. 72–76.

18. Riese, "Probleme des Kürten-Prozesses," p. 106.

19. Kürten's admission is cited by Police Commissioner Gennat, "Der Kürtenprozeß," *Kriminalistische Monatshefte* 5 (1931): 111. The quotations about Düsseldorf and the Rhineland are from a *Sonderausgabe des Kriminal-Magazins* published in 1930 in Düsseldorf. The publication is reprinted in Lenk and Kaever, *Leben und Wirken des Peter Kürten*, pp. 13–36.

20. This fact is noted in an article from the Nazi newspaper, *Der völkische Beobachter*, 31 May 1930.

21. "Rachsucht gegenüber der Menschheit," as reported in the Communist daily, *Die rote Fahne*, 27 May 1930.

22. Lenke and Kaever, *Leben und Wirken des Peter Kürten*, p. 197. To be sure, Kürten may have exaggerated the role of the public in arousing him so as to downplay the sexual release afforded by the murders.

23. Lenk and Kaever, *Leben und Wirken des Peter Kürten*, p. 36.

24. Kriminal-Polizeirat Gennat, "Die Düsseldorfer Sexualverbrechen," *Kriminalistische Monatshefte* 4 (1930): 2–7, 27–32, 49–54, 79–85; and "Der Kürtenprozeß," pp. 108–11, 130–33.

25. Berta Epstein, "Rede und Antwort: Begnadigung für Kürten," *Die Justiz* 6 (1930–31): p. 513.

26. Kiaulehn, "Der Kürten-Prozeß," p. 466.

27. Walther Riese, "Probleme des Kürten-Prozesses," p. 116. For copies of some of the letters, see Lenk and Kaever, *Leben und Wirken des Peter Kürten*, pp. 326–30.

28. The criminologist Erich Wulffen is cited by Birgit Kreutzahler, *Das Bild des Verbrechers in Romanen der Weimarer Republik: Eine Untersuchung vor dem Hintergrund anderer gesellschaftlicher Verbrecherbilder und gesellschaftlicher Grundzüge der Weimarer Republik* (Frankfurt a.M.: Peter Lang, 1987), p. 45. See also Richard Herbertz, *Verbrecherdämmerung: Psychologische Deutung und weltanschauliche Perspektiven der jüngsten Mordfälle Haarmann, Angerstein, Denke usw.* (Munich: Curt Pechstein, 1925), who speculates on the way in which criminality will produce a climate of mass hysteria in Germany.

29. Karl Berg, "Der Sadist. Gerichtsärztliches und Kriminalpsychologisches zu den Taten des Düsseldorfer Mörders," *Deutsche Zeitschrift für die gesamte gerichtliche Medizin* 17 (1931): 331, and *Frankfurter Zeitung*, 15 April 1931.

30. "Für Hochschule und Jugend. Der Fall Kürten: Ein Sensationsprozeß in Sicht," *Frankfurter Zeitung*, 13 April 1931, p. 6.

31. Theodor Lessing, *Haarmann. Die Geschichte eines Werwolfs und andere Gerichtsreportagen*, ed. Rainer Marwedel (Frankfurt a.M.: Luchterhand, 1989), p. 32. On the reception of Lessing's views, see especially Hermann Hass, *Sitte und Kultur im Nachkriegsdeutschland* (Hamburg: Hanseatische Verlagsanstalt, 1932), pp. 44–45.

32. Cited by Isabella Claßen, *Darstellung von Kriminalität in der deutschen Literatur, Presse und Wissenschaft, 1900–1930* (Frankfurt a.M.: Peter Lang, 1988), p. 246.

33. Nikki Meredith, "The Murder Epidemic," *Science 84* (December 1984): 43. Joel Norris repeatedly resorts to metaphors of contagion to describe the violence of serial murder. See especially his chapter "The Disease of Serial Murder" in *Serial Killers: The Growing Menace* (New York: Doubleday, 1988), pp. 35–44.

34. Lessing, *Haarmann*, p. 116.

35. Ibid., pp. 114, 211. See also Lessing's discussion of his dismissal from the trial in part because of his insistence on "psychoanalytic" evaluation: "Zwischenfall im Haarmann-Prozeß," *Das Tage-Buch*, 20 December 1924, pp. 1795–98. One discerning contemporary study, written by a criminologist, points out that it is precisely when serial murderers are brought to trial that psychological evaluation becomes of paramount importance. See Albrecht Wetzel, *Über Massenmörder: Ein Beitrag zu den persönlichen Verbrechensursachen und zu den Methoden ihrer Erforschung* (Berlin: Julius Springer, 1920), pp. 7–8.

36. For the citations, see the two articles "Massenmörder und Menschenfleischhändler Haarmann als Vertrauensmann der Polizei," 13 July 1924, and "Todesurteile gegen Haarmann und Grans," 19 December 1924, in *Die rote Fahne*. Hans Hyan deplored the way in which the judicial system disposed of the Kürten case, along with others, far too quickly, leaving too many unanswered questions. See "Der Düsseldorfer Polizeiskandal," in *Die Weltbühne* 27 (1931): 613–16.

37. Kiaulehn, "Der Kürten-Prozeß," p. 467. Kiaulehn reports that 150 witnesses were called. The trial was astonishingly short given the numbers of persons testifying.

38. *Berliner Lokal-Anzeiger*, 14 April 1931. Cited by Isabella Claßen, *Darstellung von Kriminalität*, p. 296.

39. For extensive excerpts from the *Berliner Tageblatt*, see Claßen, pp. 284–320.

40. "Kürten, ein Rätsel," *Frankfurter Zeitung* (Abendblatt), 23 April 1931, p. 1.

41. Franz Blei, "Der Massenmörder," *Berliner Tageblatt*, 24 July 1924, p. 2. Magnus Hirschfeld writes of the sexual torment inflicted on some men by prostitutes and differentiates between *Lustmord* and murders committed by "coarse" and "impulsive"—though

not deranged—men in response to provocative behavior on the part of women. See *Geschlecht und Verbrechen*, p. 189.

42. *Berliner Illustrirte*, 1925, pp. 765–67.

43. Otto Weininger, *Geschlecht und Charakter: Eine prinzipielle Untersuchung* (Vienna: Wilhelm Braumüller, 1903), p. 112.

44. Karl Berg, "Der Sadist," p. 277.

45. Marie-Christine Leps makes the important point that these murders "left most readers feeling safe: after all, the vast majority of them were not prostitutes in Whitechapel" (*Apprehending the Criminal*, p. 116). She implicitly refutes Judith R. Walkowitz's argument about the myth of male violence as an instrument for securing stable gender roles.

46. Kürten himself, when the verdict was announced, tried to implicate his victims by claiming that they were all too eager to pair off with him. The judge, to his credit, cut short his statement. The letter in *The Times* is cited by Marie-Christine Leps, *Apprehending the Criminal*, p. 126.

47. John Beattie, *The Yorkshire Ripper Story* (London: Quartet Books, 1981), p. 133.

48. Charles Bernheimer, *Figures of Ill Repute: Representing Prostitution in Nineteenth-Century France* (Cambridge: Harvard University Press, 1989), p. 38.

49. Isabella Claßen, *Darstellung von Kriminalität*, p. 227. Erich Wulffen describes Haarmann as a "hybrid creature, whose femininity was conjoined with intense sadistic elements." See *Kriminalpsychologie*, p. 408.

50. Lessing, *Haarmann*, pp. 59, 62.

51. George L. Mosse, *Nationalism and Sexuality: Middle-Class Morality and Sexual Norms in Modern Europe* (Madison: University of Wisconsin Press, 1985), p. 134.

52. "Irrenhaus oder Schafott? Die Wahrheit über den Massenmörder Haarmann aus Hannover" (Hanover, 1924). Cited by Isabella Claßen, *Darstellung der Kriminalität*, p. 235.

53. Cited in Plant, *The Pink Triangle*, p. 49.

54. Gennat and Berg discuss Kürten's assertion about drinking blood. See "Der Kürtenprozeß," pp. 110–11, and "Der Sadist," pp. 316–17.

55. George Godwin, *Peter Kürten: A Study in Sadism* (London: Acorn, 1938), p. 20.

56. Theodor Lessing, "Haarmann," *Das Tage-Buch*, 13 December 1924, pp. 1755–62.

57. Kürten's prison declaration is printed in *Die rote Fahne*, 28 May 1930.

58. "Nosferatu," in *Masterworks of the German Cinema*, ed. Roger Manvell (New York: Harper & Row, 1973), p. 53.

59. Ibid., p. 80.

60. Paul Coates notes the "potentially anti-Semitic elements" in the film. See *The Gorgon's Gaze: German Cinema, Expressionism, and the Image of Horror* (Cambridge: Cambridge University Press, 1991), p. 96. Siegfried Kracauer, by contrast, sees in this and other films of the time a "procession of tyrants"—all of whom anticipate the Führer of National Socialism; see *From Caligari to Hitler: A Psychological History of the German Film* (Princeton: Princeton University Press, 1947), pp. 77–87. Ernst Prodolliet endorses the view in *Nosferatu: Die Entwicklung des Vampirfilms von Friedrich Wilhelm Murnau bis Werner Herzog* (Olten: Universitätsverlag Freiburg Schweiz, 1980), pp. 29–43.

61. Lotte H. Eisner, *Murnau. Mit dem Faksimile des von Murnau beim Drehen verwendeten Originalskripts von NOSFERATU* (Frankfurt: Kommunales Kino, 1979), pp. 421, 423, 435, 440.

62. Elisabeth Bronfen, "The Vampire: Sexualizing or Pathologizing Death," in *Disease*

and Medicine in Modern German Cultures, ed. Rudolf Käser and Vera Pohland (Ithaca: Cornell Studies in International Affairs, 1990), p. 85. The connections between *Nosferatu* and the discourse on serial murderers from the 1920s became apparent to me after hearing Bronfen's paper and discussing it with her.

63. Fritz Lang, *M: Protokoll* (Hamburg: Marion von Schröder, 1963), p. 43. For an intelligent commentary on the way in which the death penalty is at odds with democratic rule, see Siegfried Kracauer, "Der Fall Kürten," *Die Neue Rundschau* 42 (1931): 142–43. The prospective description of a murderer's excution in the British *The Leader* reveals the public need to eradicate antisocial criminals: "A quantity of quick lime and a few buckets of water will be thrown in upon the felon's corpse, the earth rapidly shovelled in, and the place smoothed down to the ordinary level, so that, within a short time, not a vestige will remain of the murderer Palmer. He will have been obliterated, physically annihilated." Cited by Thomas Boyle, *Black Swine in the Sewers of Hampstead* (New York: Viking, 1989), p. 88.

64. Kracauer describes Lang's difficulties in finding studio space because of the film's title. See *From Caligari to Hitler*, pp. 218–19.

65. On this topic, see especially Sander Gilman, *Pathology and Difference: Stereotypes of Sexuality, Race, and Madness* (Ithaca: Cornell University Press, 1985).

66. On this point, see Bronfen, "The Vampire: Sexualizing or Pathologizing Death."

67. Artur Dinter, *Die Sünde wider das Blut* (Leipzig: Ludolf Beust, 1919), p. 319. Bronfen's essay drew my attention to this novel.

68. *Der ewige Jude*, dir. Fritz Hippler, Deutsche Filmgesellschaft, 1940.

69. David Welch, *Propaganda and the German Cinema, 1933–1945* (Oxford: Clarendon, 1983), p. 298.

70.
Es liegt dem Juden in dem Blut
Der Zorn, der Neid, der Haß, die Wut
Auf jedes Volk der ganzen Welt
Das nicht zum "auserwählten" zählt.

Er schächtet Tiere, schächtet Menschen
Es kennt sein Blutdurst keine Grenzen!
Es wird die Welt erst dann genesen
Wenn wir vom Juden sie erlösen.

Cited in *Der ewige Jude: Wie Goebbels hetzte. Untersuchungen zum nationalsozialistischen Propagandafilm*, ed. Yizhak Ahren (Aachen: Alano, 1990), p. 98. I have, for obvious reasons, not sought to preserve the rhymes and cadences of the original.

71. R. Po-chia Hsia, *The Myth of Ritual Murder: Jews and Magic in Reformation Germany* (New Haven: Yale University Press, 1988).

72. Sander L. Gilman, *Sexuality: An Illustrated History. Representing the Sexual in Medicine and Culture from the Middle Ages to the Age of AIDS* (New York: John Wiley & Sons, 1989), p. 258.

73. Adolf Hitler, *Mein Kampf* (Munich: Zentralverlag der NSDAP, 1939), pp. 269–70.

74. Ibid., p. 135.

75. Klaus Theweleit, *Male Fantasies*, trans. Erica Carter and Chris Turner (Minneapolis: University of Minnesota Press, 1989), 2:16; cited by Jay Geller, "Blood Sin: Syphilis and the Construction of Jewish Identity," *Faultline* 1 (1992): 21–48. Geller makes the point that the

intersection of discourses about syphilis with that used to talk about prostitutes, Jews, and diseased sexuality coded Nazi rhetoric about degeneration and reproduction with important gender, racial, and sexual dimensions.

CHAPTER FOUR
FIGHTING FOR LIFE

1. Quoted in Otto Conzelmann, *Der andere Dix: Sein Bild vom Menschen und vom Krieg* (Stuttgart: Klett-Cotta, 1983), pp. 132–33.

2. Fritz Löffler, *Otto Dix, 1891–1969* (Recklinghausen: Aurel Bongers, 1981), p. 81.

3. Quoted in Conzelmann, *Der andere Dix*, p. 133.

4. Eva Karcher sees the same effect in *Still Life with Widow's Veil* (*Stilleben mit Witwenschleier*, 1925). See her *Otto Dix, 1891–1969: Leben und Werk* (Cologne: Benedikt Taschen Verlag, 1988).

5. Barbara Johnson's "Is Female to Male as Ground Is to Figure?" (the title is a reformulation of Sherry Ortner's classic "Is Female to Male as Nature Is to Culture?") gives a full discussion of the gender problematics of the figure/ground relationship. See *Feminism and Psychoanalysis*, ed. Richard Feldstein and Judith Roof (Ithaca: Cornell University Press, 1989), pp. 255–68.

6. Cited by Eva Karcher, *Eros und Tod im Werk von Otto Dix. Studien zur Geschichte des Körpers in den zwanziger Jahren* (Münster: Lit, 1984), p. 57. On Dix's representation of war in general, see Dietrich Schubert, "Otto Dix und der Krieg," in *Otto Dix und der Krieg: Zeichnungen und Grafik, 1913–1924* (Regensburg: Veit Loers, 1981), pp. 7–17.

7. Conzelmann, *Der andere Dix*, p. 20; Karcher, *Otto Dix*, p. 44; and Jean Cassou, cited in *Otto Dix: Aquarelle, Zeichnungen, Radierfolge "Der Krieg"* (Essen: Richard Bacht, 1972), n.p. Cassou points out that the soldiers assault the very earth in which they take refuge.

8. Quoted in Karcher, *Otto Dix*, p. 43.

9. Conzelmann, *Der andere Dix*, p. 121.

10. Matthias Eberle, *World War I and the Weimar Artists* (New Haven: Yale University Press, 1985), p. 41.

11. It is telling that this painting not only positions the male counterpart to the woman in an inferior spatial location (she straddles him), but also represents him as a diminutive beast. After the birth of his second child, Dix painted a family portrait in sumptuous reds, relegating himself to a buffoonish role in the margins of a canvas dominated by Martha Dix and the two children. Once again, the male body becomes a kind of "negative space" on a canvas dominated by a fleshy female.

12. Hélène Cixous, "The Laugh of the Medusa," in *New French Feminisms: An Anthology*, ed. Elaine Marks and Isabelle de Courtivron (Amherst: University of Massachusetts Press, 1980), pp. 244–67.

13. Nancy Huston, "The Matrix of War: Mothers and Heroes," in *The Female Body in Western Culture*, ed. Susan Rubin Suleiman (Cambridge: Harvard University Press, 1985), p. 131.

14. Ernst Jünger, "Der Kampf als inneres Erlebnis," in his *Sämtliche Werke* (Stuttgart: Klett, 1980), 7:11–12.

15. Klaus Theweleit, *Male Fantasies*, trans. Erica Carter and Chris Turner (Minneapolis:

University of Minnesota Press, 1989), 2:88. The idea of war as the crucible for a "new reality," "new era," and "new man" was preached not only by Germany's poets, but also by its politicians and philosophers. The distinguished jurist Otto von Gierke, for example, described war as a creative force constituting new values—"the most powerful of all destroyers of culture is also the most intensely productive of culture." For the historians Erich Marcks and Hermann Oncken, war was celebrated as a power that not only annihilated the moribund but also quickened the life force of the strong. See Otto von Gierke, "Krieg und Kultur," in *Aufrufe und Reden deutscher Professoren im Ersten Weltkrieg,* ed. Klaus Böhme (Stuttgart: Reclam, 1975), p. 67; Erich Marcks, "Wo stehen wir? Die politischen, sittlichen und kulturellen Zusammenhänge unseres Krieges," in ibid., p. 81; and Hermann Oncken, "Die Deutschen auf dem Wege zur einigen und freien Nation," in ibid., p. 112.

16. Hermann Hesse, *Demian: Die Geschichte von Emil Sinclairs Jugend* (Frankfurt a.M.: Suhrkamp, 1981), p. 160.

17. Jane Caputi, *The Age of Sex Crime* (Bowling Green, Ohio: Bowling Green State University Press, 1987).

18. See the discussion of Klein, Horney, and Jones in Miriam M. Johnson's essay "Women's Mothering and Male Misogyny," in her *Strong Mothers, Weak Wives: The Search for Gender Equality* (Berkeley: University of California Press, 1988), pp. 71–95.

19. Dix evidently had nothing to do with the title. He prided himself on a lack of interest in politics and, when asked once if he wished to attend an evening meeting of communists, reportedly replied that he would rather go to "a whorehouse"; see Lothar Fischer, *Otto Dix: Ein Malerleben in Deutschland* (Berlin: Nikolaischeverlagsbuchhandlung, 1981), p. 30. The statement unwittingly points to Dix's passionate interest in sexual politics.

20. Linda Nochlin calls attention to the way in which "'fallen' in the masculine means killed in the war, and in the feminine given over to a particular kind of vice." See "Lost and *Found*: Once More the Fallen Woman," in *Feminism and Art History: Questioning the Litany,* ed. Norma Broude and Mary D. Garrard (New York: Harper & Row, 1982), pp. 220–45.

21. In conversation with Karl Heinz Hagen, Dix spoke of the flood of books published during the Weimar Republic that glorified a form of heroism "that had been taken ad absurdum in the trenches of World War I." Quoted by Reiner Beck, "Dix und der Krieg," in *Otto Dix, 1891–1969* (Munich: Hans Goltz, 1985), pp. 11–21.

22. ". . . dann sah man eben auch, wenn man zurückkam, seine ganze Umgebung in diesem Sinne: daß das Leben gar nicht so was Schönes und Lyrisches ist, daß das Leben auch *grausam* sein konnte. . . . Wie gesagt, 1919/20 fing ich an, ganz *grau*, ohne viel Farbe zu malen. Da es diesem Erleben, da es dem, was ich *sah*—der grauen Straße, den grauen Menschen—, am nächsten kam." Dix made the remarks in an interview with Maria Wetzel, "Prof. Otto Dix, ein harter Mann dieser Maler," in *Diplomatischer Kurier* 14 (1965): 731–45. Cited by Rainer Beck, "Krieg," in *Otto Dix, 1891–1969,* Catalog of Exhibit in the Villa Stuck Museum, 1985 (Munich: Passavia, 1985), p. 18. Beck also calls attention to the numerous allusions to Christ's passion.

23. The quotation, along with a discussion of the analogies between military service and Christ's martyrdom, appears in Paul Fussell's *The Great War and Modern Memory* (London: Oxford University Press, 1975), pp. 117–20.

24. "Ich wollte ganz einfach—fast reportagemäßig—meine Erlebnisse der Jahre 1914–18 zusammenfassend sachlich schildern und zeigen, daß echtes menschliches Heldentum in

der Überwindung des sinnlosen Sterbens besteht." Dix made this observation in conversation with Karl Heinz Hagen in 1964. It is cited by Rainer Beck, "Krieg," p. 18.

25. Fritz Löffler notes Dix's reading matter: *Otto Dix: Bilder zur Bibel und zu Legenden, zu Vergänglichkeit und Tod* (Stuttgart: Belser, 1987), p. 6.

26. Dieter Scholz, "Das Großstadt-Triptychon von Otto Dix," in *Otto Dix: Bestandskatalog* (Stuttgart: Galerie der Stadt Stuttgart, Edition Cantz, 1989), pp. 61–72. The *Self-Portrait with Carnation* also refers to Jan van Eyck's *Man with a Carnation* of 1435; see Gunter Otto, *Otto Dix: Bildnis der Eltern* (Frankfurt a.M.: Fischer, 1984), p. 15.

27. Michael Fried, *Realism, Writing, Disfiguration: On Thomas Eakins and Stephen Crane* (Chicago: University of Chicago Press, 1987).

28. Note in this context especially *Die Dirne* of 1913. Heinz Höfchen discusses these works in "Dixens frühe Werkgruppe roter Tuschzeichnungen," in *Otto Dix: Zeichnungen und Druckgraphik aus der Stiftung Walther Groz in der Städtischen Galerie Albstadt* (Kaiserslautern: Pfalzgalerie, 1987), pp. 18–26. For Carol Duncan, female nudes of this type demonstrate that "art originates in and is sustained by male erotic energy." See her essay "Virility and Domination in Early Twentieth-Century Vanguard Painting," in *Feminism and Art History: Questioning the Litany*, pp. 292–313.

29. Beth Irwin Lewis sees in Dix's images "an overpowering fear of sexuality and an obsessive dread of women." "In the midst of the profound unsettling of boundaries between the sexes that the war accelerated," she adds, "these artists' apprehension and anxiety produced vicious images that grew out of complex emotional and social responses to woman's changing role." See her "*Lustmord*: Inside the Windows of the Metropolis," in *Berlin: Culture and Metropolis*, ed. Charles W. Haxthausen and Heidrun Suhr (Minneapolis: University of Minnesota Press, 1990), p. 136.

30. Fussell, *The Great War and Modern Memory*, p. 328.

31. Ibid., p. 334.

32. *The Metamorphoses of Ovid*, trans. Mary M. Innes (Harmondsworth: Penguin, 1955), p. 231.

33. Diether Schmidt, *Otto Dix im Selbstbildnis* (Berlin: Henschel, 1978), pp. 54–56. Schmidt reproduces this self-portrait, a woodcut, and another drawing on which the words "AHOI! Das ist DIX, d.h. A + O zeit + raumlos" are found.

34. Ibid., p. 70.

35. Schmidt describes paintbrush and maulstick as "scalpel and sword," in what is decidedly not an accidental lapse into surgical and military metaphor (*Otto Dix im Selbstbildnis*, p. 84).

36. On this point, see Duncan, "Virility and Domination in Early Twentieth-Century Vanguard Painting." Anne M. Wagner gives this argument many unexpected twists and turns in "Rodin's Reputation," in *Eroticism and the Body Politic*, ed. Lynn Hunt (Baltimore: Johns Hopkins University Press, 1991), 191–242.

37. France Borel has observed that "art flirts with anatomy," but in Dix's case the flirtation turns into a full-blown love affair. See *The Seduction of Venus: Artists and Models*, trans. Jean-Marie Clarke (New York: Rizzoli, 1990), p. 160.

38. See Otto Conzelmann, *Otto Dix: Handzeichnungen* (Hanover: Fackelträger, 1968), p. 42, and Schmidt, *Otto Dix im Selbstbildnis*, p. 210.

39. The photograph is reproduced as plate 11 in Fritz Löffler's *Otto Dix: Leben und Werk* (Dresden: VEB Verlag der Kunst, 1977).

40. On this point, see Marta Weigle, *Creation and Procreation: Feminist Reflections of*

Mythologies of Cosmogony and Parturition (Philadelphia: University of Pennsylvania Press, 1989), pp. 59–61, and Gerda Lerner, *The Creation of Patriarchy* (New York: Oxford University Press, 1986).

41. Brigid S. Barton sees in the painting a reference to art, which "captures the transitory in contrast to the figures who are related to death and decay." See her *Otto Dix and Die neue Sachlichkeit* (Ann Arbor, Mich.: UMI Research Press, 1981), p. 50.

42. Dix acknowledged the confessional dimension of his artistic production. "Ich habe niemals Bekenntnisse schriftlich von mir gegeben," Dix wrote to Hans Kinkel in 1947, "da ja, wie der Augenschein Sie lehren wird, meine Bilder Bekenntnisse aufrichtigster Art sind, wie Sie sie selten in dieser Zeit finden werden." See Schmidt, *Otto Dix im Selbstbildnis*, p. 217. In this context it is pertinent to observe that one critic, who finds that Dix sought to discredit "idealized images of war, the city, and women," also finds that these "principal themes" remain "unsolved problems." See Jens Christian Jensen, ed., *Otto Dix: Zeichnungen aus dem Nachlaß, 1911–1942* (Kiel: Katalog der Kunsthalle zu Kiel und Schleswig-Holsteinischer Kunstverein, 1980), n.p.

43. Felixmüller's comment is cited by Gunter Otto, *Otto Dix: Bildnis der Eltern*, p. 21.

CHAPTER FIVE
LIFE IN THE COMBAT ZONE

1. Marty Grosz, "I Remember . . . ," in *George Grosz: The Berlin Years*, ed. Serge Sabarsky (New York: Rizzoli, 1985), p. 14.

2. M. Kay Flavell, *George Grosz: A Biography* (New Haven: Yale University Press, 1988), p. 46.

3. Lynda Nead, *The Female Nude: Art, Obscenity and Sexuality* (London: Routledge, 1992), pp. 1–2.

4. Kenneth Clark, *The Nude: A Study in Ideal Form* (Garden City, N.Y.: Doubleday Anchor, 1956), pp. 45, 23, 445.

5. George Grosz, *Ein kleines Ja und ein großes Nein: Sein Leben von ihm selbst erzählt* (Reinbek bei Hamburg: Rowohlt, 1974), p. 236.

6. Flavell, *George Grosz: A Biography*, p. 42.

7. The quotations are cited by Hans Hess, *George Grosz* (New York: Macmillan, 1974), p. 217.

8. Roland Barthes, *Sade, Fourier, Loyola* (New York: Hill and Wang, 1926), p. 151.

9. Susan Sontag, *Styles of Radical Will* (New York: Farrar, Straus and Giroux, 1969), p. 45.

10. George Grosz, *Briefe: 1913–1959*, ed. Herbert Knust (Reinbek bei Hamburg: Rowohlt, 1979), p. 58.

11. Grosz, *Ein kleines Ja und ein großes Nein*, p. 98.

12. On Grosz's misanthropy, see Beth Irwin Lewis, *George Grosz: Art and Politics in the Weimar Republic* (Madison: University of Wisconsin Press, 1971), pp. 19–21.

13. Grosz, *Briefe: 1913–1959*, pp. 46, 48, 52.

14. Ibid., pp. 194–95.

15. Cited by Martin Kane in *Weimar Germany and the Limits of Political Art: A Study of the Work of George Grosz and Ernst Toller* (Fife, Scotland: Hutton Press, 1987), pp. 42–44. The gloss appeared in the exhibition catalog for the First International Dada Fair held in Berlin in 1920.

16. Grosz, *Ein kleines Ja und ein großes Nein*, p. 29.

17. Flavell has stated that for Grosz, "sex and alcohol are seen as drugs capable of turning men into Circe's swine or into demonic murderers." See *George Grosz: A Biography*, p. 22.

18. Grosz, *Ein kleines Ja und ein großes Nein*, p. 36.

19. See the discussion of Medusa by Susan Gubar in "Representing Pornography: Feminism, Criticism, and Depictions of Female Violation," *Critical Inquiry* 13 (1987): 712–41.

20. Sigmund Freud, "Medusa's Head" (1922), in Sigmund Freud, *Sexuality and the Psychology of Love*, ed. Philip Rieff (New York: Collier, 1963), pp. 212–13.

21. Grosz, *Ein kleines Ja und ein großes Nein*, p. 34.

22. Clark, *The Nude*, p. 133.

23. Grosz, *Ein kleines Ja und ein großes Nein*, p. 35.

24. On the cultural significance of Eve, see especially John A. Phillips, *Eve: The History of an Idea* (San Francisco: Harper & Row, 1984).

25. Grosz, *Ein kleines Ja und ein großes Nein*, p. 37.

26. Nancy Chodorow, *The Reproduction of Mothering: Psychoanalysis and the Sociology of Gender* (Berkeley: University of California Press, 1978), pp. 218–19.

27. Gubar, "Representing Pornography," p. 737.

28. Grosz, *Ein kleines Ja und ein großes Nein*, pp. 18–23.

29. Uwe M. Schneede, "Infernal Apparitions of Reality," in *George Grosz: The Berlin Years*, ed. Sabarsky, p. 30.

30. Hess, *George Grosz*, p. 38.

31. Cited by Flavell, *George Grosz: A Biography*, p. 42.

32. A pen-and-ink of 1912 entitled *Crime* shows a triumphant woman of colossal proportions holding the head of a man decapitated by a baboonlike figure dressed in a suit. It is reprinted in Hess, *George Grosz*, p. 42.

33. Margaret R. Miles, *Carnal Knowing: Female Nakedness and Religious Meaning in the Christian West* (Boston: Beacon Press, 1989), p. 153.

34. See also an untitled ink drawing that depicts a brutal looking man with a reed cane standing over the corpse of a woman. The drawing is reprinted in Beth Irwin Lewis's "*Lustmord*: Inside the Windows of the Metropolis," in *Berlin: Culture and Metropolis*, ed. Charles W. Haxthausen and Heidrun Suhr (Minneapolis: University of Minnesota Press, 1990), p. 124.

35. Grosz, *Ein kleines Ja und ein großes Nein*, p. 111.

36. *Eine Jugend in Deutschland*, in Ernst Toller, *Prosa, Briefe, Dramen, Gedichte* (Reinbek bei Hamburg: Rowohlt, 1961), pp. 70–71.

37. August Stramm, "Briefe an Herwarth und Nell Walden," in *Literatur-Revolution 1910–1925: Dokumente, Manifeste, Programme*, ed. Paul Pörtner (Darmstadt: Luchterhand, 1960), p. 47.

38. Ibid., pp. 50–51.

39. Grosz, *Briefe: 1913–1959*, pp. 49–50.

40. Ibid., p. 52.

41. Grosz, *Ein kleines Ja und ein großes Nein*, p. 94.

42. Beth Irwin Lewis, "The Medical Journal of Dr. William King Thomas. U.S.A. Oct. 15 to 15 Nov. 15: Sketchbook 1915/2," in *The Sketchbooks of George Grosz*, ed. Peter Nisbet (Cambridge, Mass.: Busch-Reisinger Museum, 1993), p. 42.

43. Kathrin Hoffmann-Curtius observes that Grosz produced a postcard of Diana "hunting by day and by night." It allows the viewer to change her dress from a hunting

costume to a sheet. See "'Wenn Blicke töten könnten' oder: Der Künstler als Lustmörder," in *Blick-Wechsel: Konstruktionen von Männlichkeit und Weiblichkeit in Kunst und Kunstgeschichte* (Berlin: Dietrich Reimer, 1989), pp. 369–93.

44. Susan Griffin, *Pornography and Silence: Culture's Revenge against Nature* (New York: Harper & Row, 1981), p. 31.

45. René Girard, *Violence and the Sacred*, trans. Patrick Gregory (Baltimore: Johns Hopkins University Press, 1977), p. 286.

46. On comparisons between the two artists, see Matthias Eberle, *World War I and the Weimar Artists: Dix, Grosz, Beckmann, Schlemmer*, trans. John Gabriel (New Haven: Yale University Press, 1985), pp. 59–60.

47. Laura Mulvey, "Visual Pleasure and Narrative Cinema," *Screen* 16 (1975): 6–18.

48. Cited by Ulrich Becher, *Der große Grosz und eine große Zeit* (Reinbek bei Hamburg: Rowohlt, 1962), p. 15. The German reads: "Hör zu, du Judensau, morgen nacht kommen wir und schlachten dich samt deiner Brut."

CHAPTER SIX
THE CORPSE VANISHES

1. Charles Bernheimer, *Figures of Ill Repute: Representing Prostitution in Nineteenth-Century France* (Cambridge: Harvard University Press, 1989), p. 270.

2. Alfred Döblin, "Die Ermordung einer Butterblume," in *Die Ermordung einer Butterblume: Ausgewählte Erzählungen, 1910–1950* (Olten: Walter-Verlag, 1962), pp. 42–54.

3. The novel's subtitle was added only on the publisher's insistence. Even as late as 1987, critics are asking: "Are we . . . to be guided by the title and take the subject to be twentieth-century Berlin, or by the subtitle, which describes the novel as 'Die Geschichte vom Franz Biberkopf'?" See Osman Durrani, "The End of *Berlin Alexanderplatz*: Towards the Terminus of Döblin's Tramway," *German Life & Letters* 40 (1987): 142–50. Leo Kreutzer works out an interesting distinction between *Geschichte* (story/history) and *Abläufe* (events) in an attempt to clarify the opposition between motivated fictional biography and unmotivated montage elements. See *Alfred Döblin. Sein Werk bis 1933* (Stuttgart: Kohlhammer, 1970), pp. 125–34. The most eloquent and convincing spokesmen for the two sides of the debate are Volker Klotz, *Die erzählte Stadt. Ein Sujet als Herausforderung des Romans von Lesage bis Döblin* (Munich: Hanser, 1969), pp. 372–418; and Hans-Peter Bayerdörfer, who, like all advocates of the novel as Bildungsroman, focuses on the conclusion in "Der Wissende und die Gewalt. Alfred Döblins Theorie des epischen Werkes und der Schluß von 'Berlin Alexanderplatz,'" *Deutsche Vierteljahrsschrift für Literaturwissenschaft und Geistesgeschichte* 44 (1970): 318–53. For a critique of attempts to harmonize the relationship between biography and montage or to drive a wedge between them, see Harald Jähner, *Erzählter, montierter, souffflierter Text. Zur Konstruktion des Romans "Berlin Alexanderplatz" von Alfred Döblin* (Frankfurt a.M.: Lang, 1984), pp. 9–14. For Marilyn Sibley Fries, "city and man become equal characters, at once complementing and contradicting one another." See "The City as Metaphor for the Human Condition: Alfred Döblin's *Berlin Alexanderplatz* (1929)," *Modern Fiction Studies* 24 (1978): 62.

4. Note, in this context, Hans-Peter Bayerdörfer's characterization of the novel as a work which is "humanistic" in its content and politically "militant" ("Der Wissende und die Gewalt," p. 353). Fritz Martini turns from the term *Entwicklung*, which he sees as

applicable only in those cases where an individual operates under a degree of "intellectual and ethical freedom," and introduces the alternative terms "breakthrough" and "transformation" to characterize Biberkopf's life. Martini fails to problematize or even to define the notion of freedom in its relationship to development and makes no effort to explain what distinguishes an Agathon or Wilhelm Meister from a Franz Biberkopf. See Fritz Martini, "Berlin Alexanderplatz," in his *Das Wagnis der Sprache. Interpretationen deutscher Prosa von Nietzsche bis Benn,* 2d ed. (Stuttgart: Klett, 1956), pp. 349–50. Walter Benjamin referred to the novel as the last gasp of the bourgeois Bildungsroman in "Krisis des Romans. Zu Döblins 'Berlin Alexanderplatz,'" in *Gesammelte Schriften,* ed. Hella Tiedemann-Bartels (Frankfurt a.M.: Suhrkamp, 1972), 3:236.

5. Klaus Müller-Salget is the most energetic advocate of the novel as a meaningfully structured whole. See his *Alfred Döblin. Werk und Entwicklung* (Bonn: Bouvier, 1988), pp. 294–95. On the basis of Döblin's theories about literary composition, Winfried Georg Sebald finds a principle of discontinuity at work in the fiction and challenges the notion of unity. See *Der Mythos der Zerstörung im Werk Döblins* (Stuttgart: Klett, 1980), p. 133.

6. Minder hastened to emphasize that *Berlin Alexanderplatz,* like Döblin's other novels, cannot be seen as "a homosexual book in the traditional sense of the term" (no examples are given of the genre); he traces the source of the conflict between the two men to the structure of the German family with its powerful, authoritarian father figure. See his "Alfred Döblin," in *Deutsche Literatur im zwanzigsten Jahrhundert,* ed. Hermann Friedmann and Otto Mann, 2d ed. (Heidelberg: Wolfgang Rothe, 1956), p. 303. In a study of Döblin's imagery, Helga Stegemann emphatically demonstrates the way in which interpretations can go wrong when they ignore the gender relationships worked out in a text. While Stegemann understands that the flower in "Die Ermordung einer Butterblume" gradually takes on the attributes of a woman, she sees the story's theme as "die Unmöglichkeit des Kontaktverlustes des Ichs mit der Natur" (p. 107) and fails to recognize that Döblin presents us with a displaced "Lustmord." See her *Studien zu Alfred Döblins Bildlichkeit: "Die Ermordung einer Butterblume" und andere Erzählungen* (Bern: Lang, 1978).

7. Richard Corliss, "Germany without Tears," *Time,* 15 August 1983, p. 64. The statement is cited by Eric Rentschler in his powerful essay on Fassbinder's film, "Terms of Dismemberment: The Body in/and/of Fassbinder's *Berlin Alexanderplatz,*" *New German Critique* 34 (1985): 205.

8. The degree to which Biberkopf's efforts to remain *anständig* are not necessarily admirable is illustrated by the use of the term in a speech of 1943 delivered by Heinrich Himmler to SS leaders: "Von euch werden die meisten wissen, was es heißt, wenn 100 Leichen beisammen liegen, wenn 500 daliegen oder wenn 1000 daliegen. Dies durchgehalten zu haben, und dabei—abgesehen von Ausnahmen menschlicher Schwächen—anständig geblieben zu sein, das hat uns hart gemacht." The passage is cited by James H. Reid, *"Berlin Alexanderplatz—A Political Novel," German Life & Letters* 21 (1968): 214–23. All quotations from the novel are to Alfred Döblin, *Berlin Alexanderplatz. Die Geschichte vom Franz Biberkopf* (Olten and Freiburg i.Br.: Walter-Verlag, 1977). Page numbers are cited parenthetically in the text. The translations are my own.

9. As Ute Karlavaris-Bremer points out, the tendency of critics to identify with the narrator's observations has endowed commentaries on Döblin's work with a "'männlichen' Charakter." See her "Die Frau-Mann-Beziehung in Döblins ersten Dramen und den frühen Erzählungen," *Internationale Alfred Döblin-Kolloquien. Basel 1980—New York 1981—Freiburg i. Br. 1983,* ed. Werner Stauffacher (Bern: Peter Lang, 1986), pp. 206–13.

10. Rainer Werner Fassbinder, "Die Städte des Menschen und seine Seele. Einige ungeordnete Gedanken zu Alfred Döblins Roman 'Berlin Alexanderplatz,'" *Die Zeit*, 14 March 1980. Note also in this context Günter Grass's homage to Döblin in his essay "Über meinen Lehrer Alfred Döblin," in Alfred Döblin, *Die drei Sprünge des Wang-Lun* (Olten and Freiburg i. Br.: Walter-Verlag, 1977), pp. v–xxxi.

11. Critics who emphasize the indeterminate conclusion (indeterminate with regard to Biberkopf's mental state, not the political messages purveyed) are in the minority. For their arguments, see Otto F. Best, "Zwischen Orient und Okzident: Döblin und Spinoza. Einige Anmerkungen zur Problematik des offenen Schlusses von *Berlin Alexanderplatz*," *Colloquia Germanica* 12 (1979): 94–105; and A. F. Bance, "Alfred Döblin's *Berlin Alexanderplatz* and Literary Modernism," in *Weimar Germany: Writers and Politics*, ed. A. F. Bance (Edinburgh: Scottish Academic Press, 1982), pp. 53–64. The three quotations are from Otto Keller, *Döblins Montageroman als Epos der Moderne* (Munich: Fink, 1980), p. 192; Kathleen Komar, "Technique and Structure in Döblin's *Berlin Alexanderplatz*," *German Quarterly* 54 (1981): 322; and Klaus Müller-Salget, *Alfred Döblin*, p. 350.

12. Matthias Prangel's view is representative. He lists the various elements of Döblin's montage, then finds: "Die Harmonisierung all dieser, zum Teil im früheren Werk schon vorgeprägten Einzeltendenzen ist es letzten Endes, die 'Berlin Alexanderplatz' zu dem gelungensten aller Werke Döblins macht." See his *Alfred Döblin*, 2d ed. (Stuttgart: Metzler, 1987), p. 67. Helmut Koopmann, in associating the novel with "classical modernism," also identifies it as a work striving for "etwas Ursprüngliches und Totales" and veering away from "die Darstellung einer nur diskongruenten und dissoziierten Wirklichkeit." See his *Der klassisch-moderne Roman in Deutschland. Thomas Mann, Alfred Döblin, Hermann Broch* (Stuttgart: Kohlhammer, 1983), p. 85.

13. *The Dialogic Imagination: Four Essays by M. M. Bakhtin*, ed. Michael Holquist, trans. Caryl Emerson and Michael Holquist (Austin: University of Texas Press, 1981), p. 263. It was Bakhtin who first called attention to the "multi-voiced, multi-styled, and often multi-languaged elements" of novelistic practice, as well as to the powerful centrifugal pressure exerted on the novel by what he termed its generically determined heteroglossia. Döblin's *Berlin Alexanderplatz* mobilizes social heteroglossia in a uniquely radical fashion to construct a comprehensive picture of German urban life in the 1920s even as it relies on multiple socio-ideological languages to accelerate a relentless process of decentralization and disunification. Not only does social heteroglossia work against the notion of stable, hermetic utterances locked in monologic contexts, it also produces a double-voiced discourse that expresses both "the voice of a character who is speaking and the refracted intention of the author" (p. 324). Its very manner of construction creates an ambiguous narrative situation that in and of itself problematizes the notion of origins and agency, this time at the level of novelistic practice. "Man glaubt zu sprechen," Döblin observed in the context of observations on the writer's craft, "und man wird gesprochen, man glaubt zu schreiben und man wird geschrieben." See Alfred Döblin, "Der Bau des epischen Werks," in *Aufsätze zur Literatur* (Olten and Freiburg i.Br.: Walter-Verlag, 1963), p. 131. This abdication of authorial hegemony and construction of a double-voiced discourse makes it all the more important to bring some skepticism to almost any pronouncement made in the novel, including "authorial" ones, but it also obliges us to heed the problematics of origins and agency at both the mimetic and diegetic levels of the novel's discursive practices.

14. On the affiliation of city and prostitute, see the illuminating essay by Hanne Bergius, "Berlin als Hure Babylon," in *Die Metropole: Industriekultur in Berlin im 20. Jahrhundert*,

ed. Jochen Boberg, Tilman Fichter, and Eckhart Gillem (Munich: Beck, 1986), pp. 102–19. Alain Corbin's magisterial tome examines the historical contexts of prostitution. See his *Women for Hire: Prostitution and Sexuality in France after 1850*, trans. Alan Sheridan (Cambridge: Harvard University Press, 1990).

15. Theodore Ziolkowski, "Alfred Döblin: *Berlin Alexanderplatz*," in Theodore Ziolkowski, *Dimensions of the Modern Novel: German Texts and European Contexts* (Princeton: Princeton University Press, 1969), p. 136. Döblin's interest in Greek tragedy is further documented by the debates about Antigone staged in *November 1918*.

16. Albrecht Schöne, "Döblin: *Berlin Alexanderplatz*," in *Der deutsche Roman vom Barock bis zur Gegenwart*, ed. Benno von Wiese (Düsseldorf: August Bagel, 1963), p. 293. I am grateful to Rachel Freudenberg for drawing my attention to this point and to others in her unpublished paper "Violence and Women: Döblin's *Berlin Alexanderplatz*."

17. See Birgit Kreutzahler, *Das Bild des Verbrechers in Romanen der Weimarer Republik. Eine Untersuchung vor dem Hintergrund anderer gesellschaftlicher Verbrecherbilder und gesellschaftlicher Grundzüge der Weimarer Republik* (Frankfurt a.M.: Peter Lang, 1987), p. 328.

18. Müller-Salget, *Alfred Döblin*, p. 313.

19. On the replaying of this drama, see Susan Suleiman, "Transgression and the Avant-Garde: Bataille's *Histoire de l'oeil*," in *Subversive Intent: Gender, Politics, and the Avant-Garde* (Cambridge: Harvard University Press, 1990), pp. 72–87.

20. David Dollenmayer, "Alfred Döblin, Futurism, and Women: A Relationship Reexamined," *Germanic Review* 61 (1986): 138–45.

21. I borrow the phrase from Eric Rentschler, "Terms of Dismemberment," p. 201, which is in turn indebted to René Girard's *Deceit, Desire, and the Novel: Self and Other in Literary Structure*, trans. Yvonne Freccero (Baltimore: Johns Hopkins University Press, 1972).

22. Eve Kosovsky Sedgwick, *Between Men: English Literature and Male Homosocial Desire* (New York: Columbia University Press, 1985), p.66.

23. Alfred Döblin, "Modern," in *Jagende Rosse, Der schwarze Vorhang und andere frühe Erzählwerke* (Olten and Freiburg i.Br.: Walter-Verlag, 1981), p. 20.

24. Alfred Döblin, "Der schwarze Vorhang," in ibid., p. 170.

25. Ibid., p. 199.

26. A quotation from Döblin's "Die Memoiren des Blasierten" is apposite here: "Ich hasse die Weiber; ich hasse, hasse, hasse, sie, daß ich weinen könnte vor Wut über sie, über die Hündinnen, die verfluchten." See *Erzählungen aus fünf Jahrzehnten* (Olten and Freiburg i.Br.: Walter-Verlag, 1977), p. 95.

27. Klaus Theweleit, *Male Fantasies*, 2 vols., trans. Erica Carter and Chris Turner (Minneapolis: University of Minnesota Press, 1989). Since Theweleit sees the impulse to destroy in the writing styles of certain Freikorps-figures, it is especially interesting to draw attention to Döblin's views on the way in which the writer goes about his business: "Er muß ganz nahe an die Realität heran, an ihre Sachlichkeit, ihr Blut, ihren Geruch, und dann hat er die Sache zu durchstossen, das ist seine spezifische Arbeit" (Alfred Döblin, *Aufsätze zur Literatur*, p. 107).

28. Döblin, "Der schwarze Vorhang," p. 128.

29. The quotation is from Monique Weyembergh-Boussart, *Alfred Döblin. Seine Religiosität in Persönlichkeit und Werk* (Bonn: Bouvier, 1970), p. 133. Fassbinder presents Ida's murder in six flashbacks, thus suggesting that Franz is haunted by it. On this point, see Sally Schoen Bergman, "*Berlin Alexanderplatz*: Fassbinder's Last Masterpiece," in *National*

Traditions in Motion Pictures: Proceedings of the Third Annual Conference on Film, Kent State University, ed. Douglas Radcliff-Umstead (Kent, Ohio: Kent State University Press, 1985), pp. 85–91.

30. "Mein Buch 'Berlin Alexanderplatz,'" in *Berlin Alexanderplatz* (Munich: Deutscher Taschenbuch Verlag, 1965), p. 414. Critics like Fritz Martini take the author at his word and write about the way in which "Leiden und Dulden" constitute the challenges of life.

31. On the biblical quotations and allusions, see Erich Hülse, "Alfred Döblin, *Berlin Alexanderplatz*," in *Möglichkeiten des modernen deutschen Romans*, ed. Rolf Geissler (Frankfurt a.M.: Diesterweg, 1962), pp. 45–101; Monique Weyembergh-Boussart, *Alfred Döblin*; and Werner Stauffacher, "Die Bibel als poetisches Bezugssystem. Zu Alfred Döblins 'Berlin Alexanderplatz,'" *Sprachkunst: Beiträge zur Literaturwissenschaft* 8 (1977): 35–40.

32. Here I would take issue with Albrecht Schöne's view that the narrator's production of parallels, analogies, and similarities creates a special resonance and depth (p. 308). See "Döblin. *Berlin Alexanderplatz*," in *Der deutsche Roman*, ed. Benno von Wiese (Düsseldorf: August Bagel, 1963), 2:291–325. Erwin Kobel, on the other hand, emphasizes—though without developing the argument—that Biberkopf's story usually has only one point of contact with the biblical tales. See his *Alfred Döblin: Erzählkunst im Umbruch* (Berlin: Walter de Gruyter, 1985), p. 271.

33. Weyembergh-Boussart, *Alfred Döblin*, p. 166. On parallels between mythical figures and fictional characters, see Dieter Baacke, "Erzähltes Engagement: Antike Mythologie in Döblins Romanen," in *Text + Kritik* 13/14 (1966): 22–31.

34. The phrase is from Erich Hülse's "Alfred Döblin, *Berlin Alexanderplatz*," p. 92.

35. On critical views of Mieze, see Dollenmayer, *The Berlin Novels of Alfred Döblin* (Berkeley: University of California Press, 1988), p. 94.

36. On the way in which self and world constitute each other, see Helmut Schwimmer, "Erlebnis und Gestaltung der Wirklichkeit bei Alfred Döblin," Ph.D. diss., University of Munich, 1960.

37. For commentaries on the close association between Reinhold and Death, see Ursula R. Mahlendorf, "Schelm und Verbrecher: Döblin's *Berlin Alexanderplatz*," *Amsterdamer Beiträge zur neueren Germanistik* 20 (1985/86): 77–108, and Albrecht Schöne, "Döblin. *Berlin Alexanderplatz*," p. 321.

38. Note in this context that the French refer to one kind of brothel as a "maison d'abattage." On this point, see Alain Corbin, "Commercial Sexuality in Nineteenth-Century France: A System of Images and Regulations," in *The Making of the Modern Body*, ed. Catherine Gallagher and Thomas Laquer (Berkeley: University of California Press, 1987), pp. 209–19.

39. Rentschler, "Terms of Dismemberment," p. 200. Kaja Silverman points out that it is impossible to "forget" or "assimilate" Ida's murder. See her *Male Subjectivity at the Margins* (New York: Routledge, 1992), p. 225.

40. In celebrating Mieze's devotion to Franz and her self-sacrificial act, critics often shift the emphasis from her victimization to her martyrdom, thus turning her into the agent of her own suffering.

41. Alfred Döblin, *Karl und Rosa*, vol. 4 of *November 1918* (Munich: Deutscher Taschenbuch Verlag, 1978), p. 297.

42. Dollenmayer, *The Berlin Novels of Alfred Döblin*, p. 172.

43. Döblin, *Karl und Rosa*, p. 397.

44. Ibid., p. 90.

45. Ibid., pp. 590, 592.

46. Ibid., pp. 591, 592.

47. The letter, dated 24 December 1917, describes the torture of the buffaloes and ends with the apostrophe, quoted in the excerpt from the film, to the tortured animal. See Rosa Luxemburg, *Gesammelte Briefe* (East Berlin: Dietz, 1984) 5:349–50. Numerous passages from the letters testify to Luxemburg's feelings of empathy with tortured creatures, but also to her sense that her love for animals did not conflict with her political goals.

48. Margarethe von Trotta and Christiane Ensslin, *Rosa Luxemburg. Das Buch zum Film* (Nördlingen: Franz Greno, 1986), p. 85.

49. As numerous critics have pointed out, there is a real discrepancy between biographical accounts of Rosa Luxemburg and Döblin's fictionalized biography. See especially Heidi Thomann Tewarson, "Alfred Döblins Geschichtskonzeption in 'November 1918. Eine deutsche Revolution' dargestellt an der Figur Rosa Luxemburgs in 'Karl und Rosa,'" in *Internationale Alfred Döblin Kolloquien*, pp. 64–75; and Helmut F. Pfanner, "Sachlichkeit und Mystik. Zur Erzählhaltung in Alfred Döblins Revolutionsroman," in ibid., pp. 76–85.

50. Döblin, *Karl und Rosa*, p. 620.

51. There is a hint of this helplessness of the victim in Max Beckmann's *Martyrdom*, a drawing of Rosa Luxemburg's murder.

52. *Alfred Döblin. Im Buch—Zu Hause—Auf der Straße* (Berlin: Fischer, 1928), p. 12.

CHAPTER SEVEN
THE KILLER AS VICTIM

1. Frederick W. Ott, *The Great German Films* (Secaucus, N.J.: Citadel, 1986), p. 116.

2. Valerie Weinstein makes this point in her "Out of Uniform: Reading against the Teleology of Weimar Film History," Harvard University Senior Thesis, 1993.

3. Siegfried Kracauer, *From Caligari to Hitler: A Psychological History of the German Film* (Princeton: Princeton University Press, 1947), p. 219.

4. Interview with Gero Gandert, in "Fritz Lang über *M*," *M: Protokoll* (Hamburg: Marion von Schröder, 1963), pp. 123–24. All quotations from *M* will be taken from the screenplay in that volume and cited parenthetically in the text by page number.

5. Lotte Eisner, *Fritz Lang*, trans. Gertrud Mander (London: Secker & Warburg, 1976), p. 123.

6. Carol J. Clover, *Men, Women, and Chainsaws: Gender in the Modern Horror Film* (Princeton: Princeton University Press, 1992), p. 29.

7. To understand the "mentality" of those who murder, Lang allegedly spent many hours with psychiatrists and psychoanalysts, just as he tried to work his way into police methods by spending time at Berlin's "Alex." See his comments in an interview with Gero Gandert, "Fritz Lang über *M*," p. 124.

8. Lang, *M: Protokoll*, p. 116.

9. On this point, see Barbara Creed, *The Monstrous-Feminine: Film, Feminism, Psychoanalysis* (London: Routledge, 1993), pp. 43–58. Roger Dadoun points out that the cave at the bottom of the catacombs in *Metropolis* "obviously resembles a uterus." See his "*Metropolis:* Mother-City—'Mittler'—Hitler," *Camera obscura* 15 (1986): 143. These comparisons may seem overly facile, but to my mind Lang was consciously affiliating these underground, enclosed spaces—which are subject to flooding—with the feminine.

10. Henrik Ibsen: *Peer Gynt: A Dramatic Poem*, trans. Peter Watts (London: Penguin, 1966), p. 71.

11. Clover, *Men, Women, and Chainsaws*, p. 194.

12. Angela Carter, *The Sadeian Woman and the Ideology of Pornography* (New York: Harper & Row, 1980), p. 123.

13. I borrow the terms of the last sentence in the paragraph from Susan Rubin Suleiman's exegesis of Bataille's notion of transgression. See "Pornography, Transgression, and the Avant-Garde: Bataille's *Story of the Eye*," in *The Poetics of Gender*, ed. Nancy K. Miller (New York: Columbia University Press, 1986), pp. 117–36.

14. On the representation of women in the city's social space, see Anton Kaes, "The Cold Gaze: Notes on Mobilization and Modernity," *New German Critique* 59 (1993): 105–17. On the opposition between work and play in the initial sequence, see Thierry Kuntzel, "The Film-Work," *Enclitic* 2 (1978): 38–61. The essay originally appeared as "Le travail du film" in *Communications* 19 (1972): 25–39. Kuntzel also speculates on the significance of the following chain: "Haarmann" (the name of a murderer in a popular song), "Grossmann" (a child murderer of the 1920s), "Sandmann" (the German term for bogeyman), and "Schwarzmann" (the subject of the children's song). Interestingly, he suppresses the two terms that would disrupt the chain's continuity: "Beckmann" and "Lohmann." Kuntzel does not speculate on why Lang called the killer "Beckert" and the mother "Beckmann."

15. Kracauer formulated the "moral" of the film in the following way: "In the wake of retrogression terrible outbursts of sadism are inevitable" (*From Caligari to Hitler*, p. 222).

16. Clover discusses the way in which the monster of horror films is "constructed as feminine" (*Men, Women, and Chainsaws*, pp. 46–48).

17. Kracauer, *From Caligari to Hitler*, p. 221.

18. "Why I Am Interested in Murder," cited in Eisner, *Fritz Lang*, p. 111.

19. One such poster is reprinted in Alfred Eibel, *Fritz Lang* (Paris: Présence du Cinéma, 1964), p. 34.

20. Lotte Eisner and other critics have emphasized the sexual meaning of the figures, neglecting their other possible dimensions. See her *Fritz Lang*, p. 117.

21. Joseph S.M.J. Chang noted the comic elements in "*M*: A Reconsideration," *Literature-Film Quarterly* (1979): 300–308.

22. On connections between surveillance, military mobilization, and social control, see Kaes, "The Cold Gaze," pp. 105–17.

23. Numerous critics have pointed to the influence of Brecht, in particular of his *Dreigroschenoper*, on Lang's representation of the alliances among the police, criminals, and beggars. Lang himself was the first to acknowledge Brecht's hold on his imagination. See Gandert's interview, "Fritz Lang über *M*," p. 125. For a full discussion of the relations between the two, see Frieda Grafe, "Einen Platz, kein Denkmal," in *Fritz Lang* (Munich: Hanser, 1976), pp. 17–21.

24. "Why I am Interested in Murder," cited by Eisner, *Fritz Lang*, p. 111.

25. Eric Rhode refers to Beckert as "the lord of misrule" who ushers in a reign of irrationality. See *Tower of Babel: Speculations on the Cinema* (London: Weidenfeld and Nicolson, 1966), p. 100.

26. Many critics subscribe to this notion of the "humanization" of the killer, but perhaps none more strongly than Stanley J. Solomon, who writes about the way in which the murderer is presented in "an almost sympathetic light" and finds that the spectator is

"actually relieved to see him rescued from execution." See *The Classic Cinema: Essays in Criticism*, ed. Stanley J. Solomon (New York: Harcourt Brace Jovanovich, 1973), p. 131.

27. "Why I Am Interested in Murder," cited in Eisner, *Fritz Lang*, p. 111.

28. Cornelius Schnauber, ed., *Fritz Lang. Der Tod eines Karriere-Girls und andere Geschichten*, trans. Edda Zimmermann et al. (Vienna: Europaverlag, 1987), p. 14.

29. Eisner, *Fritz Lang*, p. 111.

30. Eisner, *Fritz Lang*, p. 128. Here, as in other contexts, Lang seems to have remained singularly blind to the visual realities of his films in his effort to present a form of enlightened "truth" to his public. The message enunciated in the film about the importance of taking care of children along with Lang's proclamations about the cruelty of capital punishment ring just as false for *M* as does the final scene of *Metropolis*, in which an enthusiastic Freder (the "heart"), in a gesture of high melodrama, joins hands with his father (the "brains") and with a foreman (the "hands") to serve as a mediator between the two.

31. One early critic of the film reproached Lang for placing on the shoulders of parents a burden that was really the responsibility of the state. See Tölle, "M: Tonfilm von Fritz Lang," *Arbeiterbühne und Film* 6 (June 1930), cited by E. Ann Kaplan, *Fritz Lang: A Guide to References and Resources* (Boston: G. K. Hall, 1981), p. 164.

32. Roger Dadoun, "Fetishism in the Horror Film," in *Fantasy and the Cinema*, ed. James Donald (London: British Film Institute, 1989), pp. 50–51.

33. *Der ewige Jude*, dir. Fritz Hippler, Deutsche Filmgesellschaft, 1940.

34. See the discussion of *Sin against Blood* in chapter 3 of this volume.

CHAPTER EIGHT

REINVENTIONS

1. Peter Selz, *German Expressionist Painting* (Berkeley: University of California Press, 1957), p. 299.

2. Hugo Bettauer, *Der Frauenmörder* (Vienna: R. Löwit, 1926). On this work, see the fascinating study by Leslie Ann Pahl, *Margins of Modernity: The Citizen and the Criminal in the Weimar Republic* (Ann Arbor: University of Michigan Press, 1991).

3. Bettauer, *Der Frauenmörder*, p. 72.

4. Jay Carr, "John Waters," *Boston Globe*, 10 April 1994.

5. Dorothea von Mücke, "History according to Theweleit," *New German Critique* 55 (1992): 139–58.

6. Klaus Theweleit, *buch der könige* (Basel: Stroemfeld/Roter Stern, 1988), 1:1049.

7. In "The Philosophy of Composition" (1846), Poe described the death of a "beautiful woman" as "the most poetical topic in the world."

8. Richard Huelsenbeck, *Doktor Billig am Ende* (Hofheim: Wolke, 1984), p. 33.

9. Theweleit, *buch der könige*, p. 396.

10. See *Paul Klee. Tagebücher, 1898–1918*, ed. Wolfgang Kersten (Stuttgart: Gerd Hatje, 1988), pp. 402, 518.

11. Wolfgang Kersten, *Paul Klee: "Zerstörung der Konstruktion zuliebe?"* (Marburg: Jonas Verlag, 1987), pp. 37–42.

12. Judith Ryan, "The Problem of Pastiche: Patrick Süskind's *Das Parfum*," *German Quarterly* 63 (1990): 396–403; Stuart Parkes, "The Novels of Patrick Süskind: A Phenome-

non of the 1980s," in *Literature on the Threshold: The German Novel in the 1980s*, ed. Arthur Williams, Stuart Parkes, and Roland Smith (New York: Berg, 1990), pp. 309–19; and Manfred R. Jacobson, "Patrick Süskind's *Das Parfum*: A Postmodern *Künstlerroman*," *German Quarterly* 65 (1992): 201–11.

13. Patrick Süskind, *Perfume: The Story of a Murderer*, trans. John E. Woods (New York: Knopf, 1986), p. 203. Subsequent citations will be to this volume and will be indicated parenthetically in the text.

14. For an astute analysis of Süskind's novel as a critique of instrumental rationality and modernist aesthetic practices, see Richard T. Gray, "The Dialectic of 'Enscentment': Patrick Süskind's *Das Parfum* as Critical History of Enlightenment Culture," *PMLA* 108 (1993): 489–505.

15. Parkes, "The Novels of Patrick Süskind," p. 319.

16. Bruce E. Fleming writes of the way in which "the definition of the self through something that self has created is the enterprise of the romantic and postromantic artist" (p. 83). See his "The Smell of Success: A Reassessment of Patrick Süskind's *Das Parfum*," *South Atlantic Review* 56 (1991): 71–86.

17. Ernst Barlach, *Das dichterische Werk*, ed. Friedrich Droß (Munich: R. Piper, 1959), 3:21.

18. Franz Marc, *Briefe 1914–1916 aus dem Felde* (Berlin: Rembrandt-Verlag, 1959), p. 68.

Index